D1581668

contents

DIANNE H. PILGRIM

Director Emeritus and Senior Advisor
for Special Projects

WHEN I BECAME DIRECTOR of the Cooper-Hewitt, National Design Museum, Smithsonian Institution in October 1988, one of my first priorities was to increase public awareness of the museum's identity and mission. Exhibitions and publications would be our chief strategic tools to illustrate that everything human-made is designed, that in design there is a goal, a process, and a final product, and that design affects our lives every second of the day.

I felt it essential that as the only museum in the United States exclusively devoted to both historical and contemporary design, we examine the pulse of the design world on a regular basis; that we reveal what is important in design at the present moment while foreshadowing new directions for the future. At the same time, we would show off the extraordinary, innovative, and diverse design talent in this country. The *National Design Triennial*, coupled with the publication of *Design Culture Now*, realizes these ideas.

What are designers interested in? How are new technologies affecting their work? How are such factors as cultural diversity, the aging of our population, globalization, and the environment influencing the theory and practice of design? In this atmosphere of accelerated change, with our world transforming so rapidly, what is it that the consumer wants or needs? This may be one of the most difficult times to be a designer, but it is also one of the most exciting, with the promise of making the world a better place—both aesthetically and functionally—for everyone.

What an auspicious time to have the first *National Design Triennial*! We have ended one century and entered another, embarking on a new millennium. Both the fear and excitement generated by such a unique occurrence are transferred to all aspects of our lives and psyches. These conflicting feelings will be expressed through design, and *Design Culture Now* will become an important record of our nation's state of mind at this extraordinary juncture.

I congratulate curators Donald Albrecht, Ellen Lupton, and Steven Skov Holt for the insightful, informative, and imaginative overview they have assembled. By allowing the designer a voice, they have given the audience a view into the process of design.

The United States, like other nations of the world, faces many social, economic, and environmental problems. As people trained to bridge the gap between technology, science, art, and the humanities, designers are in a unique position to be a powerful force for positive change.

We hope this review of recent design developments will prove informative and fascinating to both the users of the designed environment and to those who create it.

ACKNOWLEDGMENTS

DONALD ALBRECHT

ELLEN LUPTON

STEVEN SKOV HOLT

Curators

Many people and institutions helped create this book and the exhibition it accompanies. Over eighty designers and firms participated in the project, sharing their work and ideas. Our thanks goes to all of them for providing such stunning evidence of the power of design.

To produce the book and exhibition, Cooper-Hewitt, National Design Museum relied on the support of key foundations, corporations, and individuals who embraced the idea of the *National Design Triennial* and became our enthusiastic partners.

We thank Agnes Bourne, trustee of the National Design Museum, for providing financial support as well as helping us shape the exhibition's content and building excitement around it in the world of design.

BP Amoco provided primary sponsorship for the exhibition. We greatly appreciate their continued partnership, starting in 1998 with *Under the Sun: An Outdoor Exhibition of Light*, which explored solar energy as a catalyst for design.

The exhibition received crucial support from Mead Coated Papers. We thank Hilary Strauss, Director, Specification Sales, and Shawn L. Hall, Marketing Communications Manager, Mead Coated Papers; and Jerome F. Tatar, Chairman, President, and Chief Executive Officer, The Mead Corporation. Mead Coated Paper's support of the *National Design Triennial* is a fitting continuation of a rewarding series of collaborations that began in 1996 with the exhibition *Mixing Messages: Graphic Design in Contemporary Culture*.

The National Design Museum's Board of Trustees generously supported the *Triennial* through the August Heckscher Exhibition Fund. Our gratitude goes to Kathleen B. Allaire, Jorge L. Batista, Agnes Bourne, William Drenttel, Anne B. Ehrenkranz, Joanne Foster, Harvey M. Krueger (chairman), Elaine La Roche, Jeffrey T. Leeds, Barbara Riley Levin, Barbara Mandel, Nancy Marks, Richard Meier, Kenneth B. Miller, Harry G. Robinson III, Arthur Ross, Richard M. Smith, Edward A. Weinstein, Joan K. Davidson (honorary), Harmon H. Goldstone (honorary), Enid W. Morse (honorary), J. Dennis O'Connor (ex officio) and Lawrence M. Small (ex officio).

The Andy Warhol Foundation for the Visual Arts has provided generous support for the *Triennial*; we thank Pamela Clapp for her guidance. The Lily Auchincloss Foundation also has supported the *Triennial*; we are grateful to Paul and Alexandra A. Herzan for their vision and friendship. Funds from the Curator's Grant Program of the Peter Norton Family Foundation, awarded to Ellen Lupton in 1997, gave us the crucial first push that launched the exhibition. Additional support was provided by the Graham Foundation for Advanced Studies in the Visual Arts. The book was underwritten by the Andrew W. Mellon Foundation.

This publication reflects the museum's ongoing collaboration with Princeton Architectural Press. Special thanks goes to our editor, Mark Lamster, who challenged us all to write clearly.

The exhibition was designed by Michael Gabellini, who brought his keen eye to the daunting task of displaying contemporary design in the historic Carnegie Mansion. It has been a pleasure to work with him and his staff at Gabellini Associates, especially Jay Boucher, Filipe Pereira, and Fran Puglisi.

The cover of this publication was designed by Karim Rashid, who has brought the book alive as a physical object. We are grateful to him and his colleagues, Harry Chong and Hugh Phear, for their patient collaboration with the National Design Museum and Princeton Architectural Press.

The entire staff of Cooper-Hewitt, National Design Museum participated in the execution of the *Triennial*, and we offer our appreciation to everyone who contributed to the project's content, design, production, administration, development, marketing, maintenance, security, and educational programming. Above all, we are grateful to Dianne H. Pilgrim, who conceived of the *Triennial* and inspired us to take on the daunting task of surveying the vast field of contemporary design.

We also direct special thanks to several key individuals at the museum: Buff Kavelman, Special Projects, Director's Office, for her unflagging efforts with exhibition development; Steven Langehough, Associate Registrar, for organizing the shipping of objects; Barbara Livenstein, Head of Public Information, for her insightful work in promoting the exhibition to the press and public; Mei Mah, Program Coordinator, for conceiving and implementing an exciting array of educational programs; Thomas F. Reynolds of the Director's Office, for researching and writing the designers' biographies; and Susan Yelavich, Assistant Director for Public Programs, for her leadership and editorial contributions. Finally, special thanks goes to Lindsay Stamm Shapiro, Head of Exhibitions, and Jen Roos, Head of Design, along with the museum's full design and exhibitions staff, whose skills and talents helped convert our ideas into a safe, beautiful, and functional environment.

SPECIAL THANKS
FROM DONALD ALBRECHT

Natalie Shivers and Barbara Livenstein were invaluable editors, challenging my thinking, untangling my ideas, and clarifying my writing. The published essays owe a great debt to Mark Lamster, our editor at Princeton Architectural Press. All three prove the adage that books aren't written, they're edited.

Susan Yelavich offered a wise and steady hand throughout the entire project. Buff Kavelman took on the heroic task of raising funds; she also raised spirits with her wonderful humor. Thomas F. Reynolds gave of his time and expert skills. My curatorial assistant, Kristina Kaufman, easily kept the project on track through mountains of detail.

Finally, I thank my friends and family, especially my mother, who once again lived through the process of creating an exhibition.

SPECIAL THANKS
FROM ELLEN LUPTON

My curatorial assistant, Megan Searing, provided research for the book and exhibition; I would never have survived the project without her.

Susan Yelavich, Mark Lamster, and Hilary Strauss are among my most valued colleagues, and I look forward to many future endeavors.

I thank my friend, Jennifer Tobias, for sharing her love and ideas.

My family is a constant source of pleasure and inspiration. My love goes out to Jay, Ruby, and Abbott; to Mary Jane and Ken; to Bill and Shirley; to Michelle and Anwar; and to Julia, Ken, and all their children.

To avoid the appearance of any conflict of interest, I chose not to feature the work of my husband, J. Abbott Miller, in this book or the *National Design Triennial*, but I know that he should be in it.

SPECIAL THANKS
FROM STEVEN SKOV HOLT

I would like to thank my teammates at frog and frog leaders Hartmut Esslinger and Patricia Roller for their unfailing support of my efforts to address issues of culture, design, creativity, media, and technology.

Between 1997 and the present, my deepest beliefs about design were challenged by personal events. In the last two years, my first child was born, and I happily adjusted to parenthood by committing myself to working less but more effectively. During the same period, I was confronted with a series of health conditions that reflect the long-term consequences of living with only one, previously transplanted, kidney. In early 1998, after surviving a systemic viral infection, I went on the national waiting list for a new kidney transplant. Eighteen months later, I am still waiting for an organ to become available.

During this difficult period, I have been graced with extraordinary work and home environments. My colleagues at frog, the California College of Arts and Crafts, and Cooper-Hewitt, National Design Museum have supported me in an unqualified, no-questions-asked manner. On the most intimate and human level, I would like to thank them, my extended family, and especially my wife and partner Mara Holt Skov and my son Larson Burton Beck Michael Hamilton Pantani Skov Holt: she for her strength, understanding, and wisdom, and he for his inspiration, curiosity, and natural joy. Together, we dream a better world.

INTRODUCTION

SUSAN YELAVICH
Assistant Director for Public Programs

Design is that highly specialized realm of human activity that shapes virtually everything in the world. This is the paradox embraced by the Cooper-Hewitt, National Design Museum. Places, products, even cyberspace, virtually the entire spectrum of human production, are expressions of ideas about living—the results of design ideas. *Design Culture Now*, the catalog for the first *National Design Triennial*, is no less ambitious and ecumenical in scope.

The *National Design Triennial* marks the first time that an American museum is committing its energies to identifying designers whose work not only bears the hallmark of excellence, but also reflects the most innovative level of engagement with contemporary culture at large. Three curators representing three broad disciplinary territories have yielded an exponentially magnified view of the role design has played in the world over the past three years. Exploratory by nature, the projects featured here also map out new ways in which design will shape the future. Whether realized or speculative, the projects displayed here are fundamentally connected to the way people live.

Donald Albrecht, the museum's Adjunct Curator for Special Projects, canvassed the realm of architecture, landscape architecture, and environmental design. Ellen Lupton, the museum's Adjunct Curator of Contemporary Design, surveyed the fields of graphic design and new media. Steven Skov Holt, design visionary at frogdesign in San Francisco, California, reviewed the fields of product design and new media, lending a voice that complements and extends the perspective of the museum's team.

From their bicoastal bases, the trio fanned out across the country and the Internet in search of the work that defines the last moments of the twentieth century and the first moments of the twenty-first. After bringing their nominations to the table, they reviewed each other's selections and hammered out an organizational structure and a final list of participants. Their survey of the work produced in this country (citizenship was not a criterion) over the past three years yielded neither a singular conclusion nor a trinity of trends, but a "dictionary of ideas" that cuts across the disciplines of design.

The work gathered here bears witness to the fact that the boundaries between architecture, products, and graphics are eroding in this dynamic period of cross-fertilization. Buildings—often developed with the same software used to create products—are designed to be flexible, adaptable, customized, and contextualized. Graphics are becoming increasingly dimensional with architectural systems of their own. Products are both material and immaterial as they become smarter and more interactive, seamlessly integrating themselves into the environments that host them.

Taking their cues from this liberal climate of design practice, the curators devised a synthetic approach to their task. The exhibition and book both foreground the individual designers and firms—that is, after all, the main task of a triennial—and positions them within a context of ideas. The entries in this new lexicon—FLUID, PHYSCIAL, MINIMAL, RECLAIMED, LOCAL, BRANDED, NARRATIVE, UNBELIEVABLE—embody the force field of contemporary practice. Albrecht, Lupton, and Holt describe an energized cultural environment that exerts the pull of popular appetites and provides the push to move beyond the predictable nature of the marketplace. We are offered a composite portrait of design that thrives on the tension of polarities.

It is tempting to parse the categories along conventional lines of function and form. It is possible to argue that when designers are involved in branding, constructing narrative, reclaiming territory and memory, and celebrating the local, they are privileging the purposeful role of design in the broadest sense. On the other hand, designers who are chiefly engaged in the exploration of the minimal, the physical, the fluid, and the unbelievable, are on the front lines of formal and aesthetic investigation.

This line of reasoning, while not totally without basis, breaks down in the face of the work presented here. GREG LYNN's fluid structures respond to practical conditions of sunlight and temperature at the same time that they represent a new vocabulary of architectural form. MARTHA STEWART's branding success, highly directed and purposeful, depends on an aesthetic vocabulary of color and proportion. CONSTANTIN BOYM AND LAURENE LEON BOYM's reclaimed furniture converts and recycles the most ordinary and utilitarian of materials into elegant articulations of form and space.

For today's designers, the tensions between remembrance and imagination, between our attachments to the past and our need to formulate the future are more interesting than conventional form and function polarities. The century born so violently that it tried to banish evidence of history in the design of its buildings and appliances, its billboards and books, is ending with a more nuanced understanding of the essential role of memory. The designers here engage with history conceptually—building on it rather than eradicating it.

Styles and ideologies are understood as part of the collective frame of reference, which now also embraces the immediacy of the everyday and the personal. The culture wars of the 1980s and 1990s (an arguably healthy phase in the evolution of American democracy) have subverted monolithic ideas of the consumer and the audience in favor of the multicultural. Hierarchies of taste and the directional flow of ideas have become inverted, subverted, and congenitally convoluted, giving designers a richer gene pool from which to spec their products' DNA.

At the same time, developments in technology have aided and abetted (if not instigated) the evolution of cultural pluralism into niche marketing. The arrival of e-commerce has spawned companies whose core business is based on tracking consumer preferences. We are at the threshold of customization-on-demand as microscopic digital servants swiftly respond to changing conditions and appetites. It remains to be seen, however, if this new democratic model of capitalism will prove to be as socially beneficial as it is economically successful. For the time being, it seems that the divide between consumer and producer is atomizing into a millennial vapor: Consumers 'R Us.

All of this emphasis on the personal and the particular has not been lost on designers. However, instead of becoming slaves to consumer preferences, they are reinvesting value in their own personal passions. It is possible to speak of beauty and not be vain. It is possible to put the consumer first without sacrificing design expression.

The pleasure principle has new legitimacy among designers—not the narcissistic pleasure of the isolated, but the generous pleasure of the engaged. For above and beyond their celebrated individual differences, the designers in the *National Design Triennial* share a common understanding of their work as events, places, or things imbedded in an ecology of experience with all the environmental consequences entailed. *Design Culture Now* celebrates the ways in which designers contribute to our collective pleasure in the world, while at the same time sustaining their spirits and keeping their souls with a particularity of vision that sharpens our own.

collage and transformation

DONALD ALBRECHT

BUILDING CULTURE NOW

A FASCINATION WITH THE HYBRID links the architects, landscape architects, set designers, and exhibition designers in *Design Culture Now*. Indeed, the multifaceted careers of today's design professionals combine theory and practice while blurring boundaries between once autonomous arts. Projects as diverse as a casino with a Native-American theme, an acid-mine reclamation landscape, and the sets for the film *Titus* all find designers crossing over from one discipline to another, operating in territories that would have once been considered foreign or taboo. Thematically and visually complex, these projects enrich the formal components of design with references to natural history, high art, popular culture, and historical events. Are DAVID ROCKWELL's interiors architecture or theater? Are RALPH APPELBAUM's exhibitions education or entertainment? Is JULIE TAYMOR's work avant-garde or mass-market? Are her references Western or Eastern? Is she a costume designer, a mask maker, or a theater director? *Design Culture Now* asserts that there are no right answers to these questions.

The interdisciplinary approach these designers' careers follow reflects our time's increasingly crossbred culture. Consider a few events from the latter half of 1999. Donna Karan and British clothing designer Nicole Farhi opened Manhattan megastores that mixed their own fashions with other people's furnishings, trinkets, and foods. (The Farhi store was designed by MICHAEL GABELLINI.) Editor Tina Brown launched *Talk* magazine, a synergistic collaboration of Hearst and Miramax that is in part a literary testing ground for potential film projects. The entertainment industry further morphed into one media landscape encompassing film, television, video, and computer technology with the announcement that Metafilmics will produce one of the first movies created by an established filmmaker for initial distribution on the Internet.

The *Triennial*'s participants rely on a range of strategies—from collage to mutation—for construction of this contemporary hybrid. In collage, discrete elements remain visually distinct. The juxtaposition and overlap of individual parts spur fresh insight. Mutations fuse discrete elements into new entities. In the process of becoming something else, forms meld to assume identities that bear few traces of their constituent parts. Mutations are agents of change; their transformations suggest latent possibilities.

The architects RICHARD GLUCKMAN, MICHAEL GABELLINI, and WALTER HOOD demonstrate the strategy of collage in urban ensembles that knit together old and new. These architects believe that the past is a living part of the present but reject the postmodern device of historicist cosmetic reference. Hood's Macon Yards in Georgia, for example, is a hybrid landscape that reclaims and incorporates evidence of the town square's physical, cultural, and social histories into what Hood calls a "multirhythmic composition." Gabellini and Gluckman are stretching the contemporary hybrid across different disciplines, from interior design to city planning, and juxtaposing references as diverse as minimalist sculpture and cast-iron construction, sixteenth-century Italian urbanism and postwar American architecture.

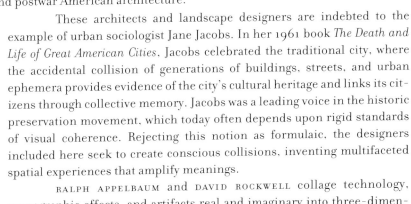

These architects and landscape designers are indebted to the example of urban sociologist Jane Jacobs. In her 1961 book *The Death and Life of Great American Cities*, Jacobs celebrated the traditional city, where the accidental collision of generations of buildings, streets, and urban ephemera provides evidence of the city's cultural heritage and links its citizens through collective memory. Jacobs was a leading voice in the historic preservation movement, which today often depends upon rigid standards of visual coherence. Rejecting this notion as formulaic, the designers included here seek to create conscious collisions, inventing multifaceted spatial experiences that amplify meanings.

RALPH APPELBAUM and DAVID ROCKWELL collage technology, scenographic effects, and artifacts real and imaginary into three-dimensional, immersive environments. Appelbaum's exhibitions and Rockwell's themed venues relate stories about history, science, and nature, often transcending the circumstances of time and place to convey larger messages about people's everyday lives. Their work reflects the power of the moving image. Rockwell conceives his interiors as cinematic scenarios to be viscerally experienced rather than static forms for passive visual pleasure. Appelbaum incorporates films, videos, and computer software as educational media throughout his exhibitions.

Architects NEIL M. DENARI and REINHOLD MARTIN AND KADAMBARI BAXI also share an interest in the movies—particularly the avant-garde cinema of the 1960s. Films such as Michelangelo Antonioni's *Blow-Up* (1967) and Orson Welles's *The Trial* (1963) appeal to these architects' concern for the open-ended and speculative. Jean-Luc Godard's *Alphaville* (1965) represents their critical approach to the future and technology—a theme evidenced in the work of LEBBEUS WOODS, who served as concept designer for the film *Alien3* (1992) as well as architect for an upcoming exhibition on the future of civilization.

HERMITAGE PERFORMANCE SPACE
Eindhoven, The Netherlands
Photograph, 1998
Architect: Lebbeus Woods

The contemporary influence of movies is part of a larger movement preoccupied with the everyday. In their fascination with vernacular architecture, today's designers are typically American. Without an elite, aristocratic tradition in design and the arts, American architects and artists have often looked to the everyday to express the country's egalitarianism. Painter Charles Sheeler celebrated the power and precision of factories, Edward Ruscha devoted whole books to gas stations and Los Angeles apartments, and FRANK O. GEHRY elevated chain-link fencing to new expressive heights in his own house in Santa Monica, California. Gehry's 1996 proposal to clad One Times Square in billowing, translucent metallic fabric is an update of this ground-breaking work.

What makes the younger *Triennial* participants unique is their interest in the ordinary architecture of postwar America—its office buildings, sports clubs, and tract housing. "As architectural fashion has freed itself from the dictates of the modernist canon and the ironies of postmodernism," historian Gwendolyn Wright recently noted, "scholarship has converged around the theme of 'everyday life'."[1] PAUL LEWIS, MARC TSURUMAKI, AND DAVID J. LEWIS, for example, provoke viewers' perceptions through a radical juxtaposition of the everyday and the strange, the rational and the irrational, the mundane and the spectacular.

In contrast to the collage approach, the architects GREG LYNN as well as SULAN KOLATAN AND WILLIAM MAC DONALD subsume individual components into new mutated forms. Inspired by the chimera, a mythological beast that is part lion, part goat, and part snake, Kolatan and Mac Donald's structures morph from the straight-edged and conventional into the fluid and experimental as they explore new domestic typologies. At the edge of theory and practice, Greg Lynn inputs mathematical coordinates and other data drawn from nontraditional contextual elements (such as local traffic patterns) to generate his designs. His Presbyterian Church of New York in Queens, commissioned by a Korean-American congregation and designed with Douglas Garofalo and Michael McInturf, features undulating forms that grow out of the structure of an abandoned factory. Defying architecture's traditional role as a metaphor for permanence and stability, the buildings created by these designers make analogies to transience, change, and the mutable body. Not unlike plastic surgeons who sculpt the human form, filmmakers who digitize it, and geneticists who try to clone it, these architects see exciting possibilities in the modern capacity to reconfigure identity and the self.

Between collage and mutation is an approach that fuses architecture, landscape architecture, and geology. MARION WEISS AND MICHAEL A. MANFREDI's Museum of the Earth, in Ithaca, New York, engages the glacial landforms of the Finger Lakes Region, merging building and topology to create an organic exhibition experience. Phoenix-based architects WENDELL BURNETT and MARWAN AL-SAYED create houses that combine the ancient traditions of adobe construction with twentieth-century features such as reflective finishes, tensile roofs, and lap pools. These architects often regard their projects as earthworks in the spirit of such land artists as Robert Smithson and James Turrell, underscoring today's interest in creating hybrids of art and architecture. And in the kitsch landscape of Las Vegas, GARY LLOYD's sky paintings are inspired by the perceptual explorations of conceptual artist Robert Irwin.

Whether collage, mutation, or a combination of the two, the hybrid approach employed by the architects, landscape architects, and designers in this book and the exhibition it accompanies shares an affinity with the work of Charles and Ray Eames. Their collagist sensibility fused old and new, foreign and familiar, in the process helping people to see beauty in the everyday. Their influence resonates in the work of the *Triennial* participants, who provoke fresh perceptions and unexpected connections, and contribute to our understanding of architecture and design as complex social and cultural activities.

HOUSINGS
Digital renderings, 1999
Architect: Kolatan/Mac Donald Studio

1. Gwendolyn Wright, "A Little Respect Please, for the Dream House," *The New York Times*, 7 February 1999, 33, 37.

fluid mechanics

ELLEN LUPTON

TYPOGRAPHIC CULTURE NOW

Fashion is another
art where soft materials
confront skeletal
structures.
GEOFFREY BEENE
uses spiralling planes
of fabric to both
reveal and contradict
the symmetrical
mechanics of shoulder,
spine, and limb.

LIQUIDITY, SATURATION, AND OVERFLOW are words that describe the information surplus that besets us at the start of the twenty-first century. Images proliferate in this media-rich environment, and so too does the written word. Far from diminishing in influence, text has continued to expand its power and pervasiveness. The visual expression of language has grown increasingly diverse, as new fonts and formats evolve to accommodate the relentless display of the word.

Typography is the art of designing letterforms and arranging them in space and time. Since its invention during the Renaissance, typography has been animated by the conflict between fixed architectural elements—such as the page and its margins—and the fluid substance of written words. Evolutions in the life of the letter arise from dialogs between wet and dry, soft and hard, slack and taut, amorphous and geometric, ragged and flush, planned and unpredicted. With unprecedented force, these conflicts are driving typographic innovation today. Typography is going under water as designers submerge themselves in the textures and transitions that bond letter, word, and surface. As rigid formats become open and pliant, the architectural hardware of typographic systems is melting down.

The flush, full page of the classical book is dominated by a single block of justified text, its characters mechanically spaced to completely occupy the designated volume. The page is like a glass into which text is poured, spilling over from one leaf to the next. By the early twentieth century, the classical page had given way to the multicolumned, mixed-media structures of the modern newspaper, magazine, and illustrated book.

Today, the simultaneity of diverse content streams is a given. Alongside the archetype of the printed page, the new digital archetype of the window has taken hold. The window is a scrolling surface of unlimited length, whose width adjusts at the will of reader or writer. In both print and digital media, graphic designers devise ways to navigate bodies of information by exploring the structural possibilities of pages and windows, boxes and frames, edges and margins.

In 1978, Nicholas Negroponte and Muriel Cooper, working at MIT's Media Lab, published a seminal essay on the notion of "soft copy," the linguistic raw material of the digital age.[1] The bastard offspring of hard copy, soft text lacks a fixed typographic identity. Owing allegiance to no font or format, it is willingly pasted, pirated, output, or repurposed in countless contexts. It is the ubiquitous medium of word-processing, desk-top publishing, e-mail, and the Internet.

1. Nicholas Negroponte and Muriel Cooper's text "Books without Pages" is cited in DAVID SMALL, "Rethinking the Book," doctoral dissertation, Massachusetts Institute of Technology, 1999.

broken windows

The finely detailed
typographic pages created by
JENNIFER STERLING
and
STEPHEN FARRELL
are hard to imagine
without the
typographic control
enabled by soft copy.

THE BURGEONING of soft copy had an enormous impact on graphic design in the 1980s and 1990s. In design for print, soft copy largely eliminated the mediation of the typesetter, the technician previously charged with converting the manuscript—which had been painstakingly marked up by hand with instructions from the designer—into galleys, or formal pages of type.

Soft copy flows directly to designers in digital form from authors and editors. The designer is free to directly manipulate the text—without relying on the typesetter—and to adjust typographic details up to the final moments of production. The soft copy revolution led designers to plunge from an objective aerial view into the moving waters of text, where they shape it from within.

Digital media enable both users and producers, readers and writers, to regulate the flow of language. As with design for print, the goal of interactive typography is to create "architectural" structures that accommodate the organic stream of text. But in the digital realm, these structures—and the content they support—have the possibility of continuous transformation.

In their essay about soft copy, Negroponte and Cooper predicted the evolution of digital interfaces that would allow typography to transform its size, shape, and color. Muriel Cooper (1925–1994) went on to develop the idea of the three-dimensional "information landscape," a model that breaks through the window frames that dominate electronic interfaces.

DAVID SMALL was among Muriel Cooper's most gifted students. He describes his hyper-linked textual landscapes: "The vision is one of an organic, reactive construct that supports both amorphous, liquid typographic forms and more rational, architectural mechanisms."
    Gigi Biederman and David Karam (POST TOOL) construct digital environments inhabited by animated letters.

SHEILA LEVRANT DE BRETTEVILLE and BJ KRIVANEK have put text into built environments, making metaphors of typographic architecture and landscape concrete.

The typeface Filosofia, designed by ZUZANA LICKO in 1996, is based on the eighteenth-century typefaces Didot and Bodoni, whose sparkling, crystalline quality results from the extreme contrast between thick and thin elements.

TIMELESS
OR
TIME & 1/2
TIME FUTURE
IS TIME PRESENT
IS TIMEPAST
IS TIME PRESENT
TIME WORN
TIMEWORN
TIME LESSEN

ED FELLA manipulates letterforms by hand. Above, he distorts the neoclassical font Bodoni by burdening it with heavy, blotchy marks.

The typeface Volgare (1996), designed by STEPHEN FARRELL, is based on a Renaissance script. It simulates the clotted flow of ink from a pen.

We can make a hand speak in a language it never knew. We can

7

liquid crystals

VIEWED FROM A DISTANCE, a field of text is a block of gray. But when one comes in close to read, the individual characters predominate over the field. Text is a body of separate objects that move together as a mass, like cars in a flow of traffic or individuals in a crowd. Text is a fluid made from the hard, dry crystals of the alphabet.

Typeface designs in the Renaissance reflected the curving lines of handwriting, formed by ink flowing from the rigid nib of a pen. The cast metal types used for printing converted these organic sources into fixed, reproducible artifacts. As the printed book became the world's dominant information medium, the design of typefaces grew ever more abstract and formalized, distanced from the liquid hand. Today, designers look back at the systematic, abstracting tendencies of modern letter design and both celebrate and challenge that rationalizing impulse. They have exchanged the anthracite deposits of the classical letter for lines of text that quiver and bleed like living things.

The distinctive use of type, which can endow a long or complex document with a sense of unified personality or behavior, also builds the identity of brands and institutions. BRUCE MAU has described identity design as a "life problem," arguing that the visual expression of a company or product should appear like a frame taken from a system in motion.

JOHN MAEDA uses text as texture, creating fields of characters that are a soft veil of gray.

MARTIN VENEZKY submits his type to bodily mutilations, treating letters as physical objects.

STEFAN SAGMEISTER generates text by hand, writing on the surface of the body, treating letters as a form of life.

KYLE COOPER'S film titles make written words seem menacingly alive.

LAURIE HAYCOCK MAKELA has described typography as the "blood" of an identity program, which flows through everything an organization publishes and displays.

MARTHA STEWART'S enormously successful brand is expressed with crisp sans serif letterforms that organically overlap.

surface tensions

THE FLAT OPACITY of the printed page has been challenged by graphic designers who use image manipulation software to embed the word within the surface of the photographic image. A pioneer of such effects in the digital realm was P. SCOTT MAKELA (1960–1999). In the early 1990s, he began using PhotoShop, a software tool that had just been introduced, as a creative medium. In his designs for print and multimedia, type and image merge in dizzying swells and eddies as letters bulge, buckle, and morph. The techniques he helped forge have become part of the fundamental language of graphic design. The linear forms of typography have become planar surfaces, skimming across and below the pixelated skin of the image.

PABLO MEDINA designs digital typefaces based on the hand-painted signs he finds in Latino neighborhoods.

PETER GIRARDI litters his Web sites with "funny garbage," making the digital world look as dirty as the real one.

CHRIS WARE dredges up the typographic culture of old magazines and mail order catalogs in order to surround his comic narratives with a manic excess of textual detail.

REBECA MENDEZ assembles diaphanous veils of image and text in her designs for books, posters, and architectural murals.

The posters and music packaging of ART CHANTRY are pieced together from visual refuse—scraps of newspaper, old book covers, faded wallpaper.

polluted waters

THE ALPHABET is an ancient form that is deeply embedded in the mental hardware of readers. Graphic designers always ground their work, to some degree, in historic precedent, tapping the familiarity of existing symbols and styles even as they invent new idioms. While some designers pay their toll to history with reluctance, others dive eagerly into the reservoirs of pop culture. Tibor Kalman (1949–1999) led the graphic design world's reclamation of visual detritus, borrowing from the commonplace vernacular of mail-order stationery and do-it-yourself signage. Designers now frankly embrace the humor and directness of everyday artifacts. In the aesthetic realm as in the economic one, pollution is a natural resource—one that is expanding rather than shrinking away.

The work of ALEXANDER GELMAN looks impossibly clean, yet its power lies in its direct link to the clichés and iconography of popular culture.

ERIK ADIGARD AND PATRICIA MCSHANE mix high technology with popular culture, creating Web sites and magazine pages that turn philosophical ideas into billboards and slogans. One sample of freeze-frame theory proclaims, "Pollution is a form of inefficiency, and inefficiency is lost profit."

solvents and solutions

THIRTY YEARS AGO, progressive design-ers often described their mission as "problem-solving." They aimed to iden-tify the functional requirements of a pro-ject and then discover the appropriate means to satisfy the brief. Today, it is more illuminating to speak of solvents than solutions. Design is often an attack on structure, or an attempt to create edi-fices that can withstand and engage the corrosive assault of content.

The clean, smooth surfaces of modernism proved an unsound fortress against popular culture, which is now invited inside to fuel the creation of new work. Image and text eat away at the vessels that would seal them shut. Forms that are hard and sharp now appear only temporarily so, ready to melt, like ice, in response to small environmental changes. All systems leak, and all waters are contam-inated, not only with foreign matter but with bits of structure itself. A fluid, by definition, is a substance that conforms to the outline of its container. Today, containers reconfigure in response to the matter they hold.

ISBN 1-56898-2

9 781568 98

beauty and the **blob** PRODUCT CULTURE NOW

WE INHABIT A TIME WHEN OBJECTS, and even images of objects, hold great sway. We have come to apotheosize all manner of consumer goods, and in the process we have created a society in which anything and everything is a product. The active consumption of products has itself become almost religious, part considered ritual and part spontaneous spectacle of existence. At the same time, those very products with the longest histories—the solid things considered the economic bedrock of the most powerful nation of the twentieth century—have evolved, mutated, shrunk, and even vanished into thin air. The need to physically travel by car, for example, has given way to the virtual presence provided by products ranging from the ubiquitous fax machines, pagers, and cell phones of today to the ascendent video conferencing systems, electronic agents, and personal digital assistants of the near future. Whole new species of products have appeared, the result of pop culture's mainline connection to a re-energized material sense of well-being.

Not surprisingly, our definition of what constitutes a product has expanded as well. In fact, products have changed more rapidly during the last three years than at any other time in American history. Did you have e-mail or a Web site at the end of 1996? Perhaps. Were you downloading MP-3 digital music three years ago? Almost certainly not. Products have become more than mere commercial goods. Today, we not only understand products tangibly, but experience them systemically.

It is an appropriate time, therefore, to look back on the "productized" output of American culture during the final years of the twentieth century—not just to draw out exemplars of creativity, but to consider the messages products deliver about our society and this particular cultural moment. We know, for example, that media-constructed, product-centric versions of the good life command an ever-increasing portion of our conscious mind. Over time, they accrete. They come to exert a psychic, unspoken level of pressure and expectation on all of us. The quest for material gain is the foundation upon which the American economy is now being built, and the troubling cycle of manufactured desire and requisite consumption driven by this reality has given product designers the greatest creative challenge in the profession's history.

21

That challenge is to balance competing demands in a way that they have never been balanced before. The commercial must be weighed against the ecological. The needs of the client must be weighed against the needs of the consumer. The urge for self-expression must be weighed against the possibility of communicating to a mass audience. Truth be told, it is not enough for the new generation of designers to weigh these options one against another, for that is already old thinking. Instead, the challenge is to bring all of these previously competing elements together into a larger, more synergistic whole. Designers have bigger, more complex problems to solve than ever before, and to solve them practitioners will have to be bolder, more courageous, and less willing to accept business-as-usual in any of its myriad guises.

Enormous opportunities for the design profession are being driven by the possibility to meaningfully combine features, objects, materials, technologies, and ideas previously considered to be separate. There are more new unions of content and commerce than at any other point in history. E-commerce is driving a whole new generation of design, and e-design is changing the world of products as we know it. As combinatory thinking becomes the new norm, design—an intrinsically hybrid practice merging the conflicting needs of art, business, and engineering—will be on its way toward total infiltration of human environments.

We are at a point in history where we can not comfortably define ourselves without the presence of products. Products help us feel more like who we believe we are, who we would like to be, and who we would like other people to think that we already are. To a large degree, we are that certain, unique combination of car, watch, sunglasses, shoes, jewelry, and whatever else we choose. On one level, such products represent the manifestation of our personal brand. On another level, they help us feel special, as if we matter. And on yet another level, they attempt to compensate for what in fact can never be compensated for—enduring feelings of inadequacy, inferiority, and an insatiable desire to belong. Designers must realize that they are complicit in this highly considered cult of consumerist experience. Perhaps the most significant challenge for today's designers is to create an atmosphere that is less about the rampant acquisition of objects and more about the possibilities that those objects present.

By creating things that people touch, and are touched by, every day, the industrial designer is becoming a new kind of hero for our time. When I became editor of *I.D.* magazine in 1983, we could barely give away ad space. But that same year the economy began to pick up, cable TV started to take hold, and graphically challenging networks such as ESPN and MTV started to assume prominence. Soon enough design was a matter of national interest, and industrial design was seen as a potential curative for a host of problems—aesthetic, financial, functional, and otherwise.

Coverage of design began to appear in the papers of record, most notably in a "Form and Function" column in the *Wall Street Journal* and in the Home and Style sections of *The New York Times*. By the late 1980s, the Industrial

Designers Society of America was annually highlighting its achievements in *BusinessWeek* in an effort to create new ways of thinking about the intersection of design and commerce. Design is also becoming ever more entwined with the electronic media. By this metric, one of 1999's pinnacle moments occurred when IDEO, a design firm represented in the Triennial, was featured as the subject of an episode of ABC's *Nightline* news program.

Despite its success, industrial design has largely failed to reach out beyond its base audience of white, middle-class males. Women, minorities, children, and the elderly have been overlooked. The profession is dominated by white male practitioners, a fact that reflects the failure of the educational system to recognize design as an area of cultural inquiry. This failure is evident both in our elementary schools and in our most ivy-clad halls. Only a handful of institutions offer classes in design—how inappropriate and ill-considered this seems at the end of the most product-intensive century in history!

There is, nonetheless, great cause for optimism. Driven by the possibilities presented by the computer, designers are in a period of unprecedented opportunity. Products have been liberated by flexible, ever-shrinking, and ever-more-powerful system-on-a-chip solutions. Materials and shapes that were inconceivable only a few years ago have become routine. Advances in tooling, manufacturing, and computer-aided software have given the designer new ways to create organic forms. Even those products that remain impossible to physically model can be virtually realized in the digital world.

Product design has been further vitalized by the astonishing development of the Internet—a participatory ecosystem replete with its own rapidly evolving digital flora and fauna. The Internet is built on the overlapping promises of near-instant communication, relationship building, pattern-based thinking, and interactive experience. The implication is clear: the Internet is first and foremost a design event. The American nation—physically fragmented into a series of micro-cultures and macro-factions—has reunited in cyberspace in the form of buddy lists, chat rooms, special interest groups, instant messages, and portal communities. The new generation of simple, smart products just emerging is symbolic of design's new frontier. Design has moved past the mere making of objects into the realm of collaboration and intellectual creativity. The Web now serves as the twentieth century's most potent symbol of how the world might yet come together willingly and peacefully in a shared realm.

Meanwhile, the old model of the designer as the singular creator of discrete objects has been supplanted by a new vision of the design professional as orchestrator of complex systems in which information, materials, sensation, and technology are in a state of flux. Design is now best understood as a team sport. What was a rarity just a few years ago—a multitasked, multidisciplinary project bringing together print, virtual, and environmental aspects of brand, media, and product—is fast becoming the norm. If anything, the need for innovation is pushing designers into the next evolution of the profession, one likely to involve trans- or extra-disciplinary creativity.

Products have become containers for stories, and designers have correspondingly become storytellers and even mythmakers. This focus on the narrative component of design has itself led to a search through both design history and material culture for elements of our physical vocabulary that can be called upon anew. Even as we have been bombarded by news, information, and an ascending cascade of consumer goods, we have seen a corresponding rise in our collective penchant for nostalgia. This has manifested itself in a surge of retro-futuristic solutions that manage to look familiar at the same time that they appear different. The exuberant forms of the 1950s, for example, have been mined for their symbolic riches. Strange time loops keep bringing back long-abandoned images, objects, and celebrities. The result is a hybrid moment where it appears easier to edit and recombine what already exists than it does to create something completely new. The sampling strategy so evident in hip-hop music provides a powerful model for all forms of design creativity, especially in consumer goods, where positive historical associations are cherished.

The free-flowing, retro-futuristic product aesthetics that have emerged over the past few years reflect both the fluidity of the design profession and the liquidity of our particular cultural moment. We are, after all, a nation of dynamists, always off somewhere in search of ourselves. Americans move about constantly—and so do the best shapes that our designers create. We are in the closing years of the Age of the Blobject, a period that began in the 1980s, when everything from the Ford Taurus to the Sony Walkman to the Tylenol caplet was designed with curved contours and swoopy silhouettes.

Since then, blobjects, along with accepted standards for good design, have become more visually evolved. In the same way that the first generation of professional industrial design pioneers, in the 1930s, focused on streamlining objects ranging from pencil sharpeners to cruise boats, the designers represented in this book are hyper-streamlining everything from motorcycles and hairbrushes to sunglasses and computers. Everything looks fast, organic, and momentary. A new-found beauty is emerging. Even as we have become a culture of products, we have found that products no longer need to be physical. Technological components will continue to shrink and become more transparent, and will soon entirely recede from view. The relevance of time, place, and space have shifted.

A cascade of goods overflows our imaginations with choices and pseudochoices. Products flood our stores and our landfills, and overwhelm our sense of what is possible. Our economy of excess simultaneously attracts and repulses. Increasingly, designers are expanding their roles to accommodate the contradictions of this economy, becoming anthropologists, psychologists, philosophers, and clairvoyants. Product designers have the ability to peer into the souls of both physical objects and the consumers that use them. Can we survive our success at consumerizing our culture and productizing our profession? Strangely, and yet somehow appropriately, the answer lies most directly in the hands of this generation's practitioners—those who will be generating this culture will be in the best position to ameliorate it.

ISBN 1-56898-15-1
55000
9 781568 982151
8 982151

This book is organized as a "dictionary
of ideas" that cuts across the many
disciplines of design today. This strategy
has allowed us to juxtapose work
produced in divergent contexts: a typeface can be seen in relation to a building,
and a chair can be viewed in proximity
to a poster or Web site.

Our dictionary proposes an open-
ended vocabulary of issues, themes, and
concepts that are shared among many
of the designers featured in the project.
Thus a designer might be presented in
a section that focuses on BRANDING, and
yet produce work that also incorporates
ideas of the PHYSICAL or the FLUID.

The roster of designers assembled
in this volume was mutually agreed upon
by the three authors, though we each
brought strong opinions to the table.
To indicate the voice behind each entry,
we have signed the following essays
with our initials.

DONALD ALBRECHT
ELLEN LUPTON
STEVEN SKOV HOLT

ISBN 1-56898

9 781568 9

fluid

Structure and surface are merging in design today. The creation of objects, buildings, and interiors consisting of complex three-dimensional curves has been enabled by advances in computer-aided design, tooling, and manufacturing. Designers are conceiving of form organically, generating fluid surfaces in place of rigid structures. Letterforms and text have become liquid materials that flow through and around such structural features as the grid of a book or the interface of a Web site. The designer has become an orchestrator of environments and experiences where materials, light, information, and imagery are in a state of flux, engaging the audience in active and intuitive ways.

TIM PARSEY B. 1960
PETER PFANNER B. 1959
TIM McKEOWN B. 1963
SCOTT WILSON B. 1969
AND TEAM

ACCO BRANDS
Lincolnshire, Illinois

ACCO's in-house-designed Swingline staplers show that even the most familiar product can be reinterpreted. Who would have thought a stapler could look good, let alone feel good? Gone are the sharp edges, the stock metal colors, and the preconceptions entrenched in the original design. The one-size-fits-all stapler has evolved into a product available in a multitude of sizes, colors, and capabilities. What once was a perfectly banal desk icon for the Organization Man has been personalized—choice has come to the desktop.

ACCO's turn-around began in 1996 with the arrival of Tim Parsey, who recruited several high-caliber design managers, including Peter Pfanner, Tim McKeown, and Scott Wilson. Pfanner lead the effort on the ground-breaking Worx "personal stapler" (1997) with London-based design consultant Ross Lovegrove.

The launch of the Worx stapler set a design standard for the company, demonstrating that office products could become alluring objects. In 1998, ACCO developed a second generation of the Worx that moved even farther away from the original's folded-metal method of fabrication.

Certain elements carried over to the Contura (1998), particularly the push for sculptural form. Thumb indentations similar to those on the underside of the Worx were also molded into the Contura. Both models were given a bright cap to dramatize the spot where the stapling action takes place. The Contura also subtly recessed the Swingline logo into its soft plastic housing. Last but not least, the Contura stands up instead of lying down, cutting a sweet profile and making the object easier to pick up. As Parsey states, "We wanted to make something that works the way that someone wants to use it."

SWINGLINE WORX
Mini stapler, 1999, injection-molded clear ABS and injection-molded PVC
Designer: Scott Wilson
Manufacturer: TSI Manufacturing for ACCO Brands
Engineers: Jim Steger and Mike Anguiano

The Worx and Contura staplers are futuristic while connecting to their forebears. Neither the staple nor the hand has changed much over the past few decades. As a result, both new and historical design solutions operate on the same principle—hand pressure. The Worx and Contura staplers satisfy what design pioneer Raymond Loewy dubbed the "MAYA Principle"—they are the "most advanced yet acceptable" designs.

Parsey created a visually rich studio environment where his design team could be surrounded by their models, product ideas, and research materials (including three composite consumers: six-year-old Danielle, teenager John, and twenty-one-year-old Philip). The result is a design group that feels it is fighting for a worthy cause—that those FLUID curves have a justification in user behavior. S.S.H.

SWINGLINE BLADE STAPLE-REMOVER AND HEAVY-DUTY STAPLE REMOVER
Staple removers, 1998, stamped cold-rolled steel and die-cast zinc
Designer: Scott Wilson
Engineers: Steve Berry and Mike Anguiano
Manufacturer: ACCO Brands

SWINGLINE CONTURA
Full-size stapler, 1998, injection over-molded, Santoprene over glass-filled nylon, and progressive die-metal stamping for mechanism
Designer: Scott Wilson
Manufacturer: ACCO Brands
Engineers: Sumir Kapur and Steve Berry

APPLE COMPUTER
Cupertino, California

Apple's compelling design heritage dates to the earliest days of its existence, when company co-founder Steven Jobs pushed the firm to create appealing, user friendly machines. Although Jobs was forced out in 1986, he returned in 1997 to reinvigorate Apple's industrial design team and pioneer a new product language with the trend-setting iMac, iBook, and G3 workstation designs (1999).

As a design statement, the egg-shaped iMac speaks volumes. After years of failed attempts to bring color and creative form to computing, Apple achieved what its competitors could not, shocking an industry consumed by technical performance. The iMac was a financial success (it sold eight-hundred-thousand units in its first year), reviving Apple. Its effect on the computing industry has been gigantic, forcing other manufacturers to rethink the nature and look of personal computing.

The iBook takes the iMac a step farther. Available in "blueberry" and "tangerine" (the iMac comes in five fruity colors), the iBook is portable and wireless. It was Jobs's insight to create a Powerbook for the backpack instead of the briefcase, but it was the industrial design team, working with Apple's hardware and software engineers, that pioneered and gave logic to the latchless close, pulsing indicator light, underside power-cord holder, molded, rubberized finish, and superstrong polycarbonate plastic housing.

Prominent handles distinguish Apple's machines. The iMac's handle makes a great ovoid gesture; in the G3 the four corners become handles; and in the iBook the handle essentially defines the product. In each case, the handle figuratively grounds the machine and calls attention to its physicality.

iMAC
Computer, 1999, translucent
plastic and rubber
Designer: Apple Industrial
Design Team
Manufacturer: Apple

While Apple has always had visionary ideas, the company's design team has closed the gap between what is conceptually possible and what can actually be realized. The iMac, iBook, and G3 have unfailingly FLUID designs. Each represents the best of what design can offer: optimism, humor, and the unleashing of the imagination. While its competitors may still be more profitable, Apple remains unparalleled in its ability to design a total user experience. Apple is the taste-maker of the computing industry, and it is moving in a most-welcome and long-overdue post-beige direction. s.s.h.

iBOOK
Computer, 1999, translucent
plastic and rubber
Designer: Apple Industrial
Design Team
Manufacturer: Apple

G3 TOWER
Computer, 1999, translucent
plastic and rubber
Designer: Apple Industrial
Design Team
Manufacturer: Apple

ERIC CHAN B.1952

ECCO
New York City

The work of Eric Chan and his product design consultancy ECCO is best characterized by its sensual physicality and a highly refined material sensibility. These are not new concerns for Chan, but represent a return to familiar territory that still holds strong appeal. Chan's 1990 design for a soft telephone covered in Santoprene, a thermoplastic rubber, and shaped in a wave-like form prefigures the FLUID organicism found in much of his work now.

ECCO's For Women Only line of semi-transparent plastic hairbrushes (1997) brought high design to a humble product at a modest price (approximately $7). The brushes pioneered the use of translucent textured plastic in mass-produced products, anticipating a dominant design direction of the late 1990s. Their continuous spiraling form provides a clever transition between the handle and the head—

it appears as if the handle was given an elegant half-turn while the plastic was still warm. Organically-shaped and comfortable in the hand, Chan's plastic form evokes natural elements such as flowing water, rounded beach pebbles, and translucent crystals.

A similar concern for translucency is evident in ECCO's Vista, a battery-operated pencil sharpener (1998). Again, a sculptural ergonomic form with an elegant look and feel was created at a modest price. The shavings reservoir is integrated into the overall form, but because the material is translucent, the user can see when it needs to be emptied. While there is a certain softness in the form, there is also a strong sense of purpose. The sharpening hole is angled slightly to give the product an eager and optimistic attitude.

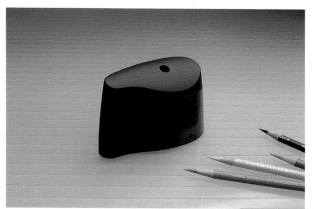

VISTA
Pencil sharpener, 1998,
injection-molded ABS
Designers: Eyal Eliav and
Fede Carandini, ECCO Design
Manufacturer: Hunt

WAVE
Bench, 1999, molded plywood
Designers: Eric Chan, Fede Carandini,
and Jeff Miller, ECCO Design
Manufacturer: R.P.I. Designs

Chan's Wave bench (1999) is an homage to the laminated plywood furniture of Charles and Ray Eames. The full length of the bench's top is curved, a gesture that is sculptural, ergonomic, and an economical use of materials.

Recently, Chan launched his largest project to date: the design of a complete furniture collection—Kiva (1999)—for Herman Miller. Designed to encourage workplace collaboration, this freestanding group of tables, peripherals, screens, and storage shells is designed to be moved rather than fixed in place. The pieces are light and have either casters or pad-like glides. There is no one way to put them into a room; instead, they afford multiple choices about placement. Multifunctional and streamlined, Kiva's Wing and Pebble tables are tapered to accommodate a seated body.

Using high-tech materials and advanced production methods, Chan grounds his designs in the physical forms of the body and nature.
S.S.H.

KIVA
Table, 1999, materials variable
Designers: Eric Chan and Jeff
Miller, ECCO Design
Manufacturer: Herman Miller

FOR WOMEN ONLY
Hairbrushes, 1997, injection-molded SAN
Designers: Eric Chan, Fede Carandini,
and Jeff Miller, ECCO Design
Manufacturer: Goody Products

NEIL M. DENARI B. 1957

Neil M. Denari Architects
Los Angeles, California

Architect Neil M. Denari is a master of three-dimensional computer modeling and animation, inventing precise and persuasive digital representations of building projects. Although his built output has thus far been limited, his computer images provide fully realized, FLUIDLY orchestrated tours of houses, urban towers, and cultural institutions. In these presentations, Denari renders the imaginary with an accuracy, intensity, and clarity that can often exceed the real.

Denari investigates a spatially complex architecture of bent and curved planes. With his high-rise Vertical Weekly Mansion project in Tokyo (1995–99), he juxtaposes solid planes and void spaces with an exposed stairway that leads to a dense honeycomb of cell-like rooms providing short-term residence for traveling businessmen. In the Beverly Hills Smooth House project

(1997–99), green metal sheathing forms a shroud that hovers ominously over the site, and large windows open into a minimal, space-age interior with criss-crossing stairways.

Denari's references to the military and aeronautics industries suggest an attraction to the enterprises that gave postwar Southern California its progressive edge. Denari further explores these associations in a proposed house for Palm Springs (1999), which features a wing-like roof of corrugated metal. Like the celebrated Palm Springs houses of modernists Richard Neutra and Albert Frey, Denari's design employs glass walls to create an indoor/outdoor continuum.

These projects also underscore Denari's fascination with cinema and its impact on contemporary architecture. Whereas David Rockwell takes cues from decorative movie scenography, Denari strives for the

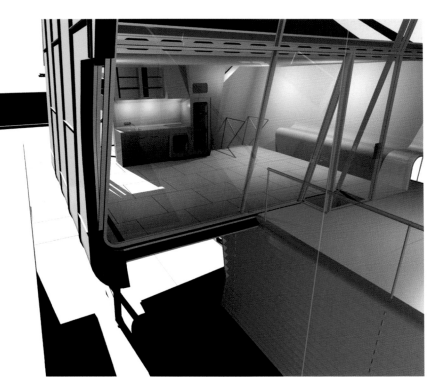

SMOOTH HOUSE
Beverly Hills, California
(unbuilt)
Digital renderings, 1999
Architect: Neil M. Denari
Architects
Team: Carsten Primdahl
(Design team); John Hartman
(Technical drawings); Andrew
Waisler (Computer graphics);
Rebecca Rudolph (Intern)

minimal effects achieved by such directors as Michelangelo Antonioni and Yasujiro Ozu. (Denari pays overt homage to Antonioni by advertising his 1967 film *Blow-Up* on the entrance marquee of the Vertical Weekly Mansion.) In these films, open-ended stories and abstract decor allow viewers to project their own imaginative speculations onto the meanings of individual scenes. Similarly, Denari's virtual buildings achieve a startling poetics of absence, exploiting light, color, texture, and space to create architectural staging platforms for unscripted futures.
D.A.

VERTICAL WEEKLY MANSION
Tokyo (unbuilt)
Digital rendering, 1999
Architect: Neil M. Denari
Team: Gunther Schatz, Angus
Schoenberger (computer graphics)

PALM SPRINGS HOUSE
Palm Springs, California
(unbuilt)
Digital rendering, 1999
Architect: Neil M. Denari
Architects
Team: Jae Shin

STEPHEN FARRELL B. 1968

Slip Studios
Chicago, Illinois

ENTROPY
Typeface, 1992
Designer: Stephen Farrell,
Slip Studios
Publisher: T-26

OSPREY
Typeface, 1993
Designer: Stephen Farrell,
Slip Studios
Publisher: T-26

An emerging voice in the field of typeface design, Stephen Farrell began exploring this medium in the early 1990s, a period when digital fonts were opening up as an accessible arena for experimental design. Farrell's typefaces Entropy (1992) and Osprey (1993), which collage elements from various sources into new characters, quickly wove their way through popular culture, from magazines to music packaging, feeding the contemporary obsession with damaged and disrupted forms.

Farrell's current work mobilizes similar strategies within a more scholarly vein, yielding results that are FLUID as well as disjunctive. Volgare (1996) was inspired by a manuscript produced in Florence in 1601 by an anonymous clerk whose ledger recorded people's names and dates of death. Farrell sliced apart letters from a reproduction of the manuscript and added penstrokes of his own, assembling over five-

hundred distinct characters, including ligatures, letters for the ends of words, and other alternate letterforms that strive to simulate the physical variations in handwriting as it flows from the human hand.

Volgare opens a fresh chapter in digital type production by turning back to an ancient and overlooked page in the history of the letter. Most script-based typefaces, such as Matthew Carter's Snell Roundhand (1966), are derived from the refined scripts of the eighteenth century, and their delicate curves emulate the character of the steel pen and the copper-plate engraving. Farrell's MSS Folio project (1996–2000) reclaimed an antique hand that appears raw and imperfect, an artifact from the past that is alien to the modern conventions of psuedo-engraved diplomas and wedding invitations.

Volgare reclaimed an antique hand that appears raw and imperfect, an artifact from the past that is alien to the modern conventions of psuedo-engraved diplomas and wedding invitations.

VOLGARE
Typeface, 1996
Designer: Stephen Farrell,
Slip Studios
Publisher: Slip Studios

Despite Volgare's historic source, Farrell deploys it in his own work without nostalgia or antiquarian fussiness. In the exhibition catalog *Mythopoeia* (1996), for example, Volgare erupts into the modern fabric of the page like an abrasion or scar. The page structure of *Mythopoeia* is dominated by an architectural "window" that visually cuts through the center of each spread. Flowing through and around this emphatic structural feature is a finely modulated body of text that incorporates various typographic styles, sizes, and alignments.

With Volgare, Farrell acknowledges both the human character of his source material and the ironic absence of its original author. "We can make a hand say things it never dreamed," Farrell writes, "in languages it never knew."

E.L.

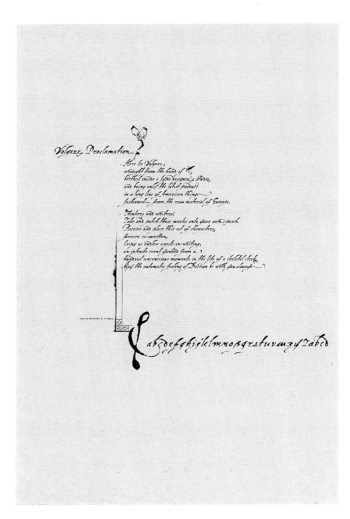

[left]
**FLORENTINE MANUSCRIPTS,
1500–1700**
Manuscript page, c. 1500, ink on vellum
Collection of Newberry Library, Chicago

VOLGARE PROCLAMATION
Prospectus, 1997, digital print
Designer: Stephen Farrell,
Slip Studios
Poet: Daniel X. O'Neil
Publisher: Slip Studios

MYTHOPOEIA
Catalog, 1996, offset lithograph
Designer: Stephen Farrell,
Slip Studios
Writer: Steve Tomasula
Publisher: Don Pollack

FROG

Austin, Texas
New York City
San Francisco, California
Sunnyvale, California

Established by Hartmut Esslinger in Germany in 1969, frog emigrated to California in 1983 to consult on the design of Apple computers. The previous year, the company had taken on its all-lowercase moniker, replacing the name of its founder. The relationship with Apple launched frog in America, and the company moved from curvaceous, swoopy products predicated on Esslinger's "form follows emotion" dictum to a more strategic approach emphasizing brand development through product design.

The Clio, an electronic writing and presentation tablet frog designed for Vadem (1997), draws inspiration from such diverse sources as women's bracelets, human bone structure, and modern sculpture. The key to Clio's design is a triple-function die-cast aluminum arm that allows the display to rotate 180 degrees so that it can be used as a tablet or sit upright. As an intimate product carried close to the body and used daily, the Clio's ability to adjust to a variety of conditions reflects what the design team described as "the human desire to customize, personalize, and effect change on the things that surround them."

Frog's designs for Moscow-based Javad, a leader in the field of global positioning system (GPS) technology, demonstrate its ability to forge an identity for a client while creating a user-friendly product. By integrating advanced Russian technology with American optimism and a particular California coolness, the frogteam created the JPS (1997), the first system to integrate a receiving antenna, processing unit, batteries, and transmitter into a single, sleek, hand-friendly object. For surveyors on the move and in the field, a single machine that could receive, compute, and transmit data proved a significant

VADEM CLIO
Computer, 1997, glass-filled
poly carbonate, and magnesium
die casting
Designer: frogteam
Manufacturer: Vadem

advantage. With its athletic aesthetic and high-visibility color scheme, the JPS has a memorable signature, insuring that it will not be left behind in the mud.

Similarly, the frogteam revamped Trimm Technologies' hot-swappable, high-speed disk drive towers—the UltraTower and Fiber-Rack Disk Drives (1997)—and in the process raised the company's profile within the computing industry. Integrated facades offer a playful, minimal, and FLUID shape that symbolically represents the flow of information while explaining the exterior mechanical workings.

These products demonstrate that user-friendly forms can be found for even the most technically esoteric products. Design is an effective strategic tool when it comes to building identity and creating a bond between consumer and product.
S.S.H.

Steven Skov Holt has worked with frog since 1992. He did not participate in the design of any of the projects presented in this volume.

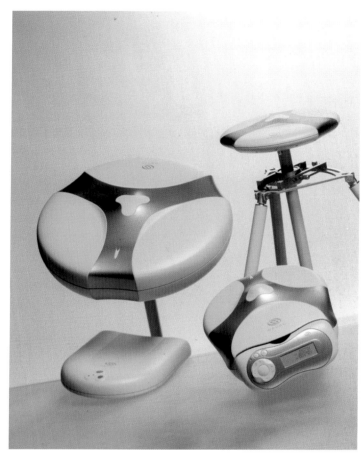

JAVAD POSITIONING SYSTEM
Global positioning
system,1997,PC/ABS,
elastometric paint, aluminum
die castings
Designer: frogteam
Manufacutrer: Javad
Positioning Systems

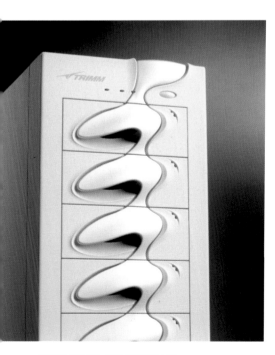

**ULTRA TOWER AND FIBERRACK
DISK DRIVES**
Computer and digital rendering, 1999,
sheet metal, glass-reinforced ABS,
ABS, lexan, and cast urethane
Designer: frogteam
Manufacturer: Trimm Technologies

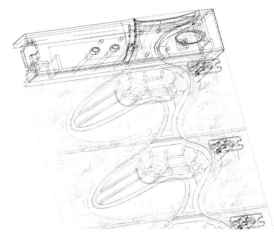

FRANK O. GEHRY B. 1929

Frank O. Gehry & Associates
Santa Monica, California

Frank O. Gehry's proposal for One Times Square, the prow-shaped tower that marks the southern end of the legendary Crossroads of the World, was commissioned as a symbolic presence for Warner Brothers and its parent company, Time Warner. Gehry's renovation of the 1903 building strips off its white marble cladding in order to expose a steel structure beneath. In Gehry's presentation of the building, a giant Calvin Klein ad tops the structure, a witty reminder of that designer's role in revealing the modern body and making underwear fashionable. Gehry clothes the building's skeleton with dramatically FLUID panels of translucent metallic fabric, a baroque descendant of the chain link fencing he wrapped around his 1977 house in Santa Monica, California, and used as a supergraphic facade at the nearby Santa Monica Place. Like a sexy gown, One Times Square's panels both reveal and conceal what lies underneath.

The building features an open public plaza off Times Square, a below-grade Warner Brothers store, and a glass-enclosed theme restaurant and bar at the top levels of the tower accessible via exterior elevators. (An armature for urban spectacle, One Times Square is also the building from which the ceremonial ball descends at midnight on New Year's Eve.) Between the underground retail store and the restaurant and bar above, an architectural attraction based on the concept of a mechanized clock tower is created by removing eight floor plates from the lower levels of the building. Visible on the exterior of the structure from Times Square and on the interior of the building from the open plaza below, animated cartoon characters such as Superman and Tweety Bird emerge hourly and

move in and around the building on a track system: modern-day media cuckoos. Accompanied by lasers, smoke machines, and other special effects, these characters dance around the building's exposed structural skeleton and metallic fabric panels, which rise like billowing stage curtains to announce their arrival.

One Times Square is just one in a long line of provocative architectural designs by Gehry, to whom young architects continuously turn for new directions. Gehry's visions may at first seem unbelievable and unbuildable. But like the architect's celebrated Guggenheim Museum in Bilbao (1997), One Times Square is a believable, metallic mirage. D.A.

ONE TIMES SQUARE
New York City (proposal)
Architect: Frank O. Gehry & Associates
Project principal: Randy Jefferson
Project designer/architect: Edwin Chan
Team: David Herrera and Leigh Jerrard

Sketch, 1996, ink on paper
Delineator: Frank O. Gehry

Model, 1996, scale 1/8":1', foam core, basswood, and fabric

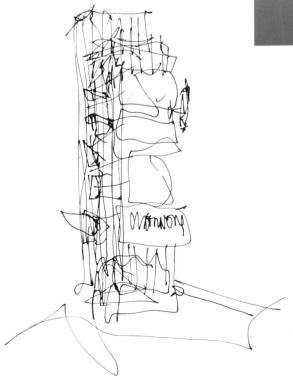

GUGGENHEIM MUSEUM BILBAO
Bilbao, Spain
Photograph, 1997
Architect: Frank O. Gehry & Associates
Team: Vano Haritunians (Project manager); Douglas Hanson (Project architect); Edwin Chan (Project designer); Rich Barrett, Karl Blette, Tomaso Bradshaw, Matt Fineout, Bob Hale, Dave Hardie, Michael Hootman, Grzegorz Kosmal, Naomi Langer, Mehran Mashayekh, Chris Mercier, Brent Miller, David Reddy, Marc Salette, Bruce Shepard, Rick Smith, Eva Sobesky, Derek Soltes, Todd Spiegel, Jeff Wauer, and Kristin Woehl

HAWORTH
Holland, Michigan

Seeing that we are in the midst of revolutionary workplace change, Haworth's industrial design team has focused on the unmet needs of today's information-oriented work force. During the last three years, the team has unleashed a torrent of solutions that seek to break workers out of their cubicles. Even in their names—Drift, Wake, Flo, and Eddy—they invoke today's FLUID, collaborative business environments.

Inspired by observational research, Drift and Wake (1996) are hand-built concept studies that address spatial organization and memory in the workplace. Drift is an organizing fixture that responds to what the designers refer to as "Post-It Note clouds" and "topographical paper piles." Its three-tiered translucent surface presents the user with a slanted rack for organizing papers and desk-top objects.

Wake consists of a horizontal, semicircular metal axis mounted on three maple legs, and plays on the idea that a thought combined with an action better lends itself to recall. The axis sprouts spiral-armed binder clips, gooseneck acrylic platforms, and jointed boxes and half-boxes so that projects can be brought forward and pushed back as needed.

Flo (1997) consists of a surfboard-like work surface with a wire mesh display area. The concept: provide a visual connection between work-in-progress and the user so that projects don't fall through the figurative cracks. Flo has several leather-wrapped flat panels that can be moved about as needed for posting information, a clamshell-shaped carryall that allows for toting, and a storage structure with coral-like cavities. Flo lets workers assign differently shaped locations to items, providing memory cues for later retrieval.

OFFICE EXPLORATIONS:
DRIFT [center]
Desk (concept), 1996, hand-laid fiberglass, aluminum tubing, tig-welded frame of butted steel tubing, and resin-cast top surface
Designer: Brian Alexander
Manager, Ideation: Jeff Reuschel
Associate industrial designer: Steve Beukema
Producer: Haworth

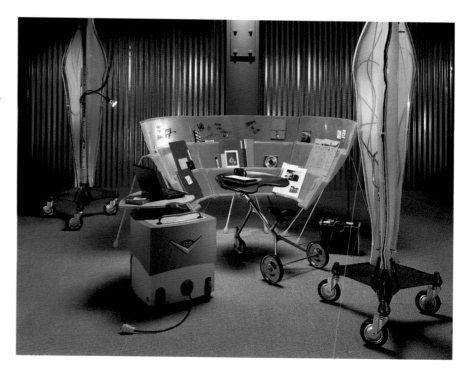

Eddy (1997) is a tiered, arena-like workspace that allows users to display reference materials that would normally end up in stacks. Its curvilinear, fiberglass levels and gooseneck fittings accommodate smaller materials and act as mental scratch pads. The folding organizers allow work to be "chunked," or put into packets of related information. The "chunk house" then provides workers with a way to organize these agglomerations.

Drift, Wake, Flo, and Eddy all enable office workers to better visualize and customize flows of information by creating an environment that serves as an extension of the mind. By embracing "cognitive ergonomics," the Haworth team is making the office function more like the brain. The ideal result is a workspace of increased productivity and reduced frustration.
S.S.H.

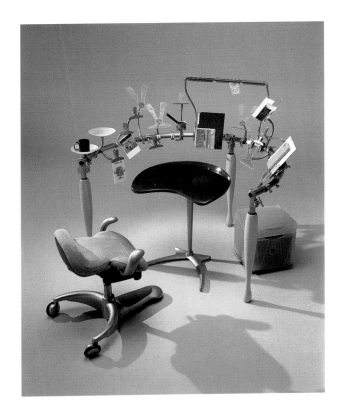

OFFICE EXPLORATIONS: WAKE
Desk (concept), 1996, acrylic, steel, cast aluminum, maple, cast resin, and silicone
Designer: Brian Alexander, Haworth
Manager, Ideation: Jeff Reuschel
Associate industrial designer: Roque Corpuz, Jr.
Producer: Haworth

OFFICE EXPLORATIONS: EDDY
Workstation (concept), 1997, polished fiberglass, Plexiglass, upholstered leather and fabric, silicone, latex rubber, steel, and water-based matte finish paint
Designers: Clarkson Thorp and Steve Beukema, Haworth
Manager, Ideation: Jeff Reuschel
Senior industrial designer: Brian Alexander
Industrial designers: Clarkson Thorp and Dan West
Associate industrial designer: Steve Beukema
Producer: Haworth

SULAN KOLATAN B. 1958
WILLIAM MAC DONALD B. 1956

Kolatan/Mac Donald Studio
New York City

The careers of Sulan Kolatan and William Mac Donald represent the FLUID nature of many contemporary design practices. The New York-based architects teach, write, practice, exhibit their work as fine art, and propose crossovers among products, architecture, and film.

Kolatan and Mac Donald's buildings are remarkably organic in form and space. Their aesthetic is evident in built projects such as the Ost/Kuttner apartment in Manhattan (1996), where curving, fiberglass planes create a fluid continuum from space to space, and the Raybould House and Garden in Fairfield County, Connecticut (1999), a curvilinear addition morphed from the forms of an existing house and landscape. The architects' theoretical project *Housings* represents their full range of investigations into new typologies. The project begins with a conventional American house type—a three-bedroom, two-bathroom colonial. Using software developed for the animation and product design fields, Kolatan and Mac Donald deform images of this traditional structure into six increasingly experimental forms. The results range from objects that look like irregularly shaped cellular telephones to computers and aircraft.

Kolatan and Mac Donald's explorations of new domestic typologies in *Housings* has segued into the production of a video. The architects manipulate the video, which comprises broadcast television programs and commercials for home mortgaging companies, seamlessly juxtaposing their own experimental architecture with images of conventional homes.

Kolatan and Mac Donald often use the Chimera—a mythological beast that is part lion, part goat, and part snake—as a metaphor for their architectural practice, a practice that is similarly more than the sum of its parts. D.A.

OST/KUTTNER APARTMENT
New York City
Photograph, 1996
Architect: Kolatan/Mac Donald Studio
Design principals: Sulan Kolatan and
William J. Mac Donald
Team: Erich Schoenenberger, Natasha
Cunningham, Steve Doub, Matt Hollis,
Rebecca Carpenter, Philip Palmgren,
and Patrick Walsch

44

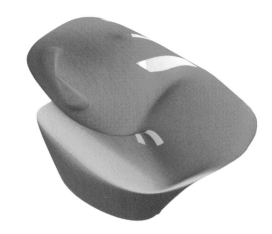

HOUSINGS

Digital renderings/video, 1999
Architect: Kolatan/Mac Donald Studio
Design Principals: Sulan Kolatan
and William Mac Donald
Team: Dean Di Simone, Stefano
Colombo (project coordinators);
Linda Malibran, Yolanda Do Campo,
Christian Ditlev Bruun, Jose
Sanchez, Maia Small, Emanuelle
Bourlier, Roger Hom, John Malley,
Mark McNamara, Aanen Olsen,
Tulya Madra, Shannon Sauceda
and Jonathan Baker

Housings is made possible
by a research grant from
Alias/wavefront, Inc.

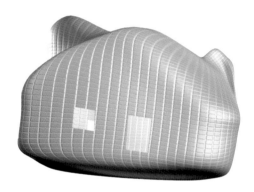

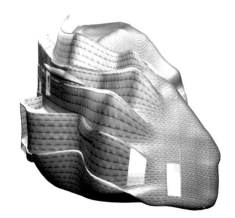

MAX YOSHIMOTO B. 1961 AND TEAM

LUNAR DESIGN
San Francisco, California

As concern for the nature of the physical interface between consumer and product has intensified, so too has the quest for more tactile materials that can make an emotional connection to the buyer. Such solutions offer the imagery of enhanced performance as well as tangible benefits.

Lunar Design's Cross-Action Toothbrush (1999) for Oral-B is a design that ultimately landed twenty-six patents. Looking into bathrooms to see people brushing became an obsession for Lunar's design team. The company's research confirmed the idea that adding size to the handle in the right places would add comfort for the brush user. Lunar tapered the handle toward the center, added ridges to facilitate grip, and used Kraton, a rubber material, on its inner and outer surfaces to increase softness. The team then reduced the impact of the added girth with

FLUID markings and a carefully considered white, blue, and green palette that connotes freshness, cleanliness, and hygiene. The head uses differently angled bristles to penetrate into the recesses of the teeth and gums, combining utility and soothing sensations with an aesthetic implying dynamism.

Lunar's Pavilion series of home/office computers for Hewlett Packard reflects the design firm's affinity for plastic form. When the series was launched in 1995, with a design by Max Yoshimoto and Yves Béhar, the Pavilion marked the company's first major step into the home PC market. The third generation (1999) takes the first-generation's curves in a more sophisticated direction, drawing on what designer Ken Wood describes as "natural and humanizing symbols as opposed to machine metaphors." The result is an object of appealing grace.

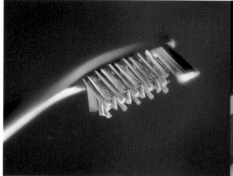

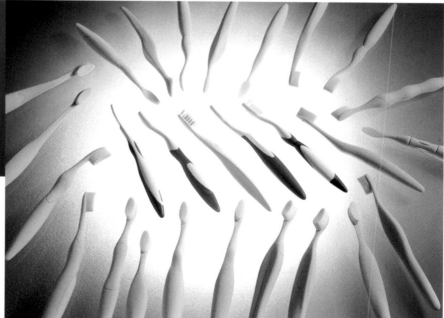

CROSS-ACTION TOOTHBRUSH

[top]
Consumer product, 1999, co-molded injection and molded plastic, and thermal-plastic elastomer

[right]
Prototypes, 1999, injection-molded ABS plastic and injection-molded rubber

Manufacturer: Gillette and Oral-B Laboratories

Designers: Max Yoshimoto and Jeffrey Salazar, Lunar Design, and Oral-B Laboratories
Imaging director: Jeff Hoefer, Lunar Design
Manager, Product Development: Donna Beals, Bill Bredall, and Brad Castillo, Oral-B Laboratories

Braun A.G.: Jurgen Greubel
Manager: Michael Roberts, The Gillette Company
Director, Corporate Product Design: Peter Schneider, Braun A.G.
Director, Product Development: Maisie Wong-Paredes, Oral-B Laboratories

Working in conjunction with Sony's West Coast Design Center, Lunar's designs for 15-inch monitors (1999) targeted what Sony considered underserved markets: young professional women and Web-savvy college students. Max Yoshimoto, Nicolas Denhez, and the Lunar team drew on the flowing lines of rave graphics and Celtic ornament. Monitor surfaces were then activated by integrating CD slots and a pegboard with hooks to hold gear like headphones and mice. Ironically, now that the days of the CRT-based display are coming to a close, consumers are finally getting distinctive monitor designs.

Using observational research, the Lunar team takes its design cues from its audience. In a language of curvy, fluid forms, Lunar's designs speak to a future when a $2 toothbrush is as carefully considered as a $2,000 computer. s.s.h.

HP PAVILION PC
Computer product, 1999, ABS
plastic enclosure and galvanized
pre-plated steel chassis
Designers: Lunar Design Team and
Hewlett-Packard Design
Manufacturer: Hewlett-Packard

SONY HMD-A100, FD TRINITRON
Computer monitor, 1999, ABS plastic
Designers: Max Yoshimoto and Nicolas Denhez,
Lunar Design, and Sony Design Center
Industrial design manager: Yutaka Hasegawa,
Sony Design Center
Director: Jim Wicks, Sony Design Center
Manufacturer: Sony

GREG LYNN B. 1964

Greg Lynn FORM
Los Angeles, California

Architect Greg Lynn investigates the FLUID, three-dimensional possibilities inherent in mathematical statistics, physics, and geometry. Lynn's so-called animate forms are based on coordinates derived from such data as local environmental forces and are modeled using computer simulation software. Lynn, Douglas Garofalo, and Michael McInturf recently completed the Presbyterian Church of New York in Queens for a large Korean-American congregation. An addition to a former laundry, the new building features undulating shapes derived from the existing structure.

Lynn develops his designs through progressive series of models made with the rapid-prototyping software used by many product designers. His forms evolve from simple to complex in response to new data such as the sun's changing positions throughout the day. The

proposed Hydrogen House (1996) for the OMV Austrian Mineral Oil Company, an exhibition pavilion for new energy systems on the outskirts of Vienna, demonstrates one of the most complete realizations of Lynn's approach. All of the building's mechanical and electrical systems are powered by a combination of passive and active solar systems and a hydrogen gas fuel cell that is currently being used by the American space program. The building's two primary facades are designed to take best advantage of the local environment—both natural and manmade. Multiple curves on the south facade are shaped to follow the sun's daily arc through the sky, optimizing the absorption of solar energy by the building's system of photovoltaic cells. The accordion-like forms of the north facade, which faces the Autobahn, were derived from the flow of daily commuter

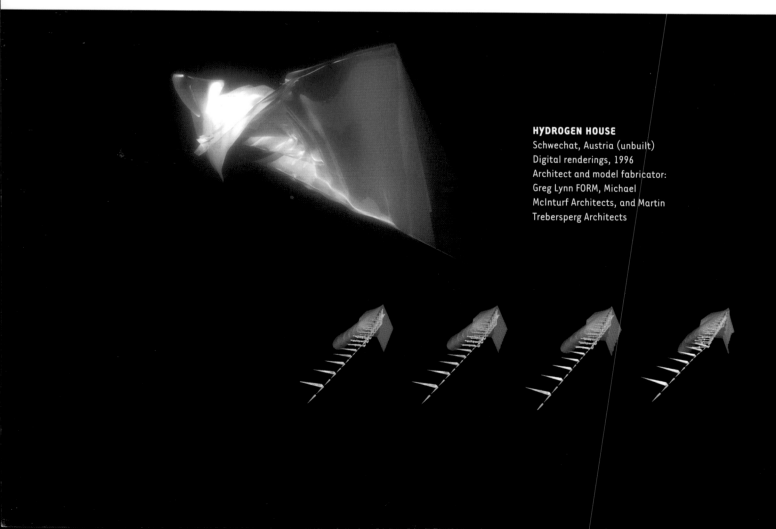

HYDROGEN HOUSE
Schwechat, Austria (unbuilt)
Digital renderings, 1996
Architect and model fabricator:
Greg Lynn FORM, Michael
McInturf Architects, and Martin
Trebersperg Architects

traffic to and from Vienna. The
windows incorporate gel coatings
that change their transparency in
response to sunlight and temperature,
regulating the interior conditions.

Lynn cites precedents for his
plastic architecture as diverse as
human anatomy and 1950s science-
fiction films like *The Blob*. He
compares his design process to that of
a naval engineer who creates the
complex shapes of a ship's hull by
studying the multiple forces of flow,
turbulence, viscosity, and drag.
By looking at sources beyond the field
of architecture, Lynn follows in the
footsteps of Le Corbusier, who, at the
beginning of the twentieth century,
modeled his own machine-age
architecture on the industrial forms
of ships and automobiles. For his
part, Greg Lynn is creating an
architecture relevant to the dynamic
forces at play at the start of the
twenty-first century. D.A.

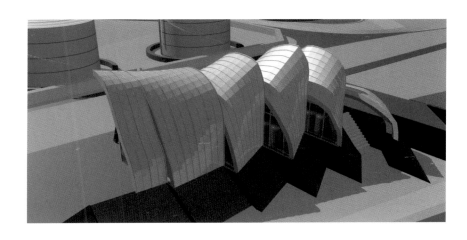

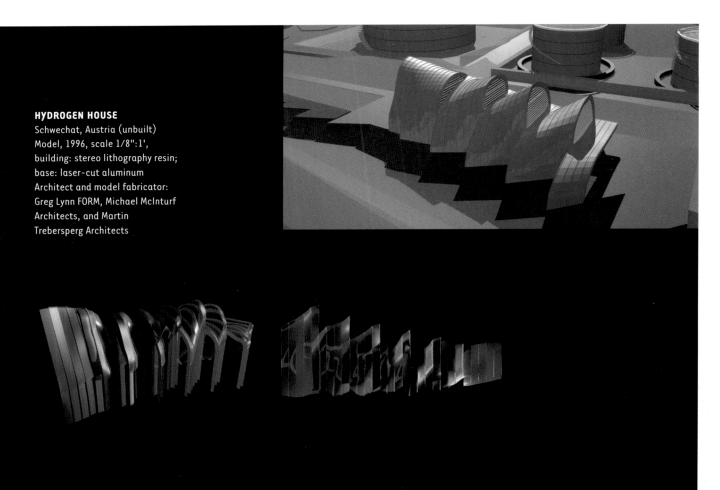

HYDROGEN HOUSE
Schwechat, Austria (unbuilt)
Model, 1996, scale 1/8":1',
building: stereo lithography resin;
base: laser-cut aluminum
Architect and model fabricator:
Greg Lynn FORM, Michael McInturf
Architects, and Martin
Trebersperg Architects

Rebeca Méndez designs complex surfaces in which images accumulate in veil-like layers. From the printed page to the architectural interior, she creates planes of imagery where hard edges give way to FLUID yet carefully controlled transitions.

Among Méndez's recent projects is a series of vast murals for the Las Vegas restaurant Tsunami, created in a 1999 collaboration with architect Thom Mayne and his office Morphosis. Tsunami's "pan-Asian" menu merges the flavors and ingredients of diverse cuisines into a free-form vocabulary. Reflecting on the themed content of the restaurant, Méndez developed narratives of visual dissolution in which discrete elements melt into each other. To produce the project, she directed an underwater film of a Japanese woman who appears to dissolve and disappear into waves of imagery.

The signage on Tsunami's storefront consists of a series of video monitors that display the restaurant's name, alternating among the roman alphabet and Asian scripts.

Méndez's environmental projects are an extension of the books and catalogs she has produced for cultural organizations such as the Art Center College of Art and Design, the Museum of Contemporary Art in Los Angeles, and the Whitney Museum of American Art. In her publication designs, Méndez develops pristine organizational structures that interact with the organic flow of content.

Méndez enables two-dimensional surfaces to harbor illusions of depth, endowing them with such physical qualities as translucency and tension. From the printed page to the architectural environment, she creates open, flowing fields for visual experience.
E.L.

TSUNAMI ASIAN GRILL
Mural and video signage, 1999
Designer: Rebeca Méndez, Rebeca Méndez
Communication Design
Architect: Thom Mayne, Morphosis
Client: Morphosis/ARK Restaurants
Assistant to Designer: Jorge Verdín
Production: Lesley Tucker, Ted Kane, Angel Go
Model: Zen
Project Manager: Adam Eeuwens
Photographers: Stuart Frolick, Rebeca
Méndez, Michael Powers, Kira Perov, Shelly
Strasiz, and Jorge Verdín

COLIN BADEN B. 1962

OAKLEY

Foothill Ranch, California

Oakley's eyewear seamlessly merges with the body. Like organic prosthetics, the glasses flow around the face in a FLUID sweep bound by the geometry of the human form. Oakley was founded in 1975 as a maker of grips for motorcycles. Its initial success led it to expand into the manufacture of motocross goggles and, by the mid-1980s, the high-performance sunglasses for which it is now best known. Since then Oakley has secured more than four-hundred patents and six-hundred trademarks, reflecting its commitment to design.

Oakley's design efforts have been led, since the mid-1990s, by Colin Baden. Trained as an architect, Baden began consulting with Oakley in 1993. He eventually joined the company as director of design and became president in 1999. Baden, a champion of diversification, has sought to extend the Oakley brand by pushing the company beyond its core eyewear business while encouraging the use of the most advanced visualization tools available—from stereo-lithography to liquid-laser prototyping—to maintain a consistent, high-tech corporate identity.

Oakley's Mars frames (1998) build on an idea of glasses as a modular system. Designed in collaboration with Oakley board member Michael Jordan, they feature circular lenses, interchangeable "nose bombs" (rubbery, detachable nose elements), and "Unobtainium" pads that allow the frame to accommodate a variety of head sizes. The product name Mars reflects the company's penchant for astronomical metaphor—its offices are known as "interplanetary headquarters."

Sculpted like the occipital orbit of the eye socket, the "air scoops"

RACING JACKET
Eyewear, 1998, O-Matter, Plutonite lens, and Unobtainium nose piece/sock
Designers: Jim Jannard, Peter Yee, and Lek Thixton
Manufacturer: Oakley

ROMEO GLASSES
Eyewear, 1996, X-Metal (titanium alloy), Plutonite lens, and Unobtainium shocks/socks
Designers: Lek Thixton, Hans Moritz, Toby Rohrbach, Peter Yee, and Jim Jannard
Manufacturer: Oakley

of Oakley's Racing Jacket shades (1998) prevent fogging and condensation. Both the liquid-looking silver frame with black iridium lenses and the more athletically assertive blue frame with red iridium lenses find inspiration in the spectacle of sport. Also anatomically derived but with a very different visual signature, the X-Metal Romeo (1996)—available with a titanium frame and gold iridium lenses—appears to be cast from some magical material.

The use of high-performance materials, the celebration of detail, and a focus on form are Oakley's trademarks. Baden hopes to push Oakley from a sunglasses company into the elite register of globally-recognized brands. Design is the tool for getting there. s.s.h.

MARS GLASSES
Eyewear, 1998, X-Metal (titanium alloy), Plutonite lens, Unobtainium shocks/socks, and leather
Designers: Colin Baden, Hans Moritz, and Jim Jannard
Manufacturer: Oakley

PRO-M FRAME
Eyewear, 1996, O-Matter frame, Plutonite lens, and Unobtainium socks
Designers: Jim Jannard and Peter Yee
Manufacturer: Oakley

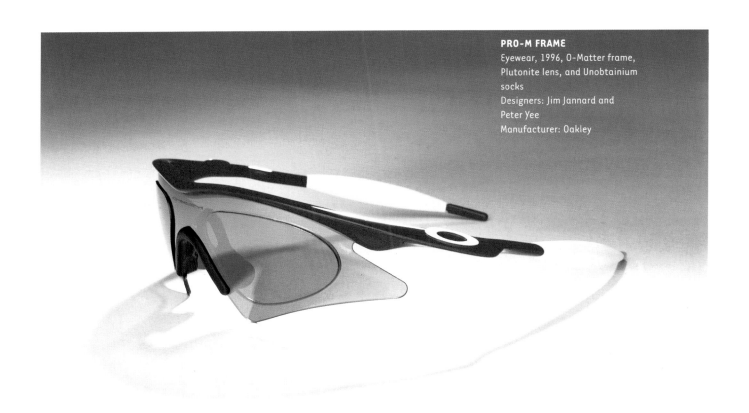

PAUL MONTGOMERY B. 1959
HERBIE PFEIFER B. 1949

Montgomery Pfeifer
San Francisco, California

While a student in the graduate program at the Cranbrook Academy of Art, Paul Montgomery explored the theory of product semantics, which approaches design as a visual language. Herbie Pfeifer brought a renegade German modernist's intensity to projects that he balanced with philosophically rich dialogs and subtle wisecracks. The two designers met while working at frog's Calfornia office in the 1980's, and they left in 1990 to establish their own firm, Montgomery Pfeifer.

Their studio now employs a dozen designers working for a variety of international clients. Combining a no-nonsense approach to problem-solving with an ambition to create visually innovative objects, they apply a vocabulary of FLUID, minimal, and understandable forms to new technologies, creating products that are easy to use and enjoyable to own.

Sun's JavaStation (1998) reveals an architectural concern for reduced form and purposeful expression. Conceptually and compositionally, it feels as if there is nothing in it that does not belong. From the start, the project aimed to materially suggest that Sun's Java system represented a dramatic difference in computer usage, fueled by Sun's proprietary programming language Java. The team envisioned the JavaStation as a physical portal to invisible networks. Study models and sketches reveal how the machine's final form found its inspiration in industrial landscapes and small scale architectural elements.

The idea behind the SunRay network terminal (1999) is that personal computers in work groups are unnecessarily bloated by software that better resides on a central server. The server is therefore tucked away, with individuals accessing it with a

SOUNDMAN X2
Speakers, 1999, ABS
Designer: Montgomery Pfeifer Design Team
Associate designer: Logitech and soundmatters
Manufacturer: Logitech

"thin client." In addition to the performance and cost benefits of eliminating the massive CPU, precious desk space is liberated for other uses. In contrast to the JavaStation, SunRay adopts a forward gesture toward the user. Although both products employ a similar design dialect, the SunRay radiates a friendlier demeanor. It is easily approachable, a personal servant standing ready to deliver information, instantly and economically.

In a 1998 project for Logitech — a subwoofer with satellite speakers— Montgomery Pfeifer found a solution in a pure cylindrical form accented with an intense blue. The confidence of the system's geometric and proportional relationships, the sureness of its detailing, and the supersaturation of its color all communicate the purity and depth of digital sound. s.s.h.

[left]

SUNRAY
Network computer, 1999, PC-ABS
Designer: Montgomery Pfeifer Design Team
Associate designer: Sun Microsystems
Manufacturer: Sun Microsystems

[right and above right]

JAVA STATION
Study models, 1998, PU foam
Designer: Montgomery Pfeifer Design Team

JAVA STATION
Network computer, 1998, PC-ABS
Designer: Montgomery Pfeifer Design Team
Associate designer: Sun Microsystems
Manufacturer: Sun Microsystems

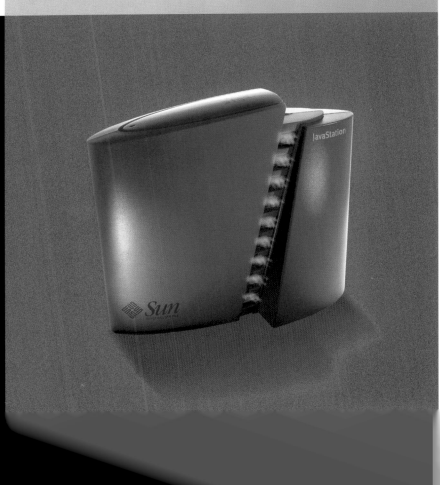

ARLEN NESS B. 1939
CORY NESS B. 1963

Arlen Ness Enterprises
San Leandro, California

Arlen Ness is a most unlikely success story. Lacking a formal design education and forbidden to own or ride a motorcycle first by his father and then by his wife, Ness has nevertheless become the premier customizer of Harley-Davidsons in the United States. Though virtually unknown in the design world, he is revered as a national treasure within the thriving subculture of easy-riding Harley enthusiasts.

Ness began transforming motorcycles in 1967, and within a few years had introduced radical frame and component design while ingeniously pairing new and old parts. His early machines had notoriously flamboyant paint jobs and attention-commanding handlebars (he was responsible for the now-iconic ram-horn motif seen on so many "hogs"). Ness's 1998 Aluminum Bike, a polished metal construction, is a study in reflection

and expressive machine imagery shaped by the FLUID lines that are now his visual signature. Over a six-month period, the Ness team (including rebuilder Jeff Border and chromer/polisher Fernando Lopez) designed and fabricated the handlebars, frame, risers, fenders, pipes, front and rear pegs, gas and oil tanks, and head and tail lights. They also reworked the electrical system and customized the assembly. A speedometer? If you need one, this isn't the bike for you.

Following in his father's tracks, in 1998 Cory Ness (with artist Carl Brouhard) created his own concept bike, a motorcycle based on a continuous radius that, in the younger Ness's words, "flows from one end to the other." The entire body is hand-formed aluminum, and the look is long, lean, and liquid. By using a mix of stock and custom components (such as gas tank,

mirrors, and grips), the team achieved a clean, dynamic aesthetic.

Both Ness bikes demonstrate the love of curvilinear form that is this father-and-son duo's trademark, and both demand to be contemplated as total design objects. Beyond their visual appeal, Ness motorcycles are meant to be heard (all feature that deep "potato-potato-potato" sound), and, most importantly, ridden. s.s.h.

CURVACEOUSNESS
Motorcycle, 1999, hand-built aluminum body, custom machine billet parts, high-gloss, and hand-rubbed parts
Designer: Cory Ness
Fabricator: Craig Naff
Paint: Jon Nelson
Assembly: Cory Ness, Jeff Border, and team
Manufacturer: Arlen Ness Enterprises

[left]
ARLEN'S ALUMINUM BIKE
Motorcycle, 1998, hand-pounded aluminum frame
Designer: Arlen Ness
Manufacturer: Arlen Ness Enterprises

Born in Egypt and raised in London and Canada, trained in Italy and now practicing in the United States, Karim Rashid practices a globally infused brand of design. American, Italian, Scandinavian, and Japanese influences seem to flow back and forth through his work like so much hot plastic in a molding machine. Liquidity is an apt metaphor for both Rashid's aesthetic and his practice; the designer's clients range from mass-market garbage-can maker Umbra to fashion innovator Issey Miyake.

Rashid's "form follows FLUID" approach arrives at a moment when the public has grown weary of the standard "black box" design of so many high-tech products. As an antidote, Rashid's "blobjects" offer a recognizable style emphasizing translucency, streamlined form, optimistic shapes, and the adroit interplay of complex curves. His sensuous designs reflect the body's contours and, not surprisingly, have connected with a broad range of consumers.

At its best, Rashid's work achieves the modernist objective of coupling elevated design with inexpensively-priced and familiar materials. Such products as a handbag for Issey Miyake (1997), the OH Chair (1999) and his titanium plastic bowls for Umbra (1999) and his mixed alloy objects for Nambé (1994–99) satisfy Rashid's criteria for good design by blurring "experience with form to the degree that the two become inseparable." Rashid has rendered these objects out of a variety of polypropylenes and polyolefines, achieving a sensual, almost edible quality. In Rashid's hands, plastic walls become taut and translucent, their skins seeming to glow from within. This tangibility is amplified by his color palette (whites,

PERFECTO BAG
Accessories, 1997, flat polypropylene sheet with injection polyolefin handle and co-extruded flourescent reversible insert
Designer: Karim Rashid
Manufacturer: Issey Miyake

blacks, and grays along with more idiosyncratic hypermodern greens, oranges, yellows, and blues) and the application of "mod" symbology.

By enabling this transformation from commonplace to precious Rashid endows ordinary objects with the status of still life subjects—making them worthy of aesthetic contemplation. s.s.h.

BOWLS FOR UMBRA
Housewares, 1999, injection-molded clear-tint and metallic polypropylene with polished finish
Designer: Karim Rashid
Manufacturer: Umbra

OH CHAIR
Furniture, 1999, injection-molded polypropylene with powder-coated steel tube legs
Designer: Karim Rashid
Manufacturer: Umbra

JIM SEAY B.1960

Premier Rides
Millersville, Maryland

We are living in a period of booming enthusiasm for roller coasters. In 1998, thirty-four new roller coaster models were introduced in North America (sixty-seven world-wide), the most since the Depression. Some of the most compelling of these theme park experiences were designed by Jim Seay and his team at Premier Rides. With their rocket-like speeds and death-defying spiral tracks, Seay's roller coasters are the darlings of thrill-seekers from Texas to Tokyo. To zoom from a dead stop to 70 miles-per-hour in under four seconds—the kind of acceleration previously reserved for race cars, elite motorcycles, and military aircraft—Seay's coasters rely on advanced propulsion technology. Seen from the ground, their spine-like structural skeletons visually celebrate FLUID dynamism.

The rides go so fast that park-goers get more of a blurred sensation of speed and acrobatic flight than a clear picture of their experience—there is little time for reflection during the ride. Whether it's at Six Flags Over Texas or Suzuka Circuitland outside Tokyo, what the rides offer passengers are a series of

MAD COBRA
Photograph, linear induction
catapult rollercoaster
Designer: Jim Seay, Premier Rides

**BATMAN™ AND ROBIN™:
THE CHILLER AT SIX FLAGS
GREAT ADVENTURE**
New Jersey
Model of rollercoaster, 1996,
aluminum and wire
Designer: Jim Seay, Premier Rides

vertigo-inducing yet fantastically FLUID inversions, banks, and twists along a spaghetti-like track. Then the ride comes to a stop, and the whole route is run again—backwards.

Looking to surpass the roller coasters that captivated him as a child, in 1996 Seay introduced aerospace technology to the theme park business. Seay's application of linear induction motors (LIMs) on a pair of rides for Paramount, erected at King's Island and King's Dominion, profoundly changed the industry, sparking a boom in coaster construction.

At Six Flags Over Texas (1998), 228 linear induction motors propel an electromagnetic wave up a tunnel, with the coaster's train riding along the path of that instant wave— eliminating the need for a chain lift. While the LIM-powered rides lack the clickety-clackety sound of old-fashioned coasters, they do allow for a maximum experience on a minimal site. On just one acre, and within 2,700 feet of track, riders may be inverted four times and put through thirty vertical curves and twenty-five compound horizontal twists—all within sixty-odd seconds.

Achieving feats that seemed impossible only a few years ago, Seay and Premier Rides are designing fluid experiences at rates of speed and force unbelievable until they are encountered. Writes Seay, "Watching park guests come off these rides open-mouthed, bug-eyed, and baffled by the experience makes months of perfecting the technology worthwhile." s.s.h.

physical

Designers engage the realm of physical experience by celebrating the play of light and shadow, juxtaposing diverse and sensual materials, or reflecting on how an object, image, or building is made. Contemporary design often reveals the trace of the hand, the grain and translucence of film, the bite of metal type or tooling, or the imperfect mixing of materials. As digital technologies have fed the burgeoning public appetite for simulation and special effects, designers have become hungry for physical making and interaction. Yet far from representing a retreat from technology, designers often employ sophisticated digital tools to express physical qualities. Physical behaviors such as tautness, adaptability, and gravitational pull can be incorporated into digital environments.

AYSE BIRSEL B.1964

Olive 1:1
New York City

Born on the Aegean coast of Turkey, Ayse Birsel came to the United States in 1986 to attend graduate school at Pratt Institute on a Fulbright fellowship. Ten years later, in conjuction with Bruce Hannah, who had been her thesis advisor at Pratt, she developed Gardens, a conceptual project with Herman Miller to explore new ideas for cable management in the office environment. Included was the sculptural Miro Pole (1996). Attached to the ceiling and floor, it supports a central power and data outlet that sprouts cables as well as other elements such as a light, fan, audio system with headphones, heater, and mirror.

Although the Gardens concepts were never further developed, Herman Miller recognized Birsel as an inventive outsider, and in June 1997, began collaborating with her on the development of Resolve, a new concept in office systems furniture.

Built on the idea that office work has greatly changed over the past decade—that it has become more technology-driven, collaborative, and multifaceted—the Resolve system uses 120 degree angles to build constellations that eliminate maze-like grids of cubicles. With its flexible PHYSICALITY and its ability to balance privacy and openness, Birsel's design offers potential liberation from the Dilbertian nightmare unwittingly created by 1960s-era office systems.

Working with Japanese bathroom manufacturing giant TOTO, Birsel created the Zoë Washlet (1995), a combination toilet seat/bidet for the American market with a built-in water feature, odor prevention system, heater, and easy-to-clean surfaces made from injection-molded ABS. Conceived as a chair, Zoë comfortably conforms to the contours of the body. The front of the seat

[above]
MIRO POLE
Office systems concept, 1996, ink, paper, modeling materials, and alias computer rendering
Designers: Ayse Birsel, Olive 1:1; and Bruce Hannah
Client: Herman Miller

[opposite page, above right]
ZOË WASHLET
Bidet-toilet combination, 1995, injection-molded ABS plastic
Designers: Ayse Birsel, Olive 1:1, and Noriko Hiraga and Jun-Ichi Tani, Toto
Engineer: Masatoshi Yada, Toto
Project leader: Alfred Polczyk, Toto
Manufacturer: Toto

curves down for proper positioning and better leg support, while large rubber bumpers underneath provide extra cushioning. The seat and lid are detachable for cleaning, while the contoured lid with a hole in the center is designed to be easy to lift. A remote control activates an aerated water jet, and an air filter operates automatically when the user sits down. Providing the advantages of both a bidet and a toilet without taking up any more room than a standard fixture, Zoë is a strikingly graceful machine that is easy to install—and given the taboos associated with these two appliances, it probably has to be. In our puritanical society, the idea of making something so practical comfortable and sculpturally beautiful is still, unfortunately, revolutionary. s.s.h.

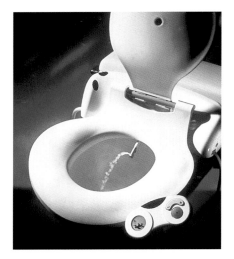

RESOLVE
Work system/office furniture, 1999, steel, aluminum, plastic, wood, and proprietary textiles
Designer: Ayse Birsel, Olive 1:1
Research and development:
concept team, Herman Miller
Senior designers: Stefanie Kubanek and Joe Stone, Olive 1:1

Strategist and writer: Allan Chochinov
Computer imaging and documentation:
Eric Ludlum, Core 77
Manufacturer: Herman Miller

MARIO GALASSO B. 1966
TOD PATTERSON B. 1958
CHRIS PECK B. 1970
AND TEAM

CANNONDALE CORPORATION
Bethel, Connecticut

In the 1980s Cannondale pioneered a new kind of road bike reliant on a fat-tube aluminum frame that was both stiffer and lighter than traditional framing systems. In the 1990s Cannondale's reputation as a design innovator continued to grow, thanks in part to sponsoring professional cyclists who pushed its bikes to their PHYSICAL limits while increasing the company's profile. Cannondale's design-forward strategy has resulted in success both on the market and on the road. The company, which went public in 1998, has established itself in difficult export markets like Japan while scoring racing victories around the world.

Frame engineer Tod Patterson has taken an iconoclastic approach to the design of the company's Super V Raven series of bicycles, which have aluminum structural skeletons wrapped by skins of carbon fiber composite. The Ravens are hard to

miss—they have no cross-bar, and instead of straight tubing, they feature an oversized, gently curving down tube that increases in diameter as it thins in wall thickness.

On the most advanced model, the Raven 2 (1998), Patterson substituted magnesium for the spine's aluminum to create a stiffer frame more than a pound lighter than other models. The Raven 2 also uses a thermoplastic carbon fiber—a thinner, lighter skin bonded to the frame with an epoxy resin.

Spurred by Mario Galasso, Cannondale has redefined the look and feel of the motocross racing motorcycle. The MX 400 (1999) has a fuel-injected, liquid-cooled engine that is both shorter and more compact than normal. Its reversed cylinder head is placed lower and farther to the rear to optimize the bike's center of gravity. The MX 400 has a lightweight aluminum frame;

RAVEN 2
Mountain bike, 1998, thermo-
plastic carbon fiber and shell with
magnesium spine
Designer: Tod Patterson
Additional designer: Mike Parkin
Manufacturer: Cannondale

the entire package weighs just 239 pounds. *Dirt Rider* named the machine its 1999 Bike of the Year even though the editors had yet to ride it. "Simply put," they said, "the MX 400 looks more like a high-dollar project from a secret division of a major automobile manufacturer than a first attempt from a leader in the pedal-power industry."

In the highly competitive fields of bicycle and motorcycle design, Cannondale has shown a strategic ability to challenge assumptions and a propensity to rethink problems that others have put aside, recognizing that aesthetics has joined performance as a keen interest for serious cyclists. s.s.h.

SAECO-CANNONDALE TEAM REPLICA
Bicycle, 1998, aluminum
(series 6061-T6)
Designer: Chris Peck
Manufacturer: Cannondale

MX 400
Off-road racing motorcycle,
1999, aluminum frame
Designer: Mario Galasso, Chris
D'Aluisio, and Cannondale
motorcycle development team
Manufacturer: Cannondale

EDWARD FELLA B. 1938

California Institute of the Arts
Valencia, California

The work of Edward Fella set the philosophical agenda for experimental typography in the 1990s. While digital publishing has enabled the quick production of slick, finished documents, Fella seeks to ground letterforms in the PHYSICAL world. Avoiding the computer altogether, he works with photocopies, rub-down type, and hand-lettering to create a typographic language that celebrates damaged and irregular forms over neat and tidy surfaces. His work has influenced a generation of designers who use digital tools to create blurred and battered typefaces and to construct page layouts that are willfully disjunctive and decentered.

Describing himself as a "former Detroit commercial artist," Fella left the arena of professional practice in 1987 to pursue his own vision of typography in the context of academia, first as a late-life graduate student at the Cranbrook Academy of Art and then as a professor at the California Institute of the Arts (Cal Arts), where he currently teaches. Fella's experimental *oeuvre* consists of a continuing series of folded posters announcing exhibitions and lectures at various venues. Often, the posters are printed after an event has taken place as documentary souvenirs—like the psychedelic posters of the 1960s—and thus have no advertising function. They serve, instead, as experiments in typographic thought.

In a poster promoting a lecture in Rotterdam, Fella reclaims the Dutch avant-garde tradition of constructing letterforms around a square grid. But Fella's postmodern variants are drawn by hand rather than built with ruler and T-square; they are deliberately imperfect and almost decorative in character.

A REALLY BIG SLY-ED SHOW & LECTURE
Poster, 1997, offset lithograph
Designer: Edward Fella
Publisher: University of California, Los Angeles

HYPE-TYPE: ROTTERDAM
Poster, 1998, offset lithograph
Designer: Edward Fella
Publisher: Edward Fella for Font Shop

To commemorate another lecture, Fella created his own version of the classical typeface Bodoni, defiling its elegant letterforms with blunt, hand-drawn serifs. Fella's poster pokes fun at the modernist myth of eternal form by following the word "timeless" with the payroll expression "time and 1/2."

Fella's sketchbooks are another serial project. Fella is fascinated with the outdoor advertising found along America's commercial streets, which he obsessively documents with a Polaroid camera. The drawings in his sketch books are often bizarre, nonsensical conglomerations of letters inspired by similar sources.

Fella's ongoing commitment to a core set of ideas is remarkable within the field of graphic design. His work, which celebrates the written word as a physical object, has had an enormous impact on contemporary typography.
E.L.

PHYSICAL—

RECLAIMED—

TIMELESS OR TIME & 1/2
Poster, 1999, offset lithograph
Designer: Edward Fella
Publisher: Edward Fella for
American Institute of Graphic Arts,
New York Chapter

LETTERING DRAWINGS
Sketchbook, 1999, ballpoint pen and
color pencil
Designer: Edward Fella

STEVEN HOLL B. 1947

Steven Holl Architects
New York City

Steven Holl forcefully expresses the PHYSICALITY of his buildings, carving a niche into a rough concrete wall with knife-like precision or converting a reflecting pool into a skylight that casts dappled sunlight onto cool underground walls. The perceptual aspects of architecture—shifting patterns of light and color—imbue his buildings with a meditative calm. It is an aesthetic of monastic minimalism. Holl's recent architecture—for example, the Museum of Contemporary Art in Helsinki (1998) or the Institute of Science at the Cranbrook Academy of Art outside Detroit (1998)——blends the humane modernism of Alvar Aalto with the plasticity of Le Corbusier's later work. In Holl's architecture, stripped-down forms are coupled with tactile surfaces and hand-crafted details.

In designing his buildings, Holl will often seek an analog in the natural world (the 1991 Stretto House, in Dallas, is in part based on a musical score, indicating that the phenomenological can also drive his design). A new scheme for a row of freshmen dormitories at the Massachusetts Institute of Technology (currently in design), for example, relates the buildings' urbanistic plan as well as their individual designs to the natural properties of honeycombs and sponges. The dorms' site along the Vassar Street Corridor is an unusually long, thin strip of land, separating MIT from the neighboring city of Cambridge. Seeking to alleviate animosities between town and gown, Holl rejected the idea of a single, impenetrable structure, instead proposing a permeable row of four individual units that would visually and physically link MIT and the adjacent neighborhood. Cut-outs

MIT RESIDENCE 2001 (SPONGE SCHEME): ATRIUM PERSPECTIVE
Cambridge, Massachusetts
Sketch, 1999, pencil and watercolor on paper
Delineator: Steven Holl
Architect: Steven Holl Architects
Project architect: Tim Bade

[right]
MIT RESIDENCE 2001 (SPONGE SCHEME): SECTION
Cambridge, Massachusetts
Sketch, 1999, pencil and watercolor on paper
Delineator: Steven Holl
Architect: Steven Holl Architects
Project architect: Tim Bade

in the buildings' facades and glass-enclosed atria open the dormitories to the outside world.

The internal organizations of two dormitories currently on the drawing board fashion a porous relationship between private and public space. Holl generated the plan and section of one building by pressing an ink-filled sponge onto sheets of paper. The sponge's solid parts comprise private spaces, such as the student rooms; its open cells suggested the location of multistoried atria. The other scheme features an interior "folded street" that ramps up the building, creating a swirl of private and public functions. In both schemes, open spaces serve as student lounges and computer workshops. Architectural lungs, they will breathe friendship, interaction, and dialog into the typically hermetic lives of contemporary college students. These spaces also underscore Holl's ambition to create buildings that are social, as well as physical, organisms. D.A.

**MIT RESIDENCE 2001
(SPONGE SCHEME)**
Cambridge, Massachusetts
Model, 1999, scale 1/16":1',
basswood, plastic, perforated
metal, and homosote
Architect: Steven Holl Architects
Project architect: Tim Bade
Model fabricator: Rong-Hui Lin
Team: Anderson Lee, Erik Langdelen,
Annette Goderbauer, Rong-Hui Lin,
Mimi Hoang, Ziad Jamaleddine,
Gabriela Barman, Steve O'Dell

**MIT RESIDENCE 2001
(SPONGE SCHEME)**
Cambridge, Massachusetts
Preliminary model, 1999, scale
1/16":1', paper and basswood
Architect: Steven Holl Architects
Project architect: Tim Bade
Model fabricator: Annette Goderbauer

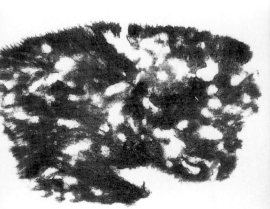

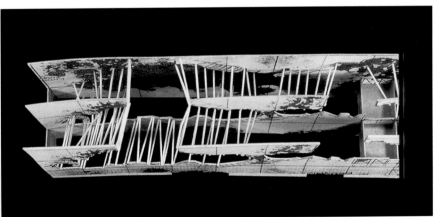

IDEO

Palo Alto, California
San Francisco, California
Chicago, Illinois
Grand Rapids, Michigan
Boston, Massachusetts
London
Milan
Tel Aviv
Tokyo

IDEO employs a user-focused approach in order to create products whose purpose and function are clear. As co-founder Bill Moggridge states, "Good design puts people first." By studying consumers' PHYSICAL and emotional interactions with products and environments, designers at IDEO often discover a solution as much as invent it.

A compelling example of IDEO's process was its one-week project to design a new grocery cart for *Nightline*, the ABC television program (1999). The IDEO team prototyped a new shopping cart that would be convenient to use and would minimize injuries—hospitals report twenty-two-thousand cart injuries each year. The design consists of a bottomless cart with drop-in baskets and hooks to attach grocery bags, it prevents tip-over when children jump in, has a kickstand to prevent parking lot runaways, and

discourages theft. The gracefully curved unit is nestable and has rubber sleeves to prevent collision damage. By challenging the cage-on-wheels standard, the IDEO team demonstrated that even the most taken-for-granted, been-there-forever products can be reinvented.

The Steelcase Q concept work-station (1997) point to a future where workers will drive enclosures through office spaces. Intended to encourage collaboration yet allow for personal privacy, the car-like furniture system is powered by a wheelchair motor and controlled by a joystick. The seat rotates around the structure, which is equipped with a four-screen display mounted on a flexible arm. Handles allow users to adjust the workstation's surfaces and to position the entire unit. Outrigger arms act as perches for chatting coworkers; video conferencing is built in for those farther away.

SHOPPING CART
Conceptual prototype, 1998,
steel tubing, high-density
urethane foam, ABS, and acrylic
Designer: Chris Flink, Jane Fulton
Suri, David Lyons, Ed Pearce,
Peter Skillman, Danny Stillion,
John Stoddard, and Alex Kazaks,
IDEO

Steelcase's Leap work chair (1999) represents a new direction in back support and office seating. The joint IDEO-Steelcase team aimed to create a chair that would change shape with the movement of the back (the spine does not move as a single unit), mimic the unique motion of the body, provide adjustable support for both the upper and lower back, and allow for reclining without change in orientation. The Leap has a design vocabulary that combines mechanical and organic references in an exposed structure with clear controls and a perforated back.

Although IDEO works almost exclusively in teams, their designs resolutely focus on the individual. Their methodology reflects the intrinsic power of collaborative thinking in which the client's project brief intersects with the "human factors of everyday life." s.s.h.

STEELCASE LEAP CHAIR
Furniture, 1999, steel, glass-filled nylon, urethane foam, urethane gel, ABS, varied fabrics
Designers: George Simons, Tom Eich, and Thomas Overthun, IDEO, and David Gresham and Kurt Heidman, Steelcase
Client: Steelcase

STEELCASE Q CONCEPT
Conceptual prototype, 1997, high-density urethane foam
Designer: Martin Bone, IDEO
Client: Steelcase

KYLE COOPER B. 1962
AND TEAM

IMAGINARY FORCES
Hollywood, California

SEVEN
Main titles, feature film, 1995
Director: Kyle Cooper,
Imaginary Forces
Designers: Kyle Cooper
and Jenny Shainin,
Imaginary Forces
Executive producer of
main titles: Peter Frankfurt,
Imaginary Forces
Director of film: David Fincher
Producers: New Line Cinema

Occasionally, a new idea changes the course of thinking within a field of art or inquiry. Such a paradigm shift occurred in 1995 with the opening titles of David Fincher's film *Seven*, designed by Kyle Cooper. In this psychological thriller a serial murderer forces each of his victims into a fatal embrace with a deadly sin, from gluttony and sloth to lust and pride. The opening titles show the villain assembling a gruesome document of his horrors. Scratched, imperfect lettering jumps and lurches to a screeching score, while rough-cut, up-close footage transforms ordinary tools of reproduction—developing trays, scissors, paper, tape—into ominous devices of torture and mutilation.

Cooper's excrutiating exploration of the PHYSICALITY of image-making had an immediate impact on the film industry, receiving more favorable publicity than the movie itself. The titles for *Seven* reflected the urge to ground text and image in physical processes, an idea that designers for print had been grappling with in response to the facile slickness of much digital design. Cooper brought a new typographic sensibility into the language of cinema—a taste for subtly deranged typographic details over large-scale special effects. *Seven* made Cooper the leading creator of motion graphics, his work widely imitated by designers for film, television, and multimedia.

Recent projects include *Mimic* (1997), a science-fiction horror film about a genetic experiment on insects that yields monstrous results. Cooper's opening sequence introduces the crisis that will prompt the ill-fated experiment. Close-up footage of bugs and butterflies—pinned for study—is intercut with newspaper clips about an insect-born epidemic and snapshots of children lost to the disease. The

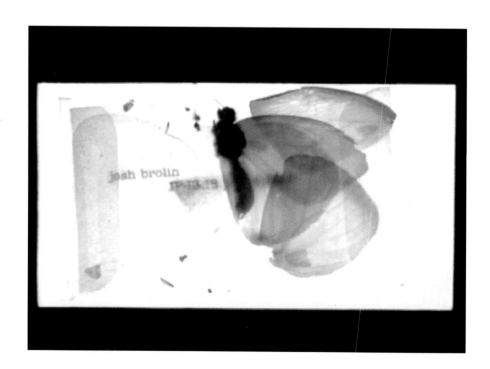

photos and news clippings are pinned and sliced into smaller segments, suggesting a ruthless course of destruction. The fluttering scraps of paper cast long, forbidding shadows, dramatizing the physical character of montage.

Although Cooper and his firm Imaginary Forces are known for dark depictions of evil, they also create titles sequences infused with humor. The typography that opens *Super Cop* (1992) makes quick leaps that synchronize with piercing kung-fu yells to comic effect. *Dead Man on Campus* (1998) begins with a meandering pan across a page of primer-style instructions for committing suicide.

During his rapid ascent within this evolving medium, Cooper has transformed the written word into a performer, and he has created filmed images that reflect their own making.
E.L.

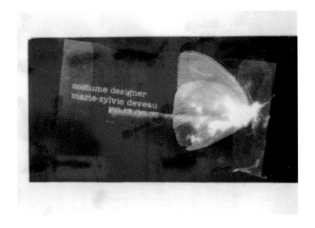

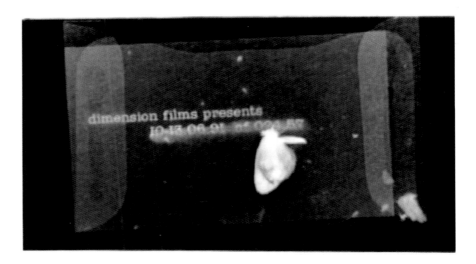

MIMIC
Main titles, feature film, 1997
Director: Kyle Cooper
Designers: Kyle Cooper, Karin Fong,
Dana Yee, Scarlett Kim, Kimberly Cooper,
Imaginary Forces
Art director: Karin Fong, Imaginary Forces
Director of film: Guillermo Del Toro
Producers: Dimension Films/Miramax

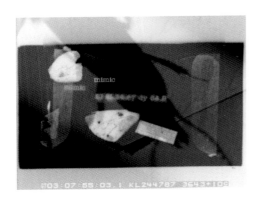

BRUCE LICHER B. 1958

Independent Project Press
Sedona, Arizona

Bruce Licher's career exemplifies the entrepreneurial, do-it-yourself ethos that many designers and artists embrace today. Working outside the metropolitan mainstream, Licher produces record and CD packaging for the independent music industry. He uses rough materials and salvaged typefaces to reveal the PHYSICAL character of print. Exploiting the potential rawness and imperfection of letterpress printing, Licher uses inks that don't completely cover his surfaces, and he allows relief characters to bite into the page.

Letterpress printing, which employs raised characters cast in lead, has been reclaimed over the past decade by artists, poets, and designers. Although this relief technique was rendered largely obsolete by offset lithography after World War II, letterpress lived on for limited edition printing in the "fine press" movement. The technique also was sustained by local print shops that produced inexpensive tickets and posters in small numbers. Licher's work, with its make-do use of available resources, is linked more to the vernacular spirit of the print shop than to the arts-and-crafts aspirations of the fine press movement.

The graphic identity for Independent Project Press revels in the material qualities of letterpress printing. Licher has made a fetish out of the routine ephemera of paper

INDEPENDENT PROJECT PRESS
Business card, 1999, letterpress on Rainbow Bristol
Designer and photographer: Bruce Licher,
Independent Project Press
Publisher: Independent Project Press

HAROLD BUDD, FENCELESS NIGHT
CD package, 1998, offset lithograph on
chipboard, plastic digipak tray
Designer: Bruce Licher, Independent
Project Press
Photographer: Harold Budd
Publisher: Polygram Music Publishing

correspondence, creating not only business cards, letterheads, and envelopes but also his own simulated postal stamps and bank checks. To create these pieces, Licher assembles minute typographic elements and prints them in multiple layers of ink. He designs a new piece when supplies run out, insuring that his brand image remains in flux—appropriately "independent"—rather than freezing into a rigid identity.

Licher's letterpress process combines mechanical and digital tools. In addition to printing letters from individual metal characters, he produces relief plates from electronic files. Licher is now translating the physical character of his letterpress work to the more commercial medium of offset lithography. A CD package for Harold Budd is printed offset on chipboard with opaque silver, gold, and orange ink— materials and colors that prevail in Licher's letterpress productions. As an alternative to the plastic "jewel box," the piece employs an all cardboard structural design created by Licher.

Letterpress is an overtly physical process that leaves its mark in the surface of printed matter. Licher uses this antiquated technology to communicate within contemporary culture. E.L.

R.E.M. 1998 HOLIDAY FANCLUB VIDEO
Video cassette package, 1998, letterpress on chipboard
Designer: Bruce Licher, Independent Project Press
Art Director: Chris Bilheimer
Publisher: R.E.M./Athens, L.L.C.

STEREOLAB, THE IN SOUND
7-inch record cover and stamps, 1999, letterpress on chipboard, vinyl
Designer: Bruce Licher, Independent Project Press
Publisher: Independent Project Records
Package based on an original design by Win Bruder for Verve Records' 1965 release of *The In Sound* by Gary McFarland, with an original cover painting by Peter Shulman. Adapted for letterpress by Bruce Licher

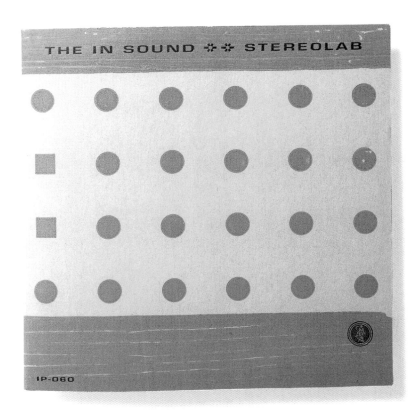

STEPHEN PEART B.1958

Vent Design
Campbell, California

Originally hired to establish frogdesign's California office in 1983, Stephen Peart set up his own firm, Vent Design, in 1987 and soon had a distinguished client base. What unites Peart's projects—including a skateboard for Santa Cruz, the Computer Cap, and an office system for Herman Miller—is an unrelenting focus on the PHYSICAL spirit of materials, a preoccupation that can be traced through much of Peart's earlier work. In his Animal wetsuit, for example (produced by O'Neil in 1992), Peart used molded neoprene rubber and thermoplastic to create a suit with accordion-like flexible sections at the joints and stress areas.

Working with Ross Lovegrove on the Surf Collection of desk accessories for Knoll (1993), Peart appropriated a heat-reactive polyurethane foam used in fighter-pilot seats. The collection's lumbar support, for example, hangs over a chair back and continually reforms itself according to the sitter's body position. Because the foam has memory, it returns to its normal shape quickly. Peart's Nuwood skateboard for Santa Cruz (1997) is formed from recycled plastic with oriented fiber strands that optimize response, feel, and sensitivity. Its virtuous, alchemical reuse of disposed materials distinguishes it from standard wood models.

Peart's materials-intensive exploration continued in a concept shoe created in 1996 for a special issue of the *New York Times Magazine*. Peart envisioned a shoe that was a living sculptural membrane, chunky and bone-like at the base, and open, thin, and tendon-like at the ankle. His Computer Cap (1996), for Virtual Vision is a see-through screen environment that sits just above the bridge of the nose like a plastic pair of glasses with an attached hat.

SANTA CRUZ NUWOOD
Skateboard, 1997, recycled "post-industrial" nylon 66 and short carbon fiber in a microcellular unidirectional matrix
Designer: Stephen Peart, Vent

It is sliced open and perforated to
insure light weight, breathability,
and economy of materials.

    Peart's string of product
innovations has redefined comfort
and performance with a newfound
"emotional ergonomics" that is
rooted in a love of materials but
makes that love contingent upon
PHYSICAL transformation. S.S.H.

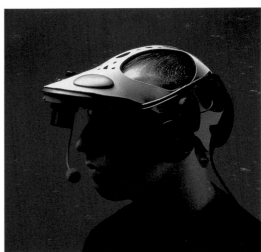

COMPUTER CAP
Prototype, 1996, closed-cell neoprene,
Lycra jersey, short carbon fiber, and
thermoplastic polyester blend
Designer: Stephen Peart, Vent
Client: Virtual Vision

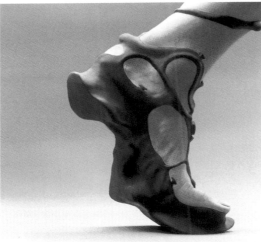

CONCEPT SHOE
Prototype, 1997, latex
Designer: Stephen Peart, Vent
Client: New York Times Magazine

RAVEEVARN CHOKSOMBATCHAI B. 1959
RALPH NELSON B. 1961

LOOM

Berkeley, California

Aptly named, the architectural firm Loom weaves together architecture's PHYSICAL and phenomenal qualities. Loom's projects are cultural artifacts as well as visceral experiences, a duality demonstrated by their 1996 Knox Garden and Playground design in Minneapolis. By painting ordinary, chain-link fences in unusual and unusually bright colors, Loom created the effect of a delicate, multihued mist, freshly presenting this everyday material to the community. Similarly, a trellis-like wall on the grounds of their Woman Suffrage Memorial (1999) at the Minnesota State Capitol in St. Paul functions as landscape sculpture and educational experience. An environmental timeline, the wall threads together vertical posts marking successive years of the suffrage movement with undulating horizontal bars describing the lives of twenty-five different suffragists.

Loom principals Ralph Nelson and Raveevarn Choksombatchai, a husband-and-wife team who have practiced architecture since 1993, were commissioned to create an installation for the *National Design Triennial*. They developed a structure that contrasts with the museum's century-old building. *Liquescence* was devised in collaboration with digital media artist Shawn Brixey and Moss Inc., the tent designer and manufacturer. It serves as a perpetual clock as well as a lightweight and ethereal foil to the landmark mansion. The title takes its name from the transitional state between solid and liquid, metaphorically calling upon the polarities of ephemerality and permanence inherent to architecture.

Occupying an outdoor courtyard adjacent to the museum's Barbara Riley Levin Conservatory, *Liquescence*

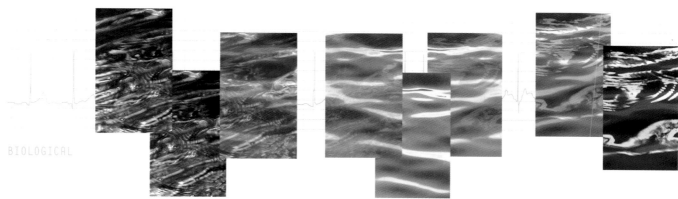

BIOLOGICAL

DIGITAL

LIQUESCENCE
Site-specific installation for the
National Design Triennial
Conceptual digital renderings, 1999
Architects: Ralph Nelson and Raveevarn
Choksombatchai, Loom in collaboration
with Shawn Brixey and Moss Inc.
Biological drawings: Alta Bates Medical
Center, Cardiology Department

comprises three tented spaces, each linked to a window overlooking the courtyard. The overall effect integrates the physical properties of natural sunlight with two kinds of artificial light—the digital glow emanating from a computer screen and the twinkling of electric bulbs pulsing at the rate of a heartbeat. All three forms of light play upon the tents' softly curved surfaces—the sun's changing orientation throughout the day registers as intense shafts of light on the tents' fabric walls, while the artificial lights subtly flicker at different speeds. The effect continually redefines the spaces within the tents, serving as a fluid marker of passing time—solar, digital, and biological. D.A.

KNOX GARDEN AND PLAYGROUND
Minneapolis, Minnesota
Photograph, 1996
Architects: Ralph Nelson and Raveevarn Choksombatchai, Loom
Construction: Ralph Nelson, Ben Awes, Tree Trust Organization, and volunteers

PHYSICAL

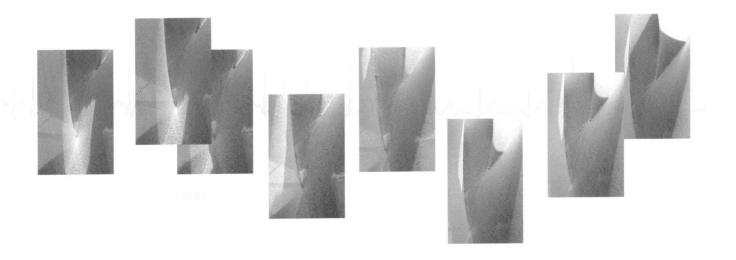

GIGI BIEDERMAN B. 1964
DAVID KARAM B. 1969

POST TOOL DESIGN
San Francisco, California

Gigi Biederman and David Karam are partners in Post Tool, located in the technology-intensive environment of San Francisco. Their projects are humorous yet thoughtful explorations of digital interactivity, as seen, for example in *Questions and Answers* (1993), a prototype for a children's museum that brings together science and poetry in a syncopated rhythm of visual and audio call and response.

Post Tool's self-published project *Cardinal Directions* explores dynamic typography in three-dimensional space. The environment is populated with four characters: a cat, a car, a rhinorceros, and bubbles. Each has its own character or behavior: the cat confronts, the car navigates, the rhino wanders, and the bubbles float. At the center is a Klein bottle, a geometric construction in which interior and exterior flow seamlessly together. The Klein bottle acts as an infinite source of energy, a perpetual motion device that is also a gravitational element pulling together this strange universe. Keyed to the cardinal directions are four words, each signifying an aspect of existence: the past, the future, the known, and the unknown. The designers explain, "As architects of a virtual environment, we reference and break the PHYSICAL laws of nature."

In addition to creating experimental works, Post Tool designs Web sites, multimedia installations, and printed matter for corporate and cultural clients. They have developed an independent voice that challenges the emerging clichés of multimedia. In place of the shiny buttons, marbelized surfaces, and rigid window frames that dominate digital design, Post Tool has created lyrical environments that are invitingly human. E.L.

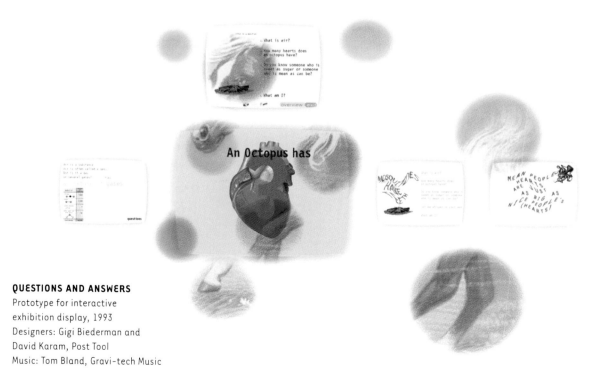

QUESTIONS AND ANSWERS
Prototype for interactive
exhibition display, 1993
Designers: Gigi Biederman and
David Karam, Post Tool
Music: Tom Bland, Gravi-tech Music

PHYSICAL

MINIMAL

Sagmeister Inc.
New York City

Stefan Sagmeister has produced a body of work that is, quite literally, embodied. Rejecting notions of design as the styling of a slick, seamless surface, Sagmeister draws on concrete events and tangible experiences. To promote a lecture about his work, Sagmeister instructed an assistant to inscribe the text of the poster into his own skin with an X-acto knife. A photograph of his bleeding body provided word and image for the final poster, conveying Sagmeister's willful embrace of typography as PHYSICAL form.

Sagmeister's work primarily serves the culture industries, especially music. He converts the cramped space of the conventional CD package into the site of an unfolding scenario, a narrative that engages the user in a series of bodily experiences and conceptual games. Sagmeister drilled a relentless grid of holes through the CD cover and booklet for Skeleton Key's *Fantastic Spikes through Balloon* (1997), and he turned David Byrne's CD *Feelings* (1997) into a multicolored, pseudoscientific "mood dial."

Other projects deploy the materials and iconography of commercial packaging in surprising contexts. To produce a promotional mailing for the fashion designer

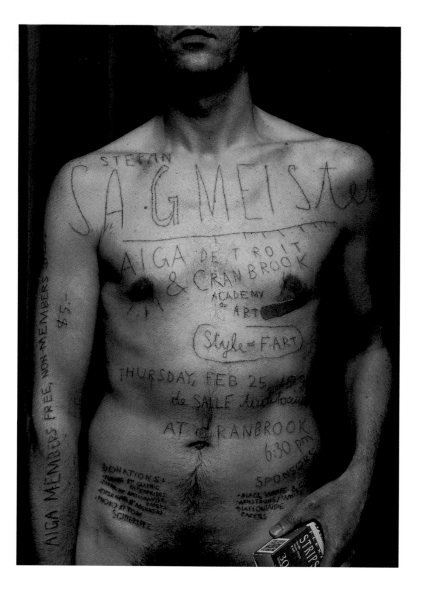

**STEFAN SAGMEISTER:
AIGA DETROIT**
Poster, 1999, offset lithograph
Art Director: Stefan Sagmeister
Designer: Martin Woodtli
Photographer: Tom Schierlitz
Publisher: AIGA Detroit

Anni Kuan, Sagmeister folded a newsprint publication over a wire hanger, shrink-wrapped the ensemble against a corrugated cardboard backing, and sent the resulting package directly through the mail. The Anni Kuan promotion reclaims lowly materials from everyday commercial culture to create an object that is both inexpensive and unforgettable. The pages within this irreverent package explore other dimensions of physicality. For one spread, Sagmeister constructed letters out of strips of fabric and laid them out on the floor to be photographed. For another, he digitally collaged Kuan's name into the storefront signage of a Manhattan dry cleaner. These experiments treat letterforms as concrete objects, earth-bound inhabitants of a three-dimensional landscape.

Sagmeister shows that as a process, design executes physical operations on materials, texts, images, and objects, and as a product, design has a physical impact on its users, its makers, and the world it occupies. E.L.

ANNI KUAN
Brochure, 1999, offset lithograph
on newsprint with corrugated board,
wire hanger, and plastic wrap
Art director: Stefan Sagmeister
Designer: Hjalti Karlsson
Photographer: Tom Schierlitz
Illustrator: Martin Woodtli
Client: Anni Kuan

ROBERT EGGER B. 19XX

SPECIALIZED BIKES
Morgan Hill, California

Specialized Bikes was founded in 1974, and one of its claims to fame is that it designed and manufactured the first production mountain bike. That 1981 model—the Stumpjumper—signaled the boom in mountain biking and the surging consumer appetite for bikes with a heartier PHYSICAL frame.

During the early 1990s, while other bicycle manufacturers were scrambling to adjust to the rise of the mountain bike and the decline of the road bike, Robert Egger and David Schultz began creating concept bikes for Specialized. Their first three bicycles changed the cycling industry. While Schultz went on to Thomson Consumer Electronics, Egger stayed at Specialized, and has since developed a series of outlandish one-off bikes in addition to complete lines of production bikes for racing, mountain, and recreation. By channeling their energy into conceptual projects and product development, Specialized has forced its competitors to change the way they think about the industry, accelerating an already competitive global market.

Egger looks to a wide range of subjects as inspiration for his whimsical bikes, from insects, cartoons, and surf culture to the horse-and-wagon. Recent bikes include the Woody and Cadillac bikes (1998). Each has a familiar reference in American automobile culture of the 1950s. Reclaiming imagery from the past, such concept bikes enlarge the possibilities for two-wheeled travel while building and expanding

the Specialized brand in a colorful
and focused way that appeals to both
hard-core cyclists and the Nintendo
generation.

Egger and his team make their
concept studies through traditional
model-making processes and guerilla
construction techniques. The
company's team of off-road riders,
Team Specialized, puts those designs
to the test. Egger's design group also
creates bikes for Specialized's
S-Works unit, which creates bikes
without limitations on materials
or price. The S-Works team car (a
hearse) and team motto ("Innovate or
Die") sum up the aggressive design
philosophy Egger has pioneered at
Specialized. s.s.h.

CADILLAC BIKE
Concept bicycle, 1998, fiberglass
Designer: Robert Egger
Manufacturer: Specialized Bikes

WOODY
Bicycle, 1999, aluminum with wood
body panels
Designer: Robert Egger
Manufacturer: Specialized Bikes

Jennifer Sterling combines an obsessively refined sense of typography with a celebration of PHYSICAL processes. Holes punch through a page of correspondence. Geometric letterforms bite into a field of velvet. Perforations divide an enormous poster into dozens of smaller parts. From the choice of paper to the selection of printing and binding methods, Sterling judges each detail for its sensual impact. She pieces together delicate lines of type with the eye of a jeweler and then drapes them with seeming abandon across the luxurious body of the page.

Sterling began her career in the San Francisco office of Steve Tolleson, where she challenged the conventions of corporate annual report design with her classical typographic ethos. Sterling established her own firm, Sterling Design, in San Francisco in 1996, where she designs annual reports as well as posters and publications for corporate and cultural clients.

The scale and texture of the book continue to pervade Sterling's work, as does evidence—real and fictional—of physical processes. A recent annual report for DSP Communications (1998) is no bigger than a trade paperback—comfortably sized to be held in the hand—and its cover appears battered and worn.

To promote photographer Marko Lavrisha and copywriter Eric La Brecque, Sterling produced a pair of slipcovered publications (1998). The covers are made of velvet flocking imprinted with large letterpress characters. The flocking accepts only a trace of ink, leaving the indentation of the letters to predominate.

A poster for a lecture series at the Southern California Institute of Architects (Sci-Arc) is also inflected by the scale and rhythm of the book (1998). In place of a single image,

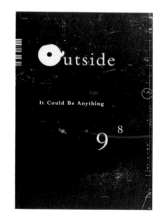

DSP ANNUAL REPORT
Annual report, 1998,
offset lithograph
Designer: Jennifer Sterling
Copywriter: Eric LaBrecque
Publisher: DSP Communications

LAVRISHA/LABRECQUE
Book with slipcover, 1998,
offset lithograph, debossed
velvet flocking
Designer: Jennifer Sterling
Publisher: Lavrisha/LaBrecque

Sterling created a grid of smaller units, each the size of a page and each framed as an independent element. Contrasts of tone, color, and scale from unit to unit makes the poster effective as a totality, while perforations invite the user to tear it apart.

For Sterling. graphic design is the shaping of physical objects. She incorporates the experience of the reader and the techniques of the maker into the content of her work.
E.L.

DIFFERENTIATED TOPOGRAPHIES
Poster, 1998, offset lithograph, perforated
Designer: Jennifer Sterling
Illustrators: Jennifer Sterling, Amy Hayson
Copywriter: Margi Reeves
Publisher: Southern California Institute of Architecture

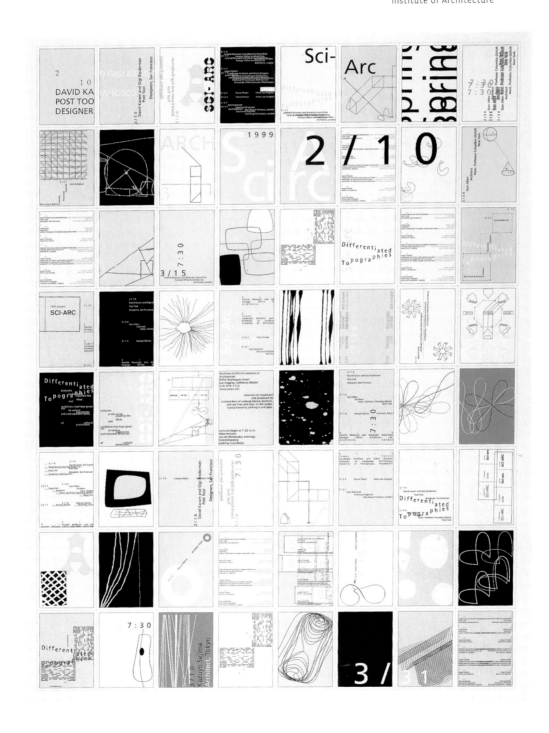

BILLIE TSIEN B.1949
TOD WILLIAMS B. 1943

Tod Williams Billie Tsien and
Associates, New York City

In the spring of 2001, the Museum
of American Folk Art will reopen on
New York City's West Fifty-third
Street, adjacent to the starkly modern
Museum of Modern Art. In contrast,
the folk art museum will be warm and
sculptural. In its powerfully PHYSICAL
expression of experimental materials
and bold forms, the museum will
exemplify the work of architects
Tod Williams and Billie Tsien. This
husband-and-wife team has
developed a mature practice that
encompasses master plans, buildings,
exhibitions, and set designs. Projects
range from a Manhattan residence
for real estate developer Jerry Speyer
and his wife Katherine Farley to
institutional buildings for Johns
Hopkins University, Princeton
University, and the Neurosciences
Research Institute in La Jolla,
California. Expanding on the legacy
of such postwar architects as Louis I.
Kahn and Carlo Scarpa, the Museum

of American Folk Art significantly
advances the ongoing dialog between
two related modernist traditions—the
machine-made and the hand-crafted.

Williams and Tsien describe
their building as a "house of art,"
acknowledging the museum's
residentially sized site (the width of
two existing townhouses) as well as
the character of its collections. Not
created for museums, folk art is often
functional, if expressive of eccentric
and obsessive visions. While not
traditionally "folksy," the new
museum will bear the dual imprint
of the everyday and the personal.
The skylit interior's domestic scale
will let visitors intimately relate to
the museum's artifacts and to the
building's sensuous materials. These
include translucent walls of blue-
and-gold iridescent fiberglass and
latticework panels of undulating wood
slats woven into what seem like giant
versions of Shaker baskets.

MUSEUM OF AMERICAN FOLK ART
New York City
Exterior wall panel studies, 1998,
Tombasil
Architects: Tod Williams and Billie Tsien
Project architect and photographer:
Matthew Baird
Associate architect: Helfand Myerberg
Guggenheimer Architects

The museum's Fifty-third Street facade contrasts two types of highly textured, hand-crafted panels of Tombasil, a variant of white bronze. Since the original idea of casting the panels on the sidewalk proved unfeasible, the architects decided to fabricate them by pouring the bronze onto coarse steel plates and the foundry's rough concrete floor, thereby imprinting them with the physical evidence of their construction. Faceted and folded inward on the facade, the panels reflect the different glows of the morning, midday, and setting sun.

Williams and Tsien have created a formidable visual juxtaposition on the streets of Manhattan—smooth versus rough, machined versus natural—while making a significant contribution to New York City's cultural landscape. The two architects have likened the facade of their museum to a cupped hand, an apt metaphor for a firm whose work offers a complex and sophisticated approach to modernism. D.A.

MUSEUM OF AMERICAN FOLK ART
New York City
Model (section from the west), 1998, scale 1/4":1', basswood
Architects: Tod Williams and Billie Tsien
Project architect: Matthew Baird
Project team: Hana Kassem, Phillip Ryan, Nina Schweiger, and Vivian Wang
Associate architect: Helfand Myerberg Guggenheimer Architects
Model fabricator: Richard Sturgeon

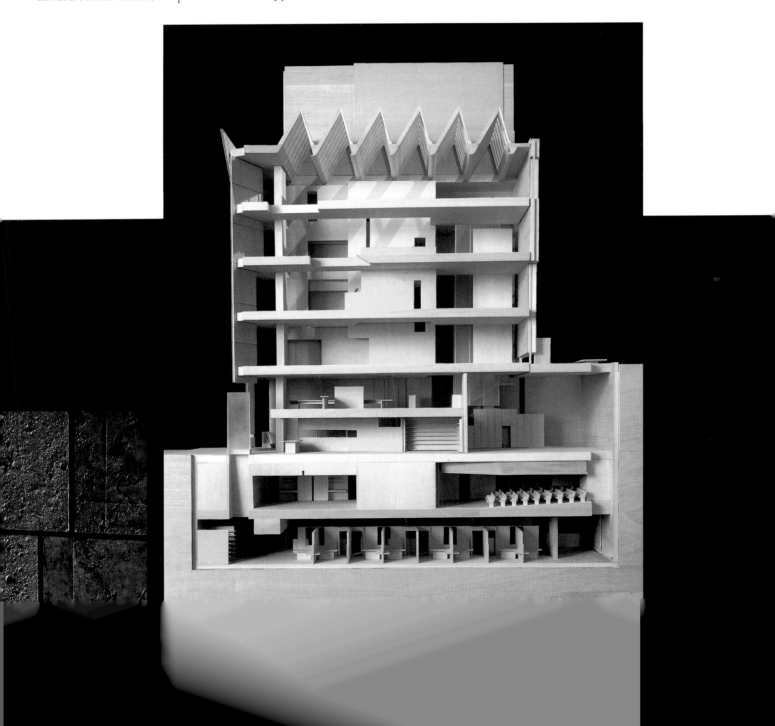

MARTIN VENEZKY B. 1957

Appetite Engineers
San Francisco, California

In Martin Venezky's designs for posters, books, magazines, and advertising, the tools of digital production collide with the PHYSICAL realm. Venezky wields camera, glue, knife, even needle and thread to ground his type and images in the material world. Venezky led a typical, service-oriented career before immersing himself in the graduate program at Cranbrook Academy of Art at the age of 35. Reborn from this experience, he committed himself to design as an experimental medium.

Among Venezky's ongoing projects is the magazine *Speak*, which serves as an open-ended laboratory for his explorations of type and image. Like *Ray Gun*, the music magazine that electrified the worlds of design and popular culture under the direction of David Carson in the early 1990s (and which Venezky briefly contributed to), *Speak* is aimed at young readers and is shaped by its visual presentation. Venezky has honed his own strategies in the pages of *Speak*, creating layouts that are at once typographically surprising and accessible to read.

Venezky began experimenting with the physical mutilation of typography in his designs for *Speak*. Working from laser prints of bold, broad-faced letters, Venezky repeatedly sliced into the characters with an X-acto blade, allowing their forms to curve, crack, and peel away. These meticulous, almost surgical procedures yielded fluid, unpredictable results, as slivers of black broke free from the letters' architecture.

Venezky extended this repertoire of typographic manipulations in an advertising campaign for Rockport, launched in 1999 in Italy by the agency Kirshenbaum Bond & Partners. Approaching the printed letter as a body to be physically

altered and adorned, Venezky subjected letterforms to a range of reconstructive surgeries and disguises. Some are cut into ribbons, while others are elaborately sewn up with thread whose loose ends unfurl like wayward hairs. Still others are wrapped in fishnet or adorned with feathers and then exposed to photographic paper, where their substance dissolves into veils of light and shadow. These elaborately cut and costumed characters were scanned for digital reproduction, becoming the principle players in a series of print ads and billboards.

Venezky fuels his work with physical materials and processes, and approaches typography as an embodied substance rather than an abstract code. E.L.

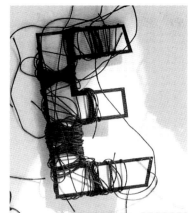

FLUID

PHYSICAL

MUTILATED LETTERS
Letterforms, 1999, mixed media
Designers: Martin Venezky and
Sara Cambridge, Appetite Engineers
Client: Letters developed for advertising
campaign, Kirshenbaum Bond & Partners
for Rockport
Art Director: U-cef Hanjani

Spare, simple forms are primary elements of the modern design tradition, which is associated with the reduction of an object to its simplest components. Designers today acknowledge that minimal solutions often require maximum attention to the details of craft and execution. The minimal object can be luxurious or economical; by reducing materials and exposing structure, designers can exalt the sensuality of what little remains or create new functional solutions that exploit lightness and portability. The modernist mantra "less is more" is being sharpened as designers seek to do "more with less."

GEOFFREY BEENE B. 1927

Geoffrey Beene Inc.
New York City

Geoffrey Beene is a singular presence in the realm of fashion, an outsider to the Seventh Avenue establishment who is nonetheless revered by his peers and by new talent. He has an unshakable coterie of women who wear his clothes—some have been doing so for three decades. *Paper* magazine, Manhattan's canny downtown arbiter of style and culture, recently dubbed Beene, at age seventy-one, the "Oldest Young Designer."

A fascination with structure recurs throughout Beene's work. Over the past two years, his collections have rigorously explored the possibilities of seams and zippers, elements of connection and closure that normally dissolve into their functional roles. Beene brings them forward as primary embellishments in a series of MINIMAL yet luxurious garments.

His Millennium winter dresses (1999) are made from wool and silk jersey, resilient, functional fabrics that are mainstays in Beene's canon of materials. In a technique called "channeling," invented by Beene, the seams become dimensional tubes spiralling around the body, slipping from thick to thin in undulating waves. The garments are conceived as continuous fluid surfaces, with front merging into back.

Beene, a great figure in the evolution of American fashion, repeatedly reinvents the structures of clothing. He shows how the archetypal vocabulary of openings and closings that make a piece of clothing can morph into new structures and configurations. E.L.

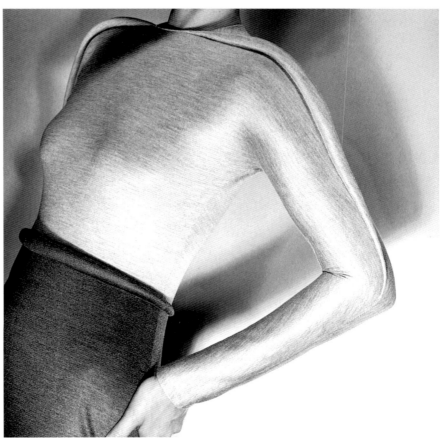

ZUZANA LICKO B. 1955
RUDY VANDERLANS B. 1955

EMIGRE
Sacramento, California

Over the past fifteen years, typeface design has been transformed from a slow-moving, capital-intensive industry into a light-footed, entrepreneurial medium. No one has had a greater role in this development than Zuzana Licko and Rudy VanderLans. Licko began creating digital fonts in 1984 for use in *Emigre*, a magazine of art and culture edited and designed by VanderLans, her husband. Typography quickly moved to the center of *Emigre*'s editorial agenda; the magazine's critical essays and interviews with designers are displayed through a changing visual structure and a flickering array of typefaces.

Emigre Graphics, headed by VanderLans, now generates books, magazines, and products as well as the magazine. Emigre Fonts publishes experimental typefaces created by Licko and other designers immersed in this newly accessible medium. Licko's first typefaces were exercises in digital MINIMALISM, embracing the coarse, blocky forms favored by early laser printers and screen displays. Although such technological limitations quickly diminished, Licko remains intrigued with building letterforms around geometric systems consisting of simple curves and angles. Her font Tarzana (1998) incorporates free-form gestures and idiosyncratic details within a relatively limited array of elements. The stable architecture of Tarzana's letter *K*, for example, is animated by the fluid sweep of its extended lower leg, while the capital *E* is constructed from two flamboyant curves.

Licko's pattern systems Whirligigs (1994) and Hypnopaedia (1997) have reclaimed the art of typographic ornament for the digital age. Hypnopaedia consists of 140 distinct pattern illustrations, each

HYPNOPAEDIA
Booklet, 1997, offset lithography
Designer: Rudy VanderLans
Pattern designer: Zuzana Licko
Publisher: Emigre Fonts

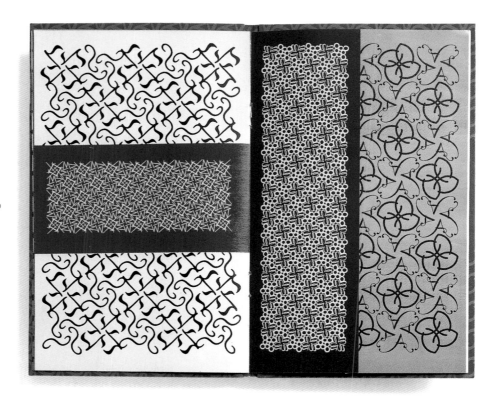

built from the concentric rotation of a letterform. The repetition of this ornamental character, which can be endlessly coupled with other ornaments from the system, yields a rich pattern in which the individual identity of the letter submits to the decorative abstraction of the field.

The Emigre brand—from its fonts to its editorial products—demonstrates the ability of two designers to plunge into a new medium at its source and to navigate its rushing waters. E.L.

Base Monospace uses the limitations of a system to generate variety and irregularity. In a monospace font, such as the familiar typewriter style Courier, all characters have the same width, unlike a traditional typeface, in which characters vary in proportion, from the narrow stalk of the letter i to the broad weave of the letter w. Ironically, a text displayed in monospace characters lacks the even, continuous gray tone sought after by classical typographers. The spotty, jittery texture that results from Base Monospace's forced regularity reflects the functional vernacular of typewriters, ticker-tapes, and bar-code labels.

BASE MONOSPACE
Typeface, 1997
Designer: Zuzana Licko
Publisher: Emigre Fonts

Tarzana incorporates free-form gestures and idiosyncratic details within a limited array of elements. **TARZANA**
Typeface, 1998
Designer: Zuzana Licko
Publisher: Emigre Fonts

PALM DESERT
Book, 1999, offset lithograph
Designer: Rudy VanderLans
Photographer: Rudy VanderLans
Typefaces: Zuzana Licko
Publisher: Emigre

GEORGE McCAIN B. 1941
JOSEPH FERRANTE B. 1952
AND TEAM

FLUKE CORPORATION
Everett, Washington

Devices that measure amperage, voltage, and wattage are generally not celebrated as design objects. But the in-house design team at Fluke has been changing that, creating tools with a consistent visual identity that is both MINIMAL and functional. Led by George McCain, Fluke's team of five industrial designers, two interaction designers, five graphic designers, and four model-makers has given routine test tools a high profile with the help of a focused design strategy.

Fluke's tools are intended for artisans, and their design solutions come from a position of deep respect for the electricians and engineers who rely on their equipment every day. The company's commitment to design extends beyond its immediately recognizable yellow and gray brand identity. Indeed, Fluke has built some of the most precise measuring tools available, and they

have done so by bringing designers and engineers together from the inception of the creative process. Discussions about shape, technology, and user behavior go hand-in-hand with discussions about how and where the various electronic components could be packaged.

Fluke products are expected to endure. The original 70 Series, described by McCain as "the Beetle of the digital multimeter world," has sold some four million units. Created in 1984, it was basic, affordable, goof-proof, and possessed what McCain describes as an "appropriate form factor." Each plastic case was imparted with a sense of consistent reliability and durability. These core ideas remain part of the evolving Fluke brand today. Fluke's no-nonsense approach has changed the very standard by which the test industry's tools are measured—and that's no accident. s.s.h.

FLUKE i410 CLAMPMETER
Electronic test tool, 1996,
case: ABS and VP-1;
overlay: reverse screened
polycarbonate (G.E. Lexan
#8B35)
Designer: Steven Fisher
Design manager: Indle King
Manufacturer: Fluke
Corporation

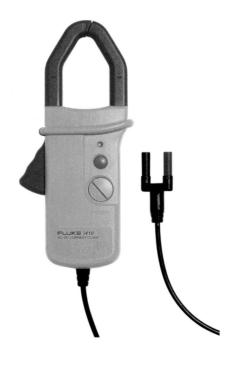

FLUKE T5 ELECTRICAL TESTER
Electronic test tool, 1998, case: Cycoloy
(ABS/PC Blend), G.E. #C2950; lens: acrylic,
Rohm & Haas #V825; boot: Santoprene 101-73,
Monsanto; overlay: reverse screened
polycarbonate (G.E. Lexan # 8B35)
Designer: Steven Fisher
User interaction design: Joseph Ferrante
Design manager: Indle King
Manufacturer: Fluke Corporation

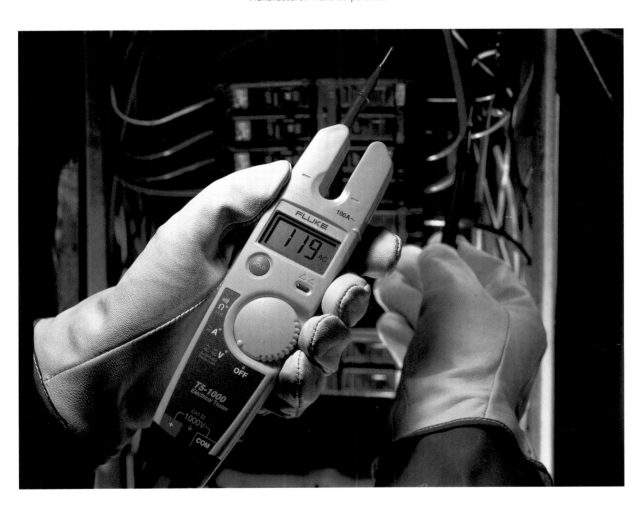

[left]
**FLUKE 89 SERIES IV TRUE RMS
MULTIMETER**
Electronic test tool, 1998,
case: Cycoloy (ABS/PC Blend), G.E.
#C2950; lens: acrylic , Rohm & Haas
#V825; overmold: SoftFlex
thermoplastic elastomer, Network
Polymers #8103
Designer: George McCain
User interaction design:
Joseph Ferrante
Manufacturer: Fluke Corporation

MICHAEL GABELLINI B. 1958

Gabellini Associates
New York City

Architect Michael Gabellini defies the reductivist connotations of the term "MINIMAL." Gabellini's store interiors and residences have many layers beneath their seemingly calm surfaces. Part of this richness comes from his modern vocabulary of pure forms and well-defined spaces, punctuated with warm colors, lavish materials, and virtuoso details. But Gabellini also draws inspiration from the worlds of theater and fine art. Like a stage director, he uses light to focus, highlight, and dramatize his spaces. "Light defines space," says Gabellini. "By shaping it and filtering it, you can articulate volume and create a sense of place." As in a well-designed museum, Gabellini's interiors form pristine backdrops for objects. His exacting curatorial eye is evident in his exhibition design for the *National Design Triennial*, where he successfully mediates the museum's historic interior and the contemporary artifacts on view by introducing a palette of industrial yet sensuous modern materials.

Gabellini's work signals a growing trend in the use of architecture and interior design in the branding of merchandise—in his case, German fashion designer Jil Sander. Gabellini and Sander have collaborated since 1991 on nearly seventy-five boutiques and showrooms in cities from Paris to Tokyo. Elements that make this worldwide network of stores identifiable include the consistent use of Spanish Arria limestone for floors and stairways, display racks made of nickel-silver, and Gabellini-designed neoclassical benches.

In addition to his work for Sander and other fashion houses, Gabellini recently won a competition to design the Piazza Isolo in Verona, Italy. Here, he has extended his knitting of old and new to the realm

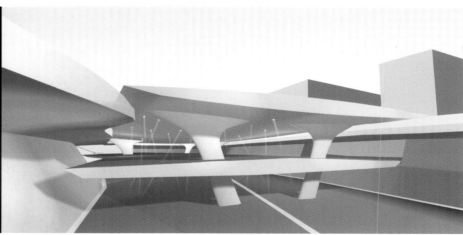

JIL SANDER BOUTIQUE
Paris
Photograph, 1993
Architect: Gabellini Associates

PIAZZA ISOLO: SECTION
Verona, Italy
Digital rendering, 1999
Architect: Gabellini Associates

of urban planning. By expressing his addition to the city in boldly modern forms, Gabellini offers a valuable model for American cities. To evoke the history of the site, which had been an island before being absorbed into Verona's fabric, Gabellini reintroduced the element of water. He designed the piazza's new public square and marketplace as trapezoidal "islands" surrounded by a shallow moat that makes the piazza appear to float within a pool of water. Around the perimeter of these islands, the moat is crossed by bridges that connect the islands to each other, to the city, and to ramps and stairways that lead down to a five-hundred-car garage. The glass-walled moat functions as a skylight, filtering light into the garage. Water also cascades down the stair walls, at times hidden to allow for only the sound of splashing water and the sight of intense shifts of light.

Gabellini's designs for the Piazza Isolo and a new residential project in Denver advance his vocabulary of curving forms. Like up-stretched arms, the columns supporting the Piazza's islands recall those designed by Eero Saarinen for Dulles International Airport, outside Washington, D.C. The Denver residence (currently under design) features wing-like roof planes that hover above glass walls and over bridges, terraces, gardens, and

pools—reminiscent of Saarinen's TWA Terminal at John F. Kennedy Airport in New York. Designed for a collector of contemporary art, the house's interior is delineated by a flexible system of lightweight, suspended walls, which slide or pivot to accommodate art. The aerodynamic forms of these projects provide an apt metaphor for Gabellini's career, moving on a trajectory—like Saarinen's—that extends beyond minimalism. D.A.

MINIMAL

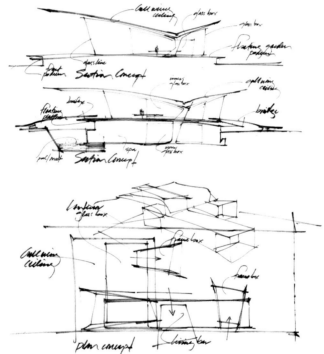

DENVER HOUSE
Denver, Colorado
Drawing, 1999,
ink on tracing paper
Delineator:
Michael Gabellini
Architect:
Gabellini Associates

PIAZZA ISOLO: AERIAL VIEWS
Verona, Italy
Digital rendering, 1999
Architect: Gabellini Associates

ALEXANDER GELMAN B. 1967

Design Machine
New York City

OBSCURE OBJECTS
Logo, 1996
Designer: Alexander Gelman,
Design Machine

The Russian-born graphic designer Alexander Gelman has revolted against both mainstream commercial design and the postmodern vanguard. Gelman's work rejects such hallmarks of hip complexity as layered texts and fragmented forms. Instead, he deploys stark typography and simple icons within flats fields of color in a willfully direct manner. Gelman's MINIMAL approach yields linguistically rich results, as seen in the logo for his self-published journal *Obscure Objects*. Two O's are represented with a square and a circle, each paired with a contrasting punctuation mark—a round period for the square and a square one for the circle. The logo converts the modernist cliché of universal geometry into a concise system of signs.

Calling himself a "subtractionist," Gelman says, "I gain by taking away. I create layers of meaning by eliminating layers of paper." In a series of posters and advertisements for the recruiting firm Janou Pakter, he uses geometric shapes and folded typography to create illusions of depth. In an advertising campaign for Dell computers, large icons of simple technologies—like a pair of scissors that pierce the surface of one ad—stand in for the functional immediacy longed for from digital tools.

Gelman puts familiar icons to work throughout his projects. To illustrate an essay about India's pursuit of nuclear testing in the Op-Ed section of the *New York Times*, for example, Gelman combined two twentieth-century archetypes—the mushroom cloud and the speech bubble—to depict a "nuclear conversation." A watch designed for Swatch features a generic, transparent wrist band and clock face. It is a Swatch watch devoid of its signature bright colors and

BE DIRECT
Advertisement, 1999, offset
lithograph
Designer: Alexander Gelman,
Design Machine
Creative Director: Eric Revels
Client: Dell Computer

NUCLEAR CONVERSATION
Illustration, 1998, offset
lithograph
Designer: Alexander Gelman,
Design Machine
Art Director: Nickolas Blechman
Publisher: The New York Times

aggressively themed graphics. Skewed across this transparent ground is a graphic image of the plain black watch that was one of Swatch's first products, introduced in the 1980s. The plain black Swatch returns here as an icon, a cultural sign.

In a society exhausted by information overload and explosions of personal style, Gelman's minimal constructions create a calm eye in the visual storm, pockets of quiet where ideas can speak. E.L.

[above right] **SIDE**
Watch, 1997, plastic, glass, watch mechanism
Designer: Alexander Gelman, Design Machine
Manufacturer: Swatch

RECRUITING THE FUTURE
Posters, 1999, offset lithograph
Designer: Alexander Gelman, Design Machine
Client: Janou Pakter

105

RICHARD GLUCKMAN B. 1947

Gluckman Mayner Architects
New York City

Richard Gluckman practices architecture as a fusion of art, fashion, theater, design, traditional urbanism, and modern global culture. Throughout his more than two-decade-long career, Gluckman has employed MINIMAL but precise architectural gestures and surprising juxtapositions to reclaim historic structures and underused neighborhoods, from New York's Chelsea to Miami's South Beach. Taking advantage of today's international network of collaborations and commissions, Gluckman has designed retail stores for Gianni Versace, a renovation of Manhattan's Second Stage Theatre with Dutch architect Rem Koolhass, and an "aesthetic enhancement" program in downtown Pittsburgh with American stage master Robert Wilson.

White-washed brick walls, polished concrete floors, and splashes of brilliant color heighten the industrial character of Gluckman's cultural projects. New York's Dia Center for the Arts (1987) and Pittsburgh's Andy Warhol Museum (1994) are two sites where the architect's factory-inspired vocabulary underscores the commercial and manufacturing-based aesthetic of the contemporary art housed in the galleries, from Dan Flavin's fluorescent-tube installations to Warhol's Brillo boxes. A more recent project, the Second Stage Theatre in Manhattan (1999), converts an old bank into a dynamic space of colored screen walls and bleacher-style seats upholstered in translucent plastic gel. With their Pittsburgh "aesthetic enhancement" project (currently under design), Gluckman and Wilson used "walls" of backlit translucent theatrical material to seductively veil the area's worn, masonry buildings. Like construction scaffolding, these glowing walls of

SECOND STAGE THEATRE: INTERIOR VIEW
New York City
Photograph, 1999
Architects: Gluckman Mayner Architects and Rem Koolhaas, Office for Metropolitan Architecture
Team: Dan Wood, OMA and Elizabeth Rexrode (Project architect), Elena Cannon, and Michael Meredith, GMA
Curtain design: Inside Outside
Acoustic consultant: Jaffe Holden Scarborough

GIANNI VERSACE BOUTIQUE
South Beach, Miami
Model, 1997, scale 3/32":1', wood, Plexiglass, vinyl, metal, and plastic
Architect: Richard Gluckman Architects
Team: Michael Hamilton, Alex Hurst, and Suzanne Song
Model fabricators: Alex Hurst and Suzanne Song

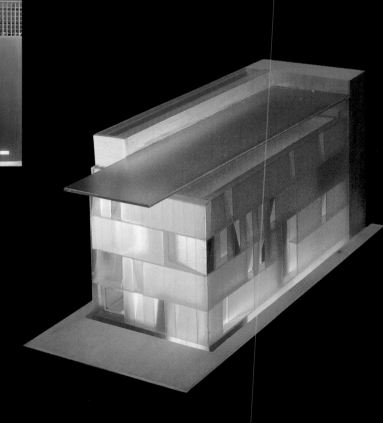

light are powerful yet provisional icons of the neighborhood's ongoing transformation.

Gluckman treats commercial goods, especially high-fashion clothing, like works of art. In his retail projects the architect consciously draws upon the uncomplicated forms and subtle manipulations of light that characterize the minimalist art displayed in the galleries and museums he designs. Meanwhile, Gluckman's stripped-down stores are stages on which to dress up. Taking his cue from Flavin, he dropped hot-pink fluorescent tubing into the street window of Versace's Madison Avenue shop (1998). In the new Helmut Lang store in SoHo (1999), Jenny Holzer's vertical zipper "sculptures" and Gluckman's new retail furnishings contrast with the building's cast-iron front, a remnant of the area's distant industrial

history. The architect's unbuilt project for a freestanding Versace store in the South Beach district of Miami dematerializes the building's mass into a multicolored, mutable light box, marrying new glass technologies with the installation strategies of conceptual artist Robert Irwin, who has employed walls of theatrical scrim and fluorescent tubes to radically change the perception of gallery spaces.

Gluckman's Zen-like affinities with artists such as Irwin run deeper than surface appearance. Like them, he rejects the notion that architects must create new and unusual forms. A low-key antidote to today's loud visual culture, Gluckman quietly yet dramatically unmasks the poetic potential of everyday places. D.A.

THE PITTSBURGH CULTURAL TRUST: ALLEYWAY WITH THEATRICAL MATERIAL
Pittsburgh, Pennsylvania
Photograph, 1999
Designers: Richard Gluckman, GMA and Robert Wilson
Team: Elizabeth Rexrode, Srdjan Jovanovic Weiss, Eric Chang, GMA and Paul Rosenblatt, John Ferri, Michelle Mondazzi, and Michael Pestel, CMU

CARLOS JIMENEZ B. 1959

Carlos Jiménez Studio
Houston, Texas

The architecture of Carlos Jiménez unites two MIMINALIST traditions in Houston.[1] Born and raised in Costa Rica, Jiménez adapts the area's Latin-American tradition of simple, stucco-clad shapes and sunlit spaces. At the same time, he builds upon the legacy of Houston's postwar modernist tradition, launched by Philip Johnson's 1950 house for Dominique de Menil, itself inspired by the work of Ludwig Mies van der Rohe. Jiménez's own house and studio compound, designed and built between 1983 and 1993, served as his training ground. (Jiménez was only twenty-three-years-old when he began the project.) Comprising four buildings, the house and studio are designed as a variation on a theme of elemental orthogonal forms that determine the shape of plans, sections, facades, as well as window and door openings. Like the sculpture of Donald Judd, the seemingly child-like simplicity of Jiménez's architecture belies a sophisticated aesthetic.

Jiménez expands upon this aesthetic in his 1999 competition entry for a proposed addition of galleries, stores, and restaurants to the Nelson-Atkins Museum of Art in Kansas City, Missouri. "As with any addition," Jiménez writes in his competition brief, "the new grows out of the existing. It must be directed toward establishing complementary yet contrasting realities to the original." Designed by Thomas Wight in 1927, the existing museum features a sequence of monumental exterior stairways and landscaped terraces—designed by modernist Dan Kiley—that run parallel to its southern facade. Jiménez echoes this concept in plan: his addition comprises a courtyard and an annex extending off the museum's northern facade and running its full width. Though similar

COMPETITION ENTRY FOR THE NELSON-ATKINS MUSEUM OF ART EXPANSION AND RENOVATION
Kansas City, Missouri
Presentation boards, 1999
Architect: Carlos Jiménez Studio
Team: Brian Burke, Gerard Chong, Emily Estes, Carlos Jiménez, Christina Lee, Alex O'Briant, and Rusty Walker

in plan, the new addition dramatically differs from the old building in appearance. Taking cues from the lacy steel framework supporting the museum's neoclassical stone facade, Jiménez designed his addition's facades in a mimimal grid of steel and glass panels. The courtyard features a dramatically swooping skylit roof that rises above the historical northern front, framing it in a contrasting modernist context.

In referring to the industrial structure under the old building, Jiménez reaches back to the early years of the twentieth century, when engineering structures inspired a new architecture. Rather than clothe their buildings in heavy masonry walls reminiscent of historical styles, progressive architects explored the simple forms and visual lightness of greenhouses and bridges. In his search for a minimal aesthetic for the twenty-first century, Carlos Jiménez seeks to reclaim the spirit of that historic moment. D.A.

1. I am indebted to architectural historian Stephen Fox for this observation.

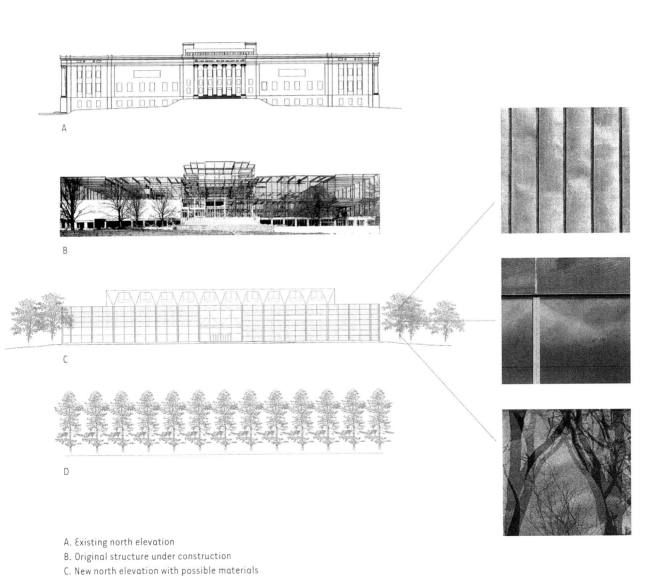

A

B

C

D

A. Existing north elevation
B. Original structure under construction
C. New north elevation with possible materials
D. Landscaping

JOHN MAEDA B. 1965

Maedastudio
MIT Media Lab
Cambridge, Massachusetts

John Maeda constructs simple graphic systems for print and screen. Avoiding the expressive gestures of personal style, he prefers to define a set of rules that interact with a limited array of elements to generate visual patterns. Trained both in the modernist tradition of graphic design and in computer science, Maeda generates his MINIMAL, intellectually rich projects with software, often using programs that he develops himself. Disenchanted with the lavishly filtered image manipulations endemic to computer-aided graphic design, Maeda builds imagery whose complexity of detail derives from data inherent to the project itself.

His *2000 Year Calendar* is a lithographic print in which the numbers 1 through 2000 are printed on a single surface that is 43 1/8 by 31 1/8 inches. Maeda developed his own software to generate this field of text, the texture of which is so fine that it cannot be deciphered with the naked eye. Maeda's calendar seeks to astound the viewer with both the vastness and containability of two-thousand years: a couple of millennia are, after all, just a blip in the history of life on earth. Conversely, the numerals, which are one point (1/72 inch) tall, produce an impenetrable field of gray that leaves one with an inescapable sense of one's own smallness.

Maeda has exercised his philosophy of design as director of the Aesthetics and Computation Group at MIT's Media Lab. Under Maeda's direction, graduate students are using computers to study the possibilities of typography and graphic systems, on the page, on the screen, and in physical space using three-dimensional interfaces. His book *Design by Numbers* (1999), teaches design principles by way of a software program created by Maeda and distributed over the Web. Readers of the book are invited to create compositions within a square field using rules that execute repetitive commands. Simple lines of computer code are used to create patterns within the square. Maeda, who employs this teaching technique in undergraduate design courses, uses it to level the playing field among students in a class, some of whom are intimidated by technology while others are already infatuated with the simulationist wonders of popular software programs like PhotoShop.

Maeda's strategy—as a teacher and practitioner—reduces design to a minimal system, promoting a structural understanding of form and programming. E.L.

2000 YEAR CALENDAR
Print, details, 1996, offset lithograph
Designer: John Maeda, Maedastudio
Manufacturer: Grapac Printing Co.

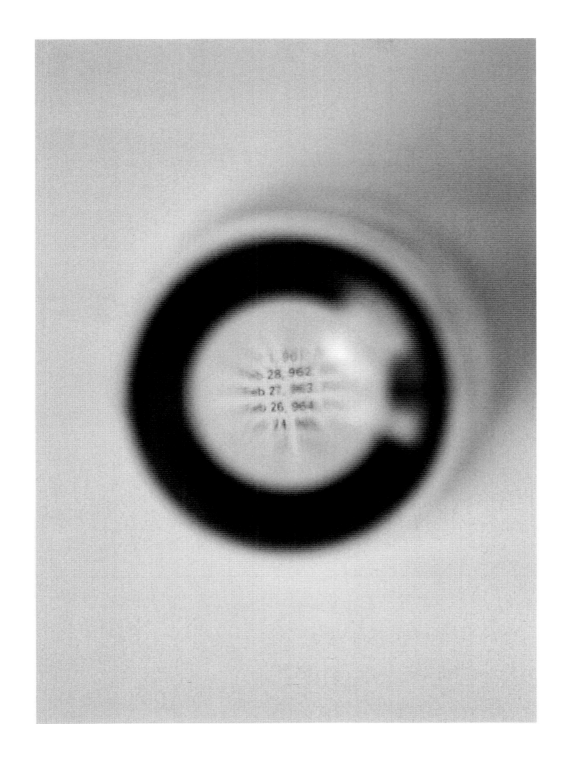

ROY McMAKIN B.1960

Domestic Furniture
Seattle, Washington

Mies van der Rohe's assertion that "less is more" has been a mantra for many twentieth-century designers. At the dawn of a new century, this spirit of distillation has been taken even farther to "doing the most with the least." No designer better exemplifies this philosophy than Roy McMakin, founder of Seattle-based Domestic Furniture. Originally headquartered in Los Angeles, Domestic was relaunched after McMakin relocated to the Pacific Northwest to pursue a program of sustainable wood harvesting. Trained as an artist, McMakin came to prominence when his work was chosen to furnish the administrative offices of the Getty Center in Los Angeles, where it serves as both complement and counterpoint to Richard Meier's architecture.

Simple but not simplistic, McMakin's designs are elusive in a way that few furniture pieces are today.

While most designers (McMakin included) opt for a signature look, these pieces inhabit a different plane as well. In McMakin's Would Seven-Drawer Hi-Boy (1998), a Shaker sensibility is visible, as are familiar-feeling touches of the Mission, Arts and Crafts, and modern styles. A nineteenth-century piece that looks amazingly fresh? An undiscovered jewel from the mid-twentieth century? McMakin's pieces are confounding hybrids of design history. Such ambiguity also invites projection—the viewer completes McMakin's work by thinking about it. Stripped clean of superfluity and edited down to the elements of edge and plane, a McMakin design is a physical *tabula rasa*. His pieces reference a simpler, pre-ergonomic time that has emotional resonance, reflecting our most basic ideas of what furniture is through MINIMAL forms.

WOULD PEDESTAL TABLE WITH BALL
Furniture, 1998, claro walnut
Designer: Roy McMakin, Domestic Furniture
Manufacturer: Big Leaf Manufacturing

The best of McMakin's pieces show a hypersensitivity to editing, process, proportion, and detail. No length, width, height, or dimension is accidental or arbitrary; a given piece looks effortless only because McMakin has expended so much effort calculating every last aspect. His pieces also evoke narratives about their origins, individual commentaries on the preciousness and physical presence of color, wood, and other natural resources. As McMakin stated in an *Architectural Record* interview, "My pieces have a clarity and a focus to them that seems to give people confidence in what I do." That literal and figurative straightforwardness is what brings deep meaning to the carefully focused designs that he envisions and creates. S.S.H.

**WOULD SEVEN-DRAWER
HI-BOY**
Furniture, 1998, claro walnut
Designer: Roy McMakin,
Domestic Furniture
Manufacturer: Big Leaf
Manufacturing

SIMPLE CHAIR
Furniture, 1989, claro walnut
Designer: Roy McMakin,
Domestic Furniture
Manufacturer: Big Leaf
Manufacturing

PALO ALTO PRODUCTS
INTERNATIONAL DESIGN TEAM

PALO ALTO PRODUCTS INTERNATIONAL

Palo Alto, California

PALM VII
Wireless PDA (personal
digital assistant), 1999,
injection-molded ABS
plastic
Designer: Dallas Grove,
Palo Alto Products
International
Mechanical engineers:
Livius Chebeleu and Hamid
Arjomand, Palo Alto
Products International,
and Kulbir Sandhu, Ed
Vertatschitsch, and Frank
Canova, 3Com
Product manager:
Joe Sipher, 3Com
Manufacturer: 3Com

Billed as a product development firm rather than an industrial design consultancy, Palo Alto Products International creates designs that can be easily manufactured, and works concurrently on aesthetic, functional, and logistical issues. This represents a new business model for designers. With the capability to develop a product from "art to part" in house, Palo Alto can develop products more quickly than those who must shuttle products between various parties. The formula works: generating the majority of its income through the manufacture of products it designs, Palo Alto has an exceptionally high revenue-per-employee rate.

The field of hand-held digital computing has seen many heroic failures, as designers and manufacturers have struggled to create a MINIMAL, portable, pocket-size information appliance that people will actually use. Palo Alto Products International's PalmPilot series, created for Palm Computing, now a division of 3Com, is a remarkable success in this rocky terrain. The company was asked to give "unconscious portability" to the Palm I "personal digital assistant" (1996), a sleek, thin, light, and low-cost unit that accomplished what previous efforts like the Apple Newton, Motorola Envoy, Sony Magic Link, and a host of others could not. A significant cluster of technologies was fit within a pleasingly curved shape that is easy to hold, stow, and operate—a design that later models have continued to refine. Since its introduction, Palo Alto Products International and 3Com have watched as Palm has turned a market toehold into a stronghold, and turned instant consumer enthusiasm into enduring brand loyalty.

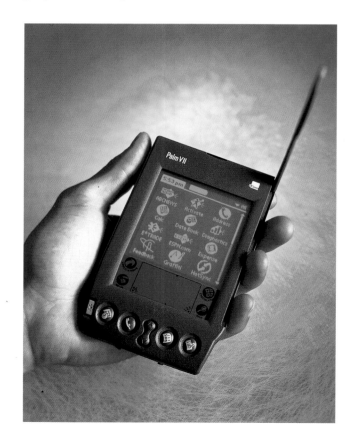

Less successful in the marketplace but more revolutionary in concept is the Rocket eBook, an electronic book. Weighing about three pounds, the unit holds thousands of pages (with graphics), and presents them on a crisp, easy-to-navigate LCD panel. Designed to have a book-like feel, the Rocket is a product for which Palo Alto Products International completely designed, engineered, tooled, and manufactured the plastic parts. The Rocket's initial list price of $599, however, has limited its audience to true early adopters, those consumer-pioneers who gravitate to the newest things, and can afford to pay for them.

Both the Palm series and the Rocket eBook point to a near-future of information products that do one or two things brilliantly rather than take the do-everything, Swiss-Army-knife-approach typical of personal computers. Palo Alto's products make information simple to access and convenient to use—no small feat in an age when knowledge is power. s.s.h.

ROCKET eBOOK
Electronic book, 1997, injection-molded ABS plastic
Designers: Ralf Grone and Dallas Grove, Palo Alto Products International
Mechanical engineers: Ricardo Penate and Livius Chebeleu, Palo Alto Products International
Manufacturer: NuvoMedia

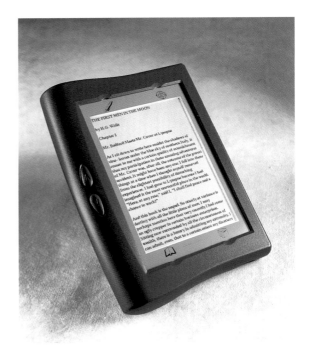

PALM III
PDA (personal digital assistant), 1998, injection-molded ABS plastic
Designer: Dallas Grove, Palo Alto Products International
Industrial designer: Jo Wollschlaeger, Palo Alto Products International
Mechanical engineers: Ricardo Penate, Palo Alto Products International, and Kulbir Sandhu and Frank Canova, 3Com
Product manager: Rob Haitani, 3Com
Manufacturer: 3Com

KATE SPADE B.1962

Kate Spade New York
New York City

With an ability to take familiar forms and make them appear both modern and simple in a single stroke, Kate Spade has changed the course of handbag design in America. In a marketplace where a designer is only as good as his or her last collection, she has built a name that stands for enhanced material and textural expectation, a trusted brand representing carefully composed yet insouciant taste.

Spade's career has now assumed the proportions of urban myth. Formerly an editor at *Mademoiselle*, she quit the magazine to produce her own handbags in 1993 with the support of her boyfriend Andy Spade (now her husband and president of the company). Their work had an immediate impact on the industry, her first bags showing that even a humble material like nylon can achieve elite status if the detailing is carefully executed. The message was that value could be added through design, not simply through expensive materials. The typical Kate Spade bag is sprightly, functional, and enduring. It uses simple, near-iconic forms, and is identified through a sewn lowercase "kate spade" nametag judiciously placed on the outside of the bag. Recent bags use a broader range of colors and materials, from two-tone canvas to red or blue suede, to offer a refreshing and contemporary classicism that is sophisticated yet retains a sense of spontaneity.

At her best, Spade achieves pocket-book quintessence, the considered rendition of a trendy object taken to a near-Platonic ideal. Her astonishing success exemplifies the emergence of a group of rare individuals capable of bringing together their professional missions with their personal passions. s.s.h.

ROSE
Handbag, 1999, cotton velvet
Designer: Kate Spade
Manufacturer: Kate Spade
New York

CAROLINE
Handbag, 1999, canvas
and gingham
Designer: Kate Spade
Manufacturer: Kate Spade
New York

reclaimed

In a culture where images and materials are continually recycled, reused, and discarded, designers today often seek to reclaim abandoned places and products. Old forms receive new uses, and familiar icons and materials are mixed and recombined. Lost artifacts and obsolete media become part of the next generation's products or entertainment. As in hip-hop music, which uses a riff from an existing song as the foundation for a new tune, a sampled approach is influencing the design of objects, graphics, and interiors, where elements of one design become the genetic basis for new work. Every material is a "raw" material, capable of being taken and manipulated to yield new results.

ERIK ADIGARD B. 1953
PATRICIA McSHANE B. 1953

M.A.D. (McShane Adigard Design)
Sausolito, California

Erik Adigard and Patricia McShane have inclusive yet critical appetites for popular culture and new technologies. Their work asserts that today all design is digital and all virtual worlds are real—places to be inhabited by both body and mind. Their projects, which range from Web sites and electronic environments to printed books and magazines, feverishly enjoy the simultaneity of multiple messages, the onslaught of icons and information, and the collapsing of word into image that characterize contemporary media culture. Adigard and McShane have orchestrated a fluid dialog between print and digital media, showing that a common—yet ever evolving—vocabulary links these seemingly disparate realms.

Adigard has produced opening spreads for *Wired* magazine since 1993. These billboard-like sequences introduce the content of the magazine in its initial pages, before the table of contents and the editorial and feature wells. Adigard's spreads RECLAIM provocative quotations from philosophical writings on technology and combine them with bold images, often dredged from the deep recesses of mass media. Adigard overlays these lush, tonal illustrations with typography and schematic symbols in compositions that invoke a vividly experienced and sharply analyzed world. The *Wired* spreads are visual essays that have the immediate impact and telescopic prose of posters.

This approach carries through to Adigard's and McShane's designs for Web sites. *LiveWired*, created while Adigard was design director at Wired Digital, features streaming news, "factoids," and images in a setting where icons, information graphics, and text mingle with rich, almost lurid images loaded with intense color and dimensional presence.

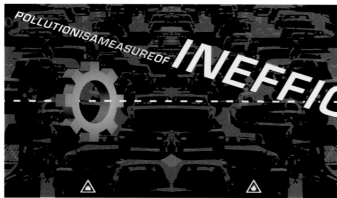

**WIRED: POLLUTION IS A MEASURE
OF INEFFICIENCY**
Magazine, 1997, offset lithograph
Designer: Erik Adigard, M.A.D.
Creative Director: John Plunkett
Publisher: Wired Ventures

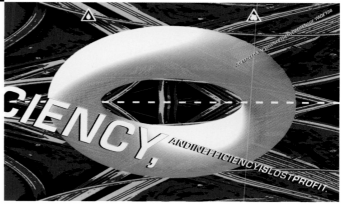

The experimental Web site *Funnel* combines a diversity of media—still and moving, verbal and pictorial—in an interactive collage of sounds, sights, and experiences. In the designers' words, *Funnel* exposes the Web as a "pond of disconnected noises that glorify our vibrant economy."

Adigard and McShane move freely between print and multimedia, and between popular culture and intellectual analysis. Their work demonstrates an expanded role for the graphic designer, who is emerging as a visual editor and cultural producer who deploys content across numerous channels.
E.L.

LIVE WIRED
Web pages, 1997
Designer: Erik Adigard, Wired Digital
Design Director: Erik Adigard
Executive Producer: Gary Wolf
Creative Director: Barbara Kuhr
Publisher: Wired Ventures

FUNNEL
Web pages, 1997
Designer: Erik Adigard and Patricia McShane, M.A.D.
Publisher: M.A.D.

BORIS BALLY B.1961

Providence, Rhode Island

Trained as a metalsmith, the son of an artist and an industrial designer, Boris Bally combines found industrial objects with elegant craftsmanship to create container-like constructions that are like nothing else in the design world today. His highly crafted bowls are formed from RECLAIMED materials like traffic signs and bottle caps. Working with a goldsmith's sensibility for material transition and detail, Bally hammers the basest of materials with the same care normally reserved for sheets of precious metal.

Recently, Bally began integrating industrial production methods with hand craftsmanship. By mixing processes such as hydraulic pressing, lathe turning, and press-die forming with hand-raising, riveting, and planishing, he formed a hybrid approach that synthesizes traditional craft and contemporary design thinking.

Bally applies these techniques to what he describes as "raw American culture." Bally believes that "garbage" is simply a resource we have yet to figure out how to use. His sampling of highway culture introduces the possibility for accidental amplitude: symbols and partial words peer out startlingly and engagingly.

In some of his bowls, Bally has reclaimed thrown-away bottle caps collected from friends, family, and colleagues. These become part of each bowl's narrative, and again reiterate Bally's commitment to taking objects that are no longer appreciated and re-animating them through the creative process. He has taken some of the most routinely authoritarian artifacts of our time—traffic signs with their relentless imperatives—and carefully refigured them to make us think as they make us smile. S.S.H.

DEFIANCE OF DIRECTION
Bowls, 1997, recycled traffic signage and brass rivets
Designer: Boris Bally
Hand-spinning: E. H. Schwab
Manufacturer: Boris Bally, Atelier

UNDER CONSTRUCTION
Bowls, 1996, recycled traffic
signage and copper rivets
Designer: Boris Bally
Hand-spinning: E. H. Schwab
Manufacturer: Boris Bally, Atelier

JULIE BARGMANN B.1958

D.I.R.T. Studio
Charlottesville, Virginia

In Southwestern Pennsylvania, deadly discharges of acid mine drainage (AMD) are spilling into streams and rivers, raising acidity levels and suffocating life forms. Abandoned coal mines and mounds of refuse— "bony piles"—are polluting and poisoning the earth. This is the late-twentieth-century legacy of the nineteenth-century mining industry. Landscape architect Julie Bargmann RECLAIMS such polluted industrial sites. To stress the value of remembering as well as reviving, Bargmann designs hybrid landscapes that blend new construction with elements that represent the physical and cultural histories of the sites at which she works.

Testing the Waters, currently under construction, is a 45-acre park for acid mine drainage and community recreation at the site of a former coal mine in Vintondale, Pennsylvania. Site architect

Bargmann assembled a multi-disciplinary design team, which included project director and historian T. Allan Comp, hydrogeologist Robert Deason, and artist Stacy Levy. Bargmann then designed the park by carving the existing topography to form a passive AMD treatment system—in effect, a giant ecological washing machine— and she invited the public to witness the cleansing process physically as well as symbolically. First, the AMD goes through a series of retention basins and spillways. As polluted water passes over this "Treatment Garden," its changing color—from acidic orange to pea green to alkaline blue-green—reflects the process of cleansing performed in each basin. The cleansing process is symbolically shown in the "Litmus Garden." The seasonal colors of bark, foliage, and fruit of alternating rows of native trees and shrubs visually represent

TESTING THE WATERS: WATER TREATMENT SYSTEM
Vintondale, Pennsylvania
Progressive photographic sequence, 1997
Site architect and photographer:
Julie Bargmann, D.I.R.T. Studio

Team: Stacy Levy (Artist); SERE Ltd.; T. Allan Comp (Community historian); Southwestern Pennsylvania Heritage Preservation Commission; Robert Deason (Hydrogeologist); Earth Tech Inc.; Anne Guillebeaux, Shelby Knox, Rob McCombie, and John Turner (Project assistants)

the treatment sequence, progressing from deep reds and oranges to cooler hues of green and blue. The flood plane of the site's creek is recontoured into a new marsh and additional wetlands for the "final rinse." After flowing through these wetland areas, water returns to the local creek in a purified state.

Bargmann's design also offers visual evidence of the site's former industrial identity. Earthen and planted forms suggest footprints of former mine buildings, and a long plinth of excavated soil and mine refuse is inscribed with black disks recalling Vintondale's 152 coke ovens. The site includes recreational amenities such as picnic grounds, play areas, and wildlife trails that serve both local and regional communities. Like its name, *Testing the Waters* combines literal and metaphorical ideas of change to form a compelling model for future industrial reclamation. D. A.

TESTING THE WATERS
Vintondale, Pennsylvania
Site map, 1999, ink and graphite
on mylar
Site architect: Julie Bargmann,
D.I.R.T. Studio

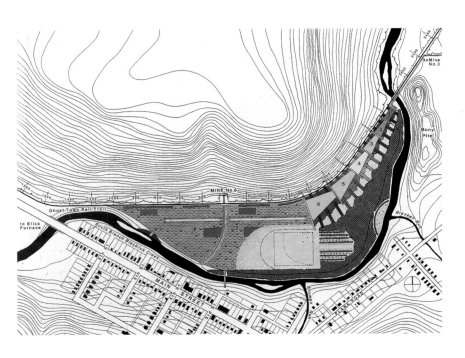

TESTING THE WATERS: PROJECT SITE
Vintondale, Pennsylvania
Photographic collage, 1997
Site architect and photographer:
Julie Bargmann, D.I.R.T. Studio

CONSTANTIN BOYM B. 1955
LAURENE LEON BOYM B. 1964

Boym Design Studio
New York City

Trained as an architect and industrial designer, Russian-born Constantin Boym has been teaching and running a small studio since 1986; Laurene Leon Boym joined him several years later in both pursuits. The two have built a reputation based on their blending of concerns from the art world (for found objects, appropriation, cultural critique) with mass-production design work. Broadly stated, the duo is interested in the "redesign" of the design profession itself—in driving it to question the nature of the very products that are its lifeblood. The two made their first public attack on the field more than ten years ago with the seminal *Recycle* exhibition (Gallery 91, New York, 1989) in which a number of throw-away items (cans, bottles, dispensers) were RECLAIMED and recontextualized in a series of framed tabletop objects.

Boym Design Studio has produced many of its iconoclastic, idea-driven projects for such mainstream corporations as Swatch, Authentics, and Alessi. For instance, they created a series of stainless steel kitchen containers for Alessi inspired by the utilitarian soup can. While Andy Warhol was captivated by the iconic simplicity of Campbell's labels, the Boyms liked what they saw when they pulled those labels off: "beautiful, perfectly machined cans."

Cloud 9 is a chunky trio of bath accessories whose wavy silhouettes refer not only to clouds but to anonymous industrial parts that might be found in an electrical substation or an old parking lot. The objects are made of bonded marble—an epoxy impregnated with marble dust—providing a nonporous surface with a permanent, classic feeling.

STRAP FURNITURE
Furniture, 1999, wood, polypropylene strapping tape
Designers: Constantin Boym and Laurene Leon Boym
Associate designers: John Lowe and Christine Warren
Manufacturer: Boym Design Studio

BUILDINGS OF DISASTER

[above]
CHERNOBYL NUCLEAR FACILITY AND ALFRED P. MURRAH FEDERAL BUILDING

[right]
UNABOMBER HOUSE
Souvenir objects, 1998-99, bonded nickel
Designers: Constantin Boym and Laurene Leon Boym
Design team: Christine Warren and Michael Gordon
Manufacturer: Souvenirs for the End of the Century
Photographer: (right) James Wojcik

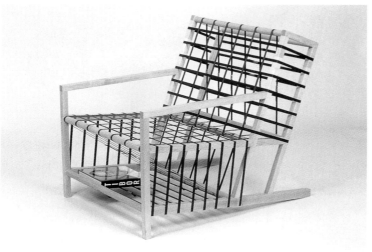

126

The pair's recent line of Strap Furniture (1999) is an experimental prototype that takes the kind of web strapping often employed by overnight delivery services as its most prominent element. Wrapped around simple wood frames, such strapping makes for a clever, end-of-the-century take on the classic mid-century webbed furniture created by Jens Risom and Alvar Aalto. Meanwhile, the appropriation of such an ordinary material gives these objects—particularly the Strap Chair—a stripped-down, almost incomplete feel, as if they had been reduced to their essential states. Cushions of air are encased in a network of lines.

Boym Design Studio's two self-produced series of limited-production, miniature-scale castings—*Missing Monuments* and *Buildings of Disaster* (1998–99) reclaim the imagery of a group of emotionally-charged structures that still exert a profound influence on our individual and collective psyches. Sold through a mail-order catalog, the *Missing Monuments* series (in bronze) includes such lamented losses as Solomon's Temple in Jerusalem (2.5-inches tall) and New York's erstwhile Pennsylvania Station (5.5-inches long). By contrast, the *Buildings of Disaster* collection (in nickel) includes the Chernobyl nuclear facility and the Alfred P. Murrah Federal Building in Oklahoma City (5- and 3-inches in height, respectively). The purpose of these toy-like terrors? "The images of burning or exploded buildings make a different, populist history of architecture, one based on emotional involvement rather than on scholarly appreciation," explain the designers.

This focus on wasted material and emotional distress seems fitting for practitioners who both literally and figuratively mine the detritus of contemporary culture. s.s.h.

CLOUD 9
Bathroom accessories, 1999, bonded marble
Designers: Constantin Boym and Laurene Leon Boym
Manufacturer: Benza

ART CHANTRY B. 1954

Seattle, Washington

The work of Art Chantry is popular in a ravenous, almost predatory way. Chantry RECLAIMS abandoned styles, faded icons, and outmoded typefaces, infusing the half-dead and the empty-hearted with his wierd energy. Chantry is self-trained and self-employed, an outsider to the mainstream design world who works largely alone in his Seattle studio, unencumbered by corporate clients, advanced technology, or a steady income. He spews out a steady stream of posters, album covers, and other ephemera for bands, music labels, theaters, and arts organizations in the Pacific Northwest.

For Chantry, the message is often in the medium—he finds humor in allowing one genre to masquerade as another. He will drop the name of a band onto an old toothpaste tube, or wrap a pulp paperback around an album cover. Chantry takes pleasure in mixing media and matching

unlikely bedfellows. To promote the band Idiot Flesh, for example, Chantry silkscreened a cartoon-style fist—emblazoned with explosive energy lines—on top of a changing series of wallpaper samples. The hyper-masculine imagery of the superhero collides ridiculously with the demure decor of the middle-class home in a juxtaposition that is direct and unlabored.

A sense of immediacy marks Chantry's posters and packages, and yet his work is, by nature, profoundly mediated. He diverts material from the slow-moving sludge of pop culture, that polluted river of images and styles that leaves its filmy residue everywhere we look. Chantry sifts through the clichés, reclaiming the material he finds by shifting its scale, reworking its frame, or changing its context. E.L.

[below and facing page]

**YOU! MUST SEE . . .
IDIOT FLESH**
Poster, 1997, silkscreen on
wallpaper
Designer: Art Chantry
Publisher: C/Z Records

RECLAIMED

**TERRIFIC! THE FABULOUS
MONO MEN AND THE MAKERS**
Poster, 1997, offset lithograph
Designer: Art Chantry
Publisher: 3B Tavern/Estrus

**BENT PAGES BY
THE MONO MEN**
12-inch record cover, 1997,
offset lithograph
Designer: Art Chantry
Publisher: Estrus/Augogo

THE VON ZIPPERS
12-inch record cover, 1997,
offset lithograph
Designer: Art Chantry
Publisher: Estrus Records

PETER GIRARDI ^{B.} 1966

FUNNY GARBAGE
New York City

Peter Girardi began his artistic career as a grafitti writer defacing New York City's subway system. He is now the founding partner of a rapidly growing multimedia firm in SoHo, serving a range of cultural and corporate clients. Funny Garbage, which Girardi directs with friend and fellow designer Chris Capuozzo, is invigorated by grafitti's wayward energy. While many designers try to endow the Web with a look of seamless technological perfection, Funny Garbage has cultivated a cheerful taste for the cast-off ephemera of popular culture, RECLAIMING the textures and iconography of comic books, candy wrappers, bar codes, and printers' waste.

Girardi has always felt at home in the narrative world of comics, and a current client is the Cartoon Network. Funny Garbage developed a Web site for this cable channel, creating not only its interface and visual identity, but developing original programming as well. The Web-based cartoon *The Pink Donkey and the Fly*, conceived and illustrated by Gary Panter in collaboration with animators and interaction designers at Funny Garbage, will soon air on cable, becoming the first cartoon to premiere on-line and then move to television. *Be Happy*, a more mature and ironic Web cartoon, was created by Mark Newsgarden and Funny Garbage. For both programs, Funny Garbage built interactive features into the narrative structure of the cartoons, so that watching them involves making choices about the direction of the story.

The company's own Web site, funnygarbage.com, is a warm and witty demonstration of the designers' visual attitude. Girardi and Capuozzo each keep notebooks full of sketches, scribbles, and scraps of paper that

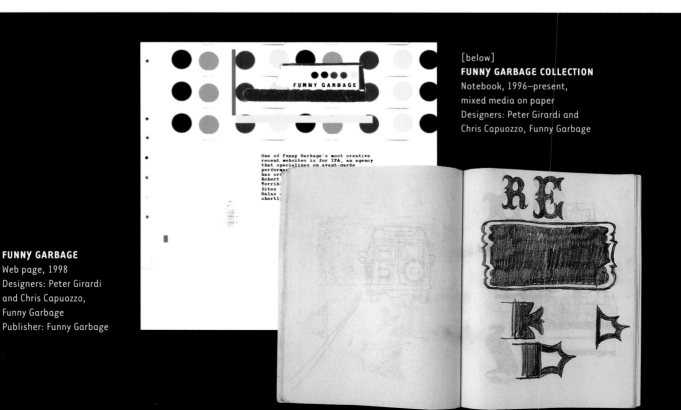

[below]
FUNNY GARBAGE COLLECTION
Notebook, 1996—present,
mixed media on paper
Designers: Peter Girardi and
Chris Capuozzo, Funny Garbage

FUNNY GARBAGE
Web page, 1998
Designers: Peter Girardi
and Chris Capuozzo,
Funny Garbage
Publisher: Funny Garbage

serve as in-house sourcebooks. Elements from this personal archive are periodically compiled on CD-ROM and distributed to designers throughout the company. Bits and pieces of discarded print culture turn up as frames, textures, buttons, and icons, while a collection of dirty backgrounds provide scuffed-up alternatives to the bland white screen that is endemic to the Web. Funny Garbage has reclaimed the gritty, everyday practice of commercial art for the digital realm, creating screen environments that are marked by physical touch. E.L.

FUNNY GARBAGE
Web pages, 1998
Designers: Peter Girardi and
Chris Capuozzo, Funny Garbage
Publisher: Funny Garbage

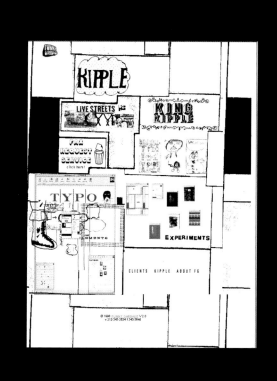

WALTER HOOD B.1958

Hood Design
Oakland, California

Like the jazz musicians that inspire him, urban designer Walter Hood is committed to densely layered experience. Jazz is an art of improvisation. Impure, quirky, and open to personal interpretations, jazz evolved from African-American spirituals and work songs into complex musical styles characterized by syncopated rhythms, ensemble playing, and complex harmonies. In creating hybrid urban landscapes, Hood similarly RECLAIMS and incorporates traces of physical, cultural, and social histories into what he calls "multirhythmic compositions." He adds new construction to create orderly environments where inhabitants are free to improvise their futures.

In 1998 Hood took first place in an invited competition for the improvement of a 180-foot-wide boulevard in the heart of downtown Macon, Georgia. Entitled Macon Yards, the project, along the slope of Poplar Street, accommodates new pedestrian amenities and vehicular traffic in a linear series of intimate spaces constituting an urban version of the domestic backyard. Based on archeologically inspired research and community interviews, Hood discovered that Poplar Street had housed markets, fire houses, cisterns, and rail lines. Remnants of these now-defunct elements are being excavated for artifacts and their boundaries marked by new paving, markets, signage, and the buildings' preserved foundation walls. The city's past is remembered as well by a wall memorializing such famous local musicians as the Allman Brothers, Little Richard, and Lena Horne. New gardens, raised seating pavilions, water pools, and an outdoor projection screen add to the enriched cacophony of the city's activities and events.

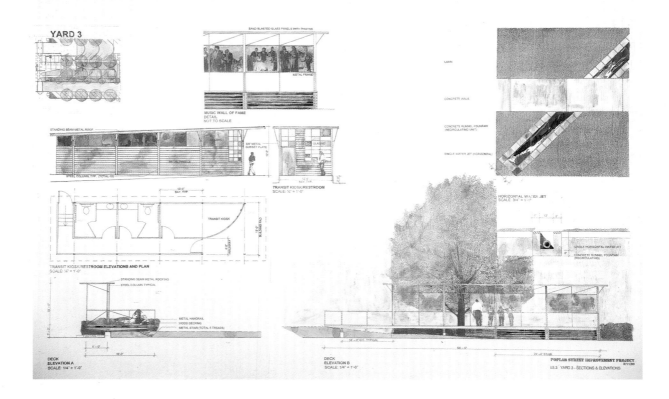

Macon Yards is one of many endeavors that present Hood's humanist vision of landscape design. As chair of the Department of Landscape Architecture and Environmental Planning at the University of California at Berkeley, Hood is currently collaborating with the office of Martha Schwartz on the Underground Railroad Museum in Cincinnati, Ohio. Hood also has articulated his ideas in two publications: *Urban Diaries* (1997), which includes his brightly colored watercolors, and the booklet *Blues and Jazz: Landscape Improvisations* (1993). The latter presents sixteen theoretical designs for a small park in West Oakland, California, each based on the personal needs and aspirations of different users, from bureaucrats to revolutionaries to chefs. Like musical notes dancing across ordered stanzas, the diverse schemes underscore Hood's commitment to improvisational design. "It is the dialog between space and order, whether planned or serendipitous," Hood writes, "that provides a proscenium for human ritual and the mundane activities of daily life."[1] D.A.

1. Walter Hood, *Blues and Jazz: Landscape Improvisations* (Berkeley, CA: Poltroon Press, 1993), np.

MACON YARDS
Macon, Georgia
Architect: Hood Design
Principal: Walter Hood
Associate Designer: Grace Lee
Design team: Anastasia Longden, Alma Du Solier, Sarah Kuehl, Rudy Widman

[left]
Drawing, 1998, collage, watercolor, and ink on paper
Delineator: Walter Hood

[above right]
Drawing (detail), 1998, photographic collage

[far right]
Models, 1998, scale 1":20', cardboard, gesso, and collage

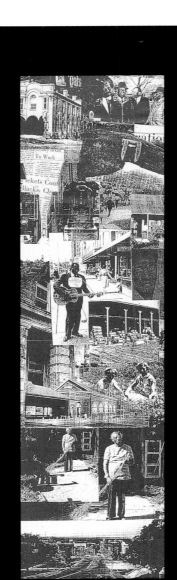

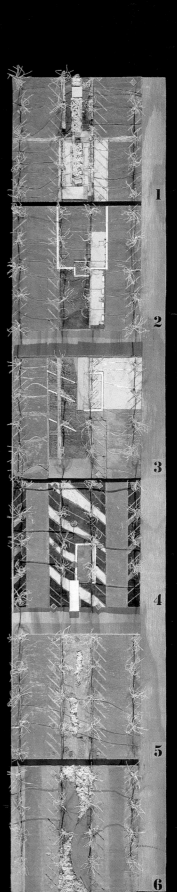

RECLAIMED

LOCAL

PAUL LEWIS B. 1966
MARC TSURUMAKI B. 1965
DAVID J. LEWIS B. 1966

Lewis.Tsurumaki.Lewis Architects
New York City

Most architects strive to impose order on a disorganized world. Lewis. Tsurumaki.Lewis, like modern-day surrealists, seek to unleash what they call "irrational desire" from apparently rational structures. All three partners graduated from Princeton University's School of Architecture and began working together in 1992. Designers of award-winning offices for a computer company, a publishing house, and a nonprofit organization, they have been engaged since founding their partnership in an ongoing theoretical practice of cultural RECLAMATION in which they rethink banal spaces— movie theaters, sports clubs, corporate office buildings—and refashion them into provocative structures that question our basic assumptions about architecture. While architects traditionally ask questions such as "How big?" or "How much?" Lewis.Tsurumaki. Lewis ask "What if?"

One such proposal is "Mies-on-a-Beam," a playful adaptation of Mies van der Rohe's Seagram Building (1958). Lewis.Tsurumaki.Lewis suggest that the ornamental bronze I-beams that extend up the full height of the building be transformed into wheel tracks for a pair of mobile grass platforms linked to window-washing hoists. Besides their intended maintenance function, the land-scaped platforms would serve as smoking terraces and putting greens. Projecting from the gridded facade of the building, which is an icon of postwar corporate America, the platforms suggest the secret desires of high-powered executives. The presentation of the project is notably witty: with the deadpan ironic realism of a Magritte painting, the detailed rendering of the building assumes the feasibility of the idea.

REFILED
Site-specific installation for the *National Design Triennial*
Digital collage (photograph and drawing), 1999
Architect:
Lewis.Tsurumaki.Lewis

SPORTS-BAR

OFFICE PARK

MIES-ON-A-BEAM

AUTO-BOARDS

VIDEO FILM-PLEX

Lewis.Tsurumaki.Lewis also confound expectations of architectural display. They present their ideas with three-dimensional installations that comprise mechanized components, photographs, drawings, and sound systems, making light of the ponderous manner in which architecture is typically presented. Their installation of five projects at the *National Design Triennial*, titled *Refiled*, is an assemblage of flat-file drawers turned on their sides, a digital answering machine, and obsolete storage systems—library card catalog drawers and index cards. Like an out-of-control cabinet of curiosities, the installation underscores the architects' commitment to meld the logical and illogical, and to take the conventional to unconventional extremes. D.A.

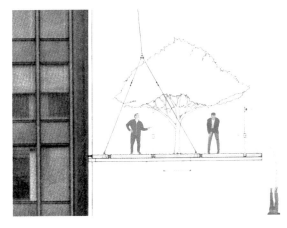

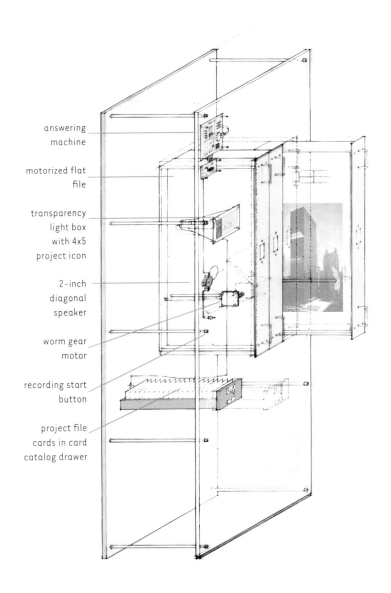

answering machine

motorized flat file

transparency light box with 4x5 project icon

2-inch diagonal speaker

worm gear motor

recording start button

project file cards in card catalog drawer

4d3.   Mies-on-a-Beam, Seagram Building, NYC.
10   **Lewis.Tsurumaki.Lewis., Mies-on-a-Beam,** collage of mobile platform and Seagram Building, (1998).

19" X 25", digital collage, color. (Testing 1,2,3...)
This landscape supplement for the Seagram Building returns function to the two anomalous, nonfunctional aspects of Mies van der Rohe's New York masterpiece: the 'ornamental' I-beams and the tree plaza. Mies-on-a-beam transforms the curtain wall I-beams into wheel tracks for a pair of mobile grass platforms linked to the window washing hoist.

see also:
1. *Situation Normal - Pamphlet Architecture 21*, Lewis.Tsurumaki.Lewis., ISBN 1-56898-154-6, p. 66 2. foliage enhanced mobile plaza (4d3.1b), 3. executive putting green (4d3.1c), 4. *Testing 1,2,3...* 5. Seagram Building.   I. Title.
○   (2)

REFILED: DETAIL OF DRAWER WITH MIES-ON-A-BEAM
Site-specific installation for the
National Design Triennial
Digital collage, 1999
Architect: Lewis.Tsurumaki.Lewis
Base photograph: © Ezra Stoller, Esto

GIUSEPPE LIGNANO B. 1963
ADA TOLLA B. 1964

LOT/EK
New York City

From Surrealist paintings to contemporary advertisements, much of twentieth-century visual culture springs from the radical juxtapositions of collage. Mixing old and new, sacred and profane, collagists make us see the world in unexpected ways. They also suggest that modern life is transitory and mutable. Marcel Duchamp transformed a urinal from a utilitarian object to a work of art by changing its context. Digitized and collaged into contemporary soft-drink commercials, old Hollywood stars magically come back to life.

Ada Tolla and Giuseppe Lignano are architectural collagists who reclaim existing objects and systems from the contemporary urban environment and make the ordinary seem extraordinary. Known together as LOT/EK, pronounced "low tech," Tolla and Lignano create architecture and furnishings that are carefully

conceived and always elegant but leave traces of their processes of fabrication, such as construction workers' notations and product labels. Transforming old uses into new programs, LOT/EK's materials and pallette combine raw and refined, soft and hard. *TV-Tank* (1998), the duo's spectacular art-cum-architecture installation, sliced an old petroleum tank into eight modules lined with sensuous black rubber tubing and outfitted with television sets. In other projects, LOT/EK has turned a stack of surplus filing cabinets into a striking, Sol Lewitt-like pattern, and converted the body of a truck into an elegant sleeping loft for a rooftop Manhattan apartment. The uncommon sculptural beauty of this apartment forces us to reconsider the seemingly ordinary appearance of adjacent water towers, roof vents, and elevator penthouses.

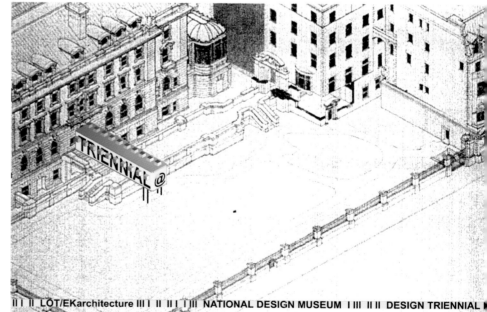

II I II **LOT/EKarchitecture** III I II II I I III **NATIONAL DESIGN MUSEUM** I III II II **DESIGN TRIENNIAL**

TV-LITE
Modular television lighting system, 1997, television sets, plastic shipping palettes, and metal rods
Architects: Giuseppe Lignano and Ada Tolla, LOT/EK
Courtesy of Henry Urbach Architecture

[above and right]
TV-TRUCK: AERIAL VIEW AND INTERIOR PERSPECTIVE
Site-specific installation for the National Design Triennial (not realized)
Digital rendering, 1999
Architects: Giuseppe Lignano and Ada Tolla, LOT/EK

LOT/EK's proposed installation for the *National Design Triennial*, entitled *TV-Truck*, converts a shipping container into a video viewing room lined with a molded-fiberglass skin like that on the interior of a refrigerator. *TV-Truck* docks at the museum's door and juts out into its garden as manufactured product, minimalist sculpture, and graphic billboard. Juxtaposing bright yellow against muted brick and stone, modern industrial forms next to classical tracery, the installation collages a vision of the future onto the museum's historic structure. Like LOT/EK's logo—a boldly abstracted version of the bar code printed on store products—the future they propose is extrapolated from our industrial and consumer-oriented present and releases the power and potential of the man-made universe around us. D.A.

[above]
TV-TANK
Installation at Deitch Projects, in collaboration with Henry Urbach Architecture, New York City
Photograph, 1998
Architects: Giuseppe Lignano and Ada Tolla, LOT/EK

III I II LOT/EKarchitecture III I II II I III NATIONAL DESIGN MUSEUM I III II II DESIGN TRIENNIAL II I II III

MICHAEL A. MANFREDI B. 1953
MARION WEISS B. 1959

Weiss/Manfredi Architects
New York City

Michael A. Manfredi and Marion Weiss practice architecture as creative archeology. Celebrated for their civic projects, they respond to local conditions representing natural and cultural histories. The firm's 1997 Women's Memorial and Education Center at Arlington National Cemetery, for example, was constructed by RECLAIMING a historic landscape and developing new spaces where the stories of female members of the armed forces are told. The memorial sits at the cemetery's ceremonial entrance, behind a 180-foot-diameter granite hemicycle, a grandiose retaining wall completing a monumental urban axis designed by the legendary firm of McKim, Mead & White in 1927. In Weiss/Manfredi's design, glass-enclosed interior stairways connect the hemicycle to an upper-level outdoor terrace defined by a curving glass skylight. The new public belvedere knits the Women's

Memorial into one of the capital's grand, symbolic axes, which stretches from the Lincoln Memorial to the John F. Kennedy grave site and Arlington House, located on the cemetery's highest promontory. The architects' scheme employs subtle yet compelling metaphors to convey the legacy of the more than two million women who have served in the military since the country's founding. For example, the four glass-enclosed stairways that lead visitors from the hemicycle to the rooftop terrace evoke the passage of servicewomen breaking through the military's male hierarchy.

Glass as a symbol of enlightenment is the terrace's most dramatic motif. Wrapping the full curve of the hemicycle are 138 glass tablets. Texts drawn from military speeches and the wartime journals of servicewomen are carved into glass panels mounted above the 240-foot-

MUSEUM OF THE EARTH
Ithaca, New York
Sketch, 1999, photographic
collage and charcoal on vellum
Delineators: Marion Weiss
and Michael A. Manfredi
Architect:
Weiss/Manfredi Architects

MUSEUM OF THE EARTH
Ithaca, New York
Model, 1999, Strathmore card stock
Architect: Weiss/Manfredi
Architects
Team: Marion Weiss and Michael A.
Manfredi (Design partners);
Christopher Ballantine (Project
manager); Armando Petruccelli
(Project architect); Lauren Crahan,
Ricky Liu, Chris Payne
Client: Paleontological Research
Institution

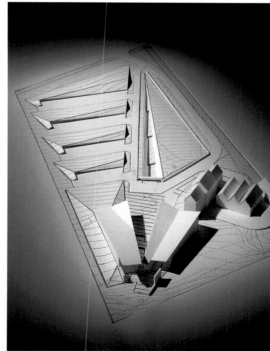

diameter skylight. Throughout the day, changing shadows cast by the skylight's inscribed texts animate the wall below with words in motion. Angled toward the city, the floating rows of tablets seem to join the servicewomen's words to those inscribed on Washington's historic monuments. Arranged in military formation, the tablets echo the cemetery's orderly rows of marble grave markers, visually integrating servicewomen into Arlington's larger community of honor and remembrance.

A new project for the Museum of the Earth in Ithaca, New York, confirms Weiss/Manfredi's allegiance to the idea of reclaiming a site's history. Commissioned by the Paleontological Research Institution, the museum is a series of tilted landforms that reflect the landscape of the local Finger Lakes Region. (The earthworks of American sculptor Robert Smithson also come to mind.) The museum's angled roofs rise like geological formations created by the glaciers that shaped the region.

Slopes for parking and water retention mimic the museum's angular forms. Inside, multistory walls of local stone display the institution's fossil collections, while large windows provide panoramas of the countryside from which these fossils were drawn. A museum of the earth situated in the earth, the structure underscores Weiss/Manfredi's ability to integrate architecture, landscape architecture, and exhibition design in buildings that make manifest the rich histories of their sites. D.A.

RECLAIMED

WOMEN'S MEMORIAL AND EDUCATION CENTER

Arlington National Cemetery
Photograph, 1998
Architect: Weiss/Manfredi Architects
Design partners: Marion Weiss and Michael A. Manfredi
Team: Michael DeCandia (Managing partner); Charles Wahl (Project architect); Christopher Ballantine, Jennifer Graessle, Karl Lehrke, and Stephen Moser (Project team); Elizabeth Corcoran, Paul Ng, Michael Levy, Ricky Liu, Paul Schulhof, and James Tilghman (Presentation)
Client: WIMSA Foundation, General Wilma Vaught USAF Ret

KADAMBARI BAXI B.1962
REINHOLD MARTIN B. 1964

Martin/Baxi Architects
New York City

Drive across the United States and look at the American landscape. Islands of dense urbanity—Chicago's Loop, for example—are surrounded by the endless blur of sprawling freeways, strip malls, suburban housing, and office parks. Reviled by historic preservationists and progressive urbanists, the indeterminate shapelessness of America's everyday landscape is ironically celebrated as an arena of open-ended possibility in *The Entropy Project* (1996–99). Created by architects Reinhold Martin and Kadambari Baxi, the conceptual project RECLAIMS buildings and media images from the seemingly utopian 1960s, a similarly technology-driven decade. These images are transformed via computer into elements of what Martin and Baxi describe as "entropic architecture," invoking a state of disorder from which they think endless possiblities may emerge.

The Entropy Project comprises three digitally-based investigations into the relationship among architecture, technology, and culture. *Homeoffice* (1996), for example, converts the 1962 First City National Bank in Houston, a model of corporate order and rationalism designed by Gordon Bunshaft, into what the architects term a "spatialized blur." The new design visually breaks down the gridded facade of the original building into a pulsating flux of surface effects. The structure's function changes as well: built exclusively for business purposes, the tower now reflects contemporary life by fluidly merging living and working in a spiraling helix.

Open House (1999) explores the instability of contemporary domestic life by increasing the spatial and formal elasticity of the 1964 New York World's Fair House by the Formica Corporation, which was clad both

THE ENTROPY PROJECT:
HOMEOFFICE
Digital renderings, 1998
Architect: Martin/Baxi
Architects

[left and right]
ENTROPIA:
HOMEOFFICE
Digital rendering, 1998
Architect: Martin/Baxi
Architects

inside and out in plastic laminate. *Embassy* (1999) addresses the paranoid legacy of the Cold War by reconfiguring the U.S. embassy in Saigon, designed by Curtis and Davis in 1965, into a windowless building that spies on itself.

From these investigations, Martin and Baxi designed *Entropia*, an interactive multimedia installation in which the three buildings from *The Entropy Project* are overlaid with materials drawn from popular culture, including film, advertising, and news footage from the 1960s. Like the shapeless American landscape—or, conversely, the computer landscape of infinite choice—navigation of the electronic project is nonlinear, allowing for unexpected relationships and juxtapositions. In *Entropia*, *Homeoffice*'s interiors form a surreal environment where the viewer is suspended between the utopian promises of advertisements and corporate promotional films and the dystopian overtones of two darkly futurist movies, Jean-Luc Godard's 1965 *Alphaville* and Orson Welles's 1963 *The Trial*.

Like their work, Martin and Baxi's careers do not fit neatly into any one category. In addition to their practice together, Baxi founded imageMachine, a multimedia design firm, and she is currently a Rockefeller Fellow working on an interactive project about the globalization of American television news. Martin is a scholar of postwar American corporate architecture and teaches architectural design and history at Columbia University. Like *Entropia*, Martin and Baxi embrace an open-ended model for the future of architectural practice D.A.

THE ENTROPY PROJECT: HOMEOFFICE
Digital renderings, 1998
Architect: Martin/Baxi Architects

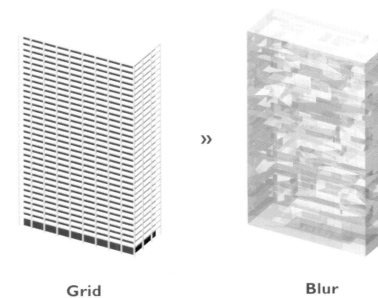

Grid » **Blur**

PABLO MEDINA B. 1960

Pablo Medina Graphic Design
New York City

Pablo Medina has always been fascinated with the hand-lettered signs found in Latino shops and neighborhoods, from North Bergen, New Jersey, where he spent time growing up, to Manhattan's East Village, where he now lives. Medina documents samples of lettering and reconstructs entire alphabets in digital form. The letters he RECLAIMS are imperfect and inconsistent. They are flamboyantly commercial, with no pretensions toward institutional neutrality or modernist simplicity.

Travelling to Spain and Latin America, Medina has discovered a remarkable continuity of Spanish-language lettering styles that appear to maintain elements of typographic identity from the Iberian peninsula to the New World, and from South to North America. The density of signs in a neighborhood—or even on a single storefront—vividly mark the identity of a place. The signage for small, Latino-owned businesses is typically hand-lettered by a local sign painter.

Medina's typeface Cuba (1997) is based on flat letters that are given dimension by shadows and planes of color, an effect Medina has translated into linear black-and-white. For Vitrina (1997), a font based on the looping forms of script, Medina has emphasized the irregularity of the curves and curlicues found in his source material. Sombra (1997) has decorative dimples of flesh pinched out from its limbs, sometimes in such unpredictable spots as the extended right leg of the letter *K*. The typeface 1st Ave (1998) is based on neon lettering, in which repeated stripes of tubing build up the body of the character—an uneven texture results as lengths of tubing double back on each other. Pursuing a less decorative idiom, Medina created the sans serif font North Bergen (1997), with soft,

inconsistent silhouettes that make the letters appear slightly out of focus.

Medina's typefaces, which have been used by such well-known designers as David Carson, Chip Kidd, and Helene Silverman, reflect the contemporary desire for imperfect, vernacular forms in the face of an increasingly homogeneous consumer landscape. Pablo Medina has reclaimed aspects of his own cultural history and made it available for use within modern forms of media and reproduction. E.L.

VITRINA, NORTH BERGEN, CUBA, SOMBRA
Typefaces, 1997
Designer: Pablo Medina
Publisher: Medina Design

1ST AVE.
Typeface, 1998
Designer: Pablo Medina
Publisher: Medina Design

LATIN TYPOGRAPHY
Photographs, 1997
Photographer:
Pablo Medina

RECLAIMED

LOCAL

local

Many architects draw from local forms and materials, local building traditions, and the immediate conditions of a site. Other designers draw on social and cultural history and seek to incorporate the voices and experiences of lost or overlooked populations. Design is conceived in response to its cultural environment.

In the fields of architecture and landscape architecture, a new model of design as an intervention within a specific context is replacing the ideal of the monument or freestanding object imposed upon a place. Many architects are aiming to merge their buildings with their surroundings, collapsing the contained and container, figure and ground. In the field of industrial design, devices such as walkie-talkies facilitate local communication, connecting people by condensing distances.

MARWAN AL-SAYED B. 1962

Marwan Al-Sayed Architects
Phoenix, Arizona

The power and beauty of Marwan Al-Sayed's architecture is rooted in its engagement with elemental, physical forces such as the sun, rain, and water. The diverse palette of his work ranges from translucent fabric roofs to Aegean-white earthen walls and sea-green glass. Al-Sayed manipulates these hues to call attention to the changing effects of nature and light.

Abundant sun and unique views of the LOCAL Sonoran desert inspired Al-Sayed's design for the McCue House in Phoenix, which the architect calls "the house of earth and light." The house (designed with Janet Fink) comprises two solid rectangular volumes supporting a glass-enclosed bridge spanning a natural desert wash. As visitors approach, they see the mountains to the north reflected in a moat-like lap pool through a break in the unadorned exterior. The house's

thick walls rise seamlessly out of the dry desert floor, suggesting ancient ruins. Elongated windows cut into the walls reveal their thickness (18 inches) and solidity. Al-Sayed dramatically contrasts these archaic walls with modern, lightweight steel trusses that support an undulating roof of tensile fabric. Natural light filters through three layers of fabric, which the architect compares to a permanent cloud or "sky painting" floating over the house, filling the interior with varied and fluidly changing desert colors and shadows. "Shade in the desert," Al-Sayed says, "is a most precious commodity, like water and light, and is the driving aesthetic concept of this project."

Born in Baghdad, Al-Sayed has lived around the world. "I've visited and studied some of the most magical cities," he says, referring to the oasis towns in the North African Sahara. "To me it has to do with the ingenuity

HOUSE OF EARTH AND LIGHT: McCUE HOUSE
Phoenix, Arizona
Digital renderings, 1999
Architect: Marwan Al-Sayed Architects
with Janet Fink
Artist: Mies Grybaitis
Computer renderer: Nathan Koren
Assistants: James O'Leary and Michael Powell

with which they're built. Theory tends to divorce you from that. The theory that informs architecture should revolve around life and desire." Ultimately, Al-Sayed seeks to develop what he terms a "nomadic form of practice, a mobile architecture studio" that would be international in scope yet local in its approach to specific projects. Whether designing a Manhattan penthouse or a desert house in Arizona, Al-Sayed says that he is motivated by two desires: to realize the potentials of light and to "restore a modern grandeur and elegance to construction, similar to what the ancients accomplished."
D.A.

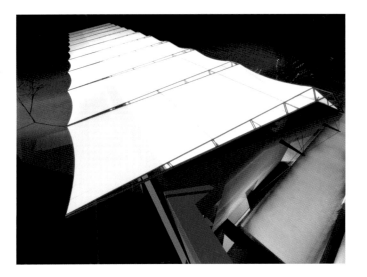

WENDELL BURNETTE B. 1962

Wendell Burnette Architects
Phoenix, Arizona

There is nothing timid about architect Wendell Burnette's approach to the desert landscape of Arizona. Rather than relating scenographically to their LOCAL context, like Taco Bells with their stucco walls and Mission-style clock towers, Burnette's buildings distill the desert's bold natural forms and materials into powerful abstract shapes and spaces.

Burnette's sophisticated aesthetic is evident in a recent pair of private houses: the architect's own home and studio, completed in 1995, and the 1998 proposal for the Tocker/McCormack House. Both residences feature living spaces raised above the landscape and facades that alternate large expanses of glass with solid walls. The houses function like full-scale telescopes, focusing their inhabitants' attention on dramatic vistas while shutting out views of neighboring structures.

In both houses, Burnette has orchestrated spatial sequences with special attention to desert light. Visitors to his own house emerge from the bright sunlight and enter through a cool, dark carport, located under the living section, then climb steel stairs into a narrow, canyon-like entry court. The working and living spaces of the house flank the court; both enclosed spaces are wedged between two parallel walls of 8-inch-thick insulated concrete blocks set 16 feet apart that rise from the ground like the desert geology of nearby mountains. Within the house, thin slots between the monoliths direct sharp slivers of intense light into the rooms, charting the sun's path during the day.

A similarly dramatic sequence characterizes the Tocker/McCormack House. Working with a steeply descending site, Burnette located the main house—a simple box raised on a

McLAUGHLIN ESTATE: WINTER VIEW
Skull Valley, Arizona
Digital rendering, 1998
Architect: Wendell Burnette Architects
Team: Wendell Burnette, Christopher Alt,
Michael LeBlanc

pinwheel of masonry walls—on the plot's highest point, overlooking a panoramic view of downtown Phoenix. Two axes extend from the house into the landscape. One links the house with a cactus garden and parking area. The other projects to a narrow flight of stairs that leads down to a swimming pool enclosed by high, whitewashed walls.

The proposed McLaughlin Estate in Skull Valley, Arizona (1998), extends Burnette's site-derived aesthetic into virgin land. The estate is a V-shaped formation of two wings—a main residence and a stable with a guest house—that reach like outstretched arms into the landscape from a distinctive boulder grouping. Seeking to establish a visual dialog between the wings, Burnette has designed the stable as an open, fence-like structure of silver-gray lath through which air can easily pass for ventilation. In contrast, the

demands of insulating the large and luxurious main house against the area's cold climate led Burnette to use magenta-plum walls of cast earth. The estate's magenta-plum and silver-gray coloring is derived from the palette of manzanita shrubs that blanket the site. Burnette describes the main house as "a dark mass receding back into the land radiating warmth to its inhabitants." Like all of his architecture, the design of the McLaughlin Estate addresses the civilized desires of contemporary city-dwellers as well as their primal needs. D.A.

TOCKER/McCORMACK HOUSE: POOL PAVILION
Phoenix, Arizona
Digital rendering, 1998
Architect: Wendell Burnette Architects
Team: Wendell Burnette, Christopher Alt, and Michael LeBlanc

McLAUGHLIN ESTATE
Skull Valley, Arizona
Model, 1998, scale 3/32":1',
chipboard and basswood
Architect and model fabricator:
Wendell Burnette Architects
Team: Wendell Burnette, Christopher Alt

COLEMAN COKER B. 1951
SAMUEL MOCKBEE B. 1944

Rural Studio at
Auburn University
Auburn, Alabama

Mockbee/Coker Architects
Memphis, Tennessee

Believing that architecture is the most site-specific of the arts, Samuel Mockbee and Coleman Coker focus their work on the needs and circumstances of LOCAL people and places. "To build," the architects state, "means to bring the human condition onto the site."

In 1993 Mockbee established the Rural Studio at Auburn University to enable his students to design and build with a "moral sense of service to a community." Each academic year, three undergraduate studio classes work with Mockbee in an intensive design/build program in Hale County, Alabama, one of the poorest regions in the United States. Students become acquainted with a family, then construct a homestead for them. They often reclaim disposable materials to create housing customized to its users' needs and tastes. The Bryant House (1994), for example, features a concrete shard

wall inset with bottles and a curved roof of exposed recycled signs. Students also undertake a series of community-service projects, from repairing existing structures (such as trailers and roofs) to building new structures (recent projects have included an open-air pavilion, a new playground, and a chapel).

Mockbee and Coker are committed to designing buildings that reflect the changes—natural and manmade—that a site experiences over the course of its history. Mockbee/Coker's design for the ReyRosa Ranch House in Ellis County, Texas (1999), for example, was inspired by two naturally occurring edges on the site—the places where change is most perceptible. The house's sprawling forms are nestled against one edge, the limestone bluff that rises from a lake. The building's angular architectural forms reflect the bluff's contours, as a new alum-

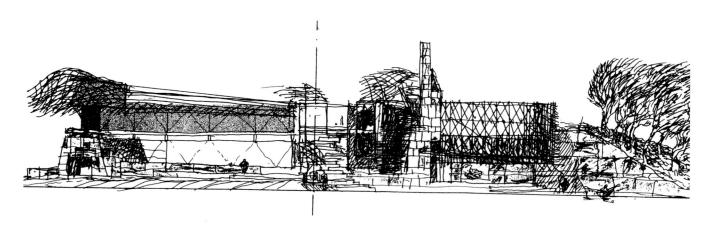

REYROSA RANCH HOUSE
Ellis County, Texas
Sketch, 1998, pen and ink on paper
Architect: Mockbee/Coker Architects
Team: John Tate, Vince Bandy, and
Carl Batton Kennon
Landscape architect: Ed Blake
Delineator: Samuel Mockbee

150

inum-clad wall rising from the lake mirrors the bluff's steep cliffs. The bluff acts as a constant reminder of the site's past. What is now the ranch was many millions of years ago immersed under a shallow, temperate ocean. "It stands there before us," Mockbee and Coker write about the bluff, "eons of tangible evidence, a distinct edge." The other edge is located at the top of the site, where an open field meets the tree line. The architects use this edge to define the road visitors travel on their approach to the house.

Although Mockbee and Coker defer to nature as the primary inspiration for their work, they realize that nature alone cannot accommodate human habitation. "To thoughtfully build," they conclude, "means to critically consider the site's conditions as they are restructured, reconstituted, and rearranged." D. A.

BRYANT HOUSE
Hale County, Alabama
Photographs, 1994
Architect: Samuel Mockbee and the
Rural Studio at Auburn University

SHEILA LEVRANT DE BRETTEVILLE B. 1940

The Sheila Studio
Hamden, Connecticut

Over the past two decades, Sheila Levrant de Bretteville has pioneered a form of public art that actively engages LOCAL communities. In place of a single image or object, de Bretteville's projects integrate a variety of elements into an existing site. Her work enlivens such functional features as railings and sidewalks with images, words, and textures. By weaving visual and verbal narratives into the fabric of public places, this approach runs counter to the established practice of erecting a large-scale sculpture in the center of a plaza, or filling a wall with a mural and leaving its site bare.

In Los Angeles's Little Tokyo neighborhood, de Bretteville embedded a timeline of quotes and facts about Japanese-Americans along the doorways of a historic block (*Omoide no Shotokyo*, 1997). In a New Haven neighborhood, she documented the lives of local citizens—past and present—with stars sunk into the sidewalk (*Path of Stars*, 1994). In the risers of the granite steps of a new library in Queens, New York, she cut titles of books and stories about the process of quest and migration (*Search: Literature*, 1998).

De Bretteville's most recent undertakings include *At the start... At long last...*, completed in the summer of 1999. Here, de Bretteville sought to humanize a dismal subway station in Inwood, a diverse neighborhood at Manhattan's uppermost tip. The 207th Street station terminates the A train, New York's longest subway line and the subject of an American jazz classic. The phrases "At the start..." and "At long last...," referring to the beginning and end of a journey, are embedded in the floor as well as in broken-mirror mosaics on the wall. Incised in the railings that lead passengers in and out of the station

SEARCH: LITERATURE
Flushing, New York
Permanent installation, 1998,
carved granite
Designer: Sheila Levrant de
Bretteville, The Sheila Studio

152

are the lyrics for Billy Strayhorn's song "Take the A Train."

De Bretteville's projects, which involve intense research into the surrounding neighborhood, often record the statements of residents. *At the start... At long last...* includes glazed subway tiles bearing quotations by 207 local people—individuals whose families have resided in the area for generations as well as recent immigrants from the Dominican Republic and other Carribean islands. The quotes express a range of attitudes toward newcomers, crime, friendship, music, and subway travel. De Bretteville's use of mirror reflects the Taino art traditions local to the Carribean, and her symbol for the A train is derived from a Dominican petroglyph.

On both coasts of the United States, de Bretteville has used typography and environmental design to enhance communities. Her aesthetically rich, metaphoric projects are meaningful to a diverse range of local populations. E.L.

AT THE START . . . AT LONG LAST . . .
New York City
Permanent installation, commissioned 1995, completed 1999, mosiac murals, broken mirror and silver tessere, terrazzo floor pieces, etched stainless steel handrail
Designer: Sheila Levrant de Bretteville, The Sheila Studio
Client: New York City Metropolitan Transportation Authority and the Inwood community
Manufacturers: Miotto Mosaics, D. Magnan Terrazzo, Signs of Success
Design assistants: Debra Drodvillo, Jamie Oliveri, John Gambell, Heather Corcoran

B. J. KRIVANEK B. 1953

B. J. Krivanek Art + Design
Chicago, Illinois

Community Architexts
Chicago, Illinois and
Los Angeles, California

By integrating the written word into built environments, B. J. Krivanek adds public and poetic dimensions to the flood of commercial messages in the modern urban landscape. Krivanek, founder of Community Architexts, a nonprofit organization based in Chicago and Los Angeles, creates typographic interventions in response to the LOCAL conditions of a site—from its architectural features to the communities that use it. His projects enrich people's experiences of the places they inhabit.

Krivanek generates the narrative content of his projects from the history of a site and through outreach to community members. *Strands of History* (1999) is located at the new central administration complex of the twenty-three-campus California State University system in Long Beach. The project includes a timeline listing the social, economic, and commercial issues that have shaped California

culture, from theme parks to World War II internment camps. With its surprising conjunction of ideas, this list reads more like a poem than a conventional timeline.

Currently under development is *Family Voices/Austin* (anticipated completion, December 2000), a project in a depressed neighborhood in Chicago that will adapt local storefronts and the sign structures attached to them. Krivanek will incorporate the voices of mothers and caregivers from the community into these reclaimed commercial facilities, which later will be returned to small businesses in their refurbished states, complete with effective supports for new signage. These changes in the urban fabric aim to spur local commercial growth.

Krivanek's work revives the tradition of architectural inscription. For centuries, public buildings in the classical style have featured texts that

STRANDS OF HISTORY
Long Beach, California
Permanent installation, 1999,
aluminum, stainless steel, glass
Design Director: BJ Krivanek
Environmental Designer: Joel Breaux
Historian: Lillian Jones
Landscape Architect: Joseph Yee, LPA
Client: California State University

serve to memorialize and instruct. The use of generously spaced capital letters throughout Krivanek's work makes reference to this tradition, but whereas classical inscriptions reflect the beliefs and values of the dominant social groups that commission civic buildings, Krivanek's work presents counternarratives and alternative viewpoints, given solemn credence by their carefully considered visual presentation.

Krivanek builds upon the character of local sites, combining typographic forms and architectural structures to let those places speak. E.L.

RECONFIGURATION

METAPHORIC
-STRUCTURE-

PUBLIC
VOICES

SELENA
**YOU NEED
MONEY
EVERY DAY**

ADAPTED TO 10
SITES ALONG CHICAGO
AVENUE

REFURBISHED
STRUCTURE

-COMMUNICATION-
INFRASTRUCTURE

APPROPRIATION

SIGN
PROVIDES
A PUBLIC VOICE
FOR A
SPECIFIC
MOTHER

FAMILY VOICES/AUSTIN
Concept proposal for permanent installation, projected completion December 2000, aluminum, structural steel, acrylic, die-cut vinyl
Artistic director: B. J. Krivanek, Community ArchiTexts
Environmental Designer: Joel Breaux
Arts Outreach Coordinator: Jennifer Van Winkle

SCOTT RICHARDS B. 1959
FRANK M. TYNESKI B. 1968
AND TEAM

MOTOROLA
Plantation, Florida

Everyone remembers the clunky, chunky walkie-talkie of childhood. It was almost easier to hear the person yelling from the backyard than it was to use the toy itself. So it should not be surprising that when the in-house design staff at Motorola began researching walkie-talkies, they found that people perceived them as distinctly "uncool." Taking this as a sign of opportunity, they challenged themselves to create a product that would be just the opposite. Even Motorola management was skeptical—hip and visually persuasive prototypes were required to convince executives that the project was anything but hopeless.

In need of some youthful inspiration, the Motorola team sponsored walkie-talkie projects at Brigham Young University in Salt Lake City, Utah, and Universidad Iberoamericano in Mexico City. As expected, the students' forays energized the corporate team. The result is the TalkAbout (1998), a two-way radio with a 2-mile range, a beefed-up gadget creating a LOCAL zone of communication. The in-house team reinvented the walkie-talkie with an attention-grabbing design language that was half-tool, half-toy. Brightly colored (yellow-and-blue and gray-and-green) and with the rugged look common to extreme gear, the TalkAbout found a market in kids and parents looking for each other at the mall, ballpark, and ski slope.

Whereas the TalkAbout does one thing exceptionally well, the iDEN i1000 telephone (1998) is an all-purpose communications device that functions as a speakerphone, cell phone, pager (with a text reader), and two-way radio. It's no toy, a fact that becomes clear with one look at its compact, contoured body of molded polycarbonate (it weighs only 6 ounces). Building on the flip-phone

TALKABOUT SLK
Wireless telephone/radio, 1998, high-impact plastic/rubber, and electronic components
Designer: Frank M. Tyneski
Director, industrial design:
Bruce Claxton
Principal staff engineer:
Billy Robertson
Lead industrial designer:
Mike Page
Industrial designer: Glen Oross
Manufacturer: Motorola

concept that has been Motorola's hallmark, the i1000's see-through cover sits atop a gently curved row of raised oval keys. Two buttons protrude through the cover via small openings, allowing access to radio, directory, and other functions without opening the phone. A paradigm for telecommunications devices, the i1000, though small, has pushed back against the phone's relentless miniaturization, achieving an optimal size and ergonomic configuration for a hand-held device.

While the TalkAbout has an element of whimsy and can-do optimism, the i1000 embraces a deep-set functionalism true to Motorola's technological roots.

The success of these two "cool tools"—the i1000, for example, has sold over one million units—augers well for a future in which communications devices respond to the physical and emotional demands of the people who use them. s.s.h.

i1000 WIRELESS DIGITAL COMMUNICATOR
Wireless telephone/radio, 1998 insert molded polycarbonate, Elastomeric keypad, and high-density interconnect circuitry
Designers: Scott Richards and Craig F. Siddoway
Mechanical designers: Wille Kottke and William Steinhoff
Manufacturer: Motorola

b®anded

Corporate identity systems have become powerful forms of currency—both cultural and economic. A brand is a family of images and values that can encompass a vast series of products. Designers develop distinctive uses of color, form, materials, letterforms, and language as well as attitudes towards function and content that bring a brand to life. They embed logotypes, taglines, and phrases directly into the body of objects, resulting in a kind of consumer tatooing of goods and services. A product is more than a concrete object: it is endowed with authority and familiarity by the power of its brand.

When Michael Jordan and Tinker Hatfield began rethinking the athletic shoe in the early 1980s, they knew that sneakers for basketball could be different and better. Their collaboration, and the work of Hatfield's design team at Nike, demonstrates the effect that visionary design can have on brand development. Indeed, the Air Jordan line of shoes became a catalyst for a global phenomenon.

Despite Nike's prominence, the people who create the BRAND experience are essentially invisible. Hatfield—largely unknown to the consumer—has emerged as the world's most influential designer of athletic footwear. His insight into the consumer mindset as well as his ability as a designer helped him to create truly lusted-after products.

Trained as an architect, Hatfield joined Nike in 1981 and has designed the last thirteen of the annual Air Jordan models. He is responsible for Nike's flagship Air Jordan sneaker, the shoe that launched Nike's extraordinary growth in the 1980s and still defines its image. In designing the shoes, Hatfield has found inspiration in everything from fighter planes to panthers to Michael Jordan himself. Jordan's black Ferrari 550 is the source for the 1998–99 Air Jordan XIV, which features a Ferrari-style shield (with the Jumpman logo in place of the carmaker's horse), a metallic paint job on the sole, and a vent detail evocative of the Ferrari's door. In a more unlikely appropriation, the Air Jordan XII includes details reclaimed from old-fashioned wing-tip shoes.

TINKER HATFIELD B. 1952

Nike
Beaverton, Oregon

MICHAEL JORDAN
Photograph
Courtesy Nike

**REAR ELEVATION:
AIR JORDAN XIV**
Digital rendering, 1998
Designer: Tinker Hatfield
Client: Michael Jordan
Manufacturer: Nike

As Michael Jordan the athlete became Michael Jordan the superbrand, Hatfield recognized the demand for designed accessories. Brand Jordan now comprises a wide array of shoes along with a full complement of hats, jerseys, t-shirts, warm-ups, and shorts. The brand is treated by Nike as its own company. In no small part, the success is due to Hatfield's ability to pioneer a design language that both asserts and fuels the mythology of the Jordan brand.
S.S.H.

[right]
INSPIRATION DRAWING: AIR JORDAN XII
Rendering, 1995, pen, ink, collage
Designer: Tinker Hatfield
Client: Michael Jordan
Manufacturer: Nike

BRANDED

24.5 HEEL KICK

[left]
OUTSOLE: AIR JORDAN XIII
Rendering, 1997, mixed media
Designer: Tinker Hatfield
Client: Michael Jordan
Manufacturer: Nike

The Martha Stewart BRAND has evolved from a one-woman catering operation in Westport, Connecticut, to an extensive enterprise with over four-hundred employees. Nearly half of them are creative staff, including graphic designers, textile designers, art directors, product developers, and editors for photography, style, food, and gardening. Directing design for this formidable network of media and merchandise is Gael Towey. She oversees the look and feel of the Martha Stewart brand, whose hallmarks include crisp, minimal typography; soft, organic colors; atmospheric photographs that seek to capture the effects of natural light; and a reverence for functional objects grounded in the American domestic vernacular. This compelling brand image resonates not only across the ever-expanding range of Martha Stewart goods and services, but has influenced the catalogs and product offerings of America's most successful home furnishing merchants.

An educational, almost evangelistic ethos animates the Martha Stewart brand, which aims to bring aesthetic enlightenment and instructional guidance to a mass audience. At the core of the empire is the magazine *Martha Stewart Living*, founded in 1990. With a circulation over 2.1 million, the magazine presents a mix of articles—at once explanatory and sensual—on the arts of living, from planting bulbs to icing a cake. Many of the articles are presented in an almost scientific

MARTHA STEWART B. 1941
GAEL TOWEY B. 1952

MARTHA STEWART LIVING OMNIMEDIA

New York City

MARTHA STEWART EVERYDAY: POISON-FREE WASP & HORNET KILLER
Packaging, 1999, offset lithograph on metal container
Creative director: Gael Towey, Martha Stewart Living Omnimedia
Designer: Stephen Doyle, Doyle Partners
Manufacturer: Wood Stream Corporation

fashion, with an approach that combines luxurious photography and rational, diagrammatic layouts.

The magazine's editorial content fuels the company's product development. When *Martha Stewart Living* ran a cover story about hydrangeas and then featured them on Stewart's television show in 1994, nurseries across the U. S. sold out of the shrubs. Gardening products are part of the Martha Stewart Everyday sub-brand, a family of goods sold at K-Mart that ranges from bed linens to bug spray. Because K-Mart stores reach such an enormous market—seventy-one million shoppers—Martha Stewart can affect not just the *demand* for specific products, but also the *supply*. By introducing a line of packaged seeds that includes over four hundred varieties of flowers and vegetables, Martha Stewart Everyday has induced growers to produce a bigger supply and a more

sophisticated array of seeds than ever before available to a mass market. Each package features original photography, produced with the soft naturalism that defines the Martha Stewart look; the idea of showing flowers and vegetables held in someone's hands stems from a recurring visual theme in the magazine.

Manufacturing executives are willing to take a leap of faith—often risking millions of dollars—when Martha Stewart proposes a design idea. She has used the authority of her brand to improve the range of products offered in one of the nation's largest marketplaces. E.L.

[left]
MARTHA STEWART LIVING: CAMELIAS
Magazine, 1997, offset lithograph
Creative director: Gael Towey, Martha Stewart
Living Omnimedia
Design director: Eric A. Pike
Designer: Claudia Bruno
Photographer: Gentl & Hyers
Publisher: Martha Stewart Living Omnimedia

[above]
MARTHA STEWART LIVING: ALLIUMS
Magazine, 1994, offset lithograph
Creative director: Gael Towey,
Martha Stewart Living Omnimedia
Art director: Anne Johnson
Photographer: Victor Schrager
Publisher: Martha Stewart Living
Omnimedia

[left]
MARTHA STEWART EVERDAY PICKLING CUCUMBERS
Packaging, 1999, offset lithograph
Creative director: Gael Towey,
Martha Stewart Living Omnimedia
Designer: Stephen Doyle, Doyle
Partners
Photographer: Lisa Hubbard
Manufacturer: Burpee

163

LAURIE HAYCOCK MAKELA B. 1956
P. SCOTT MAKELA 1960–1999

Words + Pictures for Business + Culture
Bloomfield Hills, Michigan

P. Scott Makela and Laurie Haycock Makela have had a pervasive influence on the field of graphic design through their work as designers and educators. Deploying digital technologies with a visceral, physical passion for form and communication, they have confronted design as a chaotic force of nature, an object of conquest that can never be fully domesticated. Their designs for print and multimedia embrace the liquid, transformable surfaces of images and letterforms.

P. Scott Makela died suddenly in May 1999, cutting short a life still in its ascendency. At the time of his death, the Makelas' studio was creating an advertising campaign for the snowboard manufacturer Rossignol. The campaign sought to dramatize the Rossignol BRAND through a series of compelling images and copy lines.

In Scott Makela's concept proposals, which landed the account, the text is spiritual—even religious—in its euphoric embrace of the bright and dangerous landscape of snowboarding. Flat, geometric letters glide transparently across glittering inclines of snow. The Rossignol product is pushed into the extreme foreground, suggesting the vantage point of the snowboarder, whose vertiginous view is partially eclipsed by the equipment of the sport.

Laurie Haycock Makela and her colleagues at the studio Words + Pictures for Business + Culture continued to develop the Rossignol campaign after Scott Makela's death, producing a broad range of advertisements and product promotions. The early concept proposals, which provided genetic material for an evolving brand image, are among Scott Makela's final works.

Laurie and Scott Makela were chairs of the two-dimensional design program at the Cranbrook Academy of Art, a post that Laurie Makela now carries forward on her own. Both designers had attended the school in the early 1990s, where they avidly engaged the atmosphere of technological discovery and cultural critique that has made Cranbrook a controversial center for design discourse since the 1970s.

The Makelas' studio continues to use typography and images in ways that are sensual, mystical, and sublime. Scott Makela's energy lives on in the work of his collaborators and students. Through them, the projects left unfinished and the ideas left nascent continue to take shape.

E.L.

AROUSE AND GRATIFY
Advertisement, 1999,
digital print
Art director: Laurie Haycock
Makela, Words + Pictures
for Business + Culture
Designer: Brigid Cabry
Development team:
Brigid Cabry, Paul Schneider,
Warren Corbit, Kurt Miller
Photographer:
Greg Von Doersten
Client: Rossignol Ski and
Snowboard

FAITH IN ACTION
Concept proposal, advertising
campaign, 1999, digital print
Designer: P. Scott Makela,
Words + Pictures for Business
+ Culture
Client: Rossignol Ski and
Snowboard, Inc.

GOD IS CLOSE TO YA
Concept proposal, advertising
campaign, 1999, digital print
Designer: P. Scott Makela,
Words + Pictures for Business
+ Culture
Client: Rossignol Ski and
Snowboard, Inc.

FLUID

PHYSICAL

BRANDED

165

In 1985 Bruce Mau began working with Zone Books, a not-for-profit venture launched by a group of writers who wished to publish scholarly texts outside the university press system. Mau's work for Zone, which features refined but idiosyncratic typography, intense colors, and inventive book-binding details, opened up a new vein of experimental graphic design. Mau eschewed layering, fragmentation, and digital special effects in favor of an intense visual engagement with editorial content.

The impact of Zone was not neatly contained, however, within the narrow field of book design. Mau and his collaborators had created a BRAND, and in so doing, they were challenging not only the conventions of academic publishing but identity design as well. Zone had transformed scholarly publishing into a dynamic, seductive medium, converting objects whose visual character was typically dull and formulaic into prestige objects. The Zone brand became a flexible framework into which flowed a stream of new publications, each having its own personality as well as a palpable genetic link to its kin.

Mau calls identity design a "life" problem. An institution, place, or product is an evolving organism that responds to input from its environment—from users, from competing goods and services, from shifts in the culture. According to Mau, the visual features of a brand, expressed through typography, color, materials, and language, should be mutable and liquid rather than fixed in time. Mau's logo for the industrial design firm Void, for example, consists of a series of deformed O's, each different from the others. The mark expresses the company's desire to temper the rational character of technology with values of singularity and change.

To create a typographic identity for Frank O. Gehry's Walt Disney Concert Hall in Los Angeles, Mau developed a font that typographically interprets the wit and humanity of Gehry's building. Using computer animation techniques, Mau clipped the ends and altered the contours of sans-serif letterforms, yielding fluid characters that seem altered by wind, water, or time.

For Mau, the identity of a place or product should feel, at any given moment, like a frame arrested from a system in flux. His broad-based work as the author and editor of visual identities has inflected the notion of the stable brand with a sense of fluid transformation. E.L.

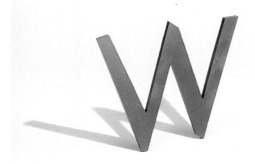

[above]
WALT DISNEY CONCERT HALL
Los Angeles, California
Letter for architectural signage, 1991–present
Designer: Bruce Mau with Chris Rowat,
Greg Van Alstyne, Robert Soar
Architect: Frank O. Gehry and Associates

[left]
THE LIBERTINE READER
Book, 1997, offset lithograph
Designer: Bruce Mau with Chris Rowat
and Barr Gilmore
Publisher: Zone Books

VOID
Identity design, 1998
Designer: Bruce Mau with Nancy Nowacek
Client: Void Office of Industrial Design

JEFFREY DACHIS B. 1966
CRAIG KANARICK B. 1967
AND TEAM

RAZORFISH
New York City

The digital communications consultancy Razorfish, founded by Jeffrey Dachis and Craig Kanarick in 1995, has ridden the rushing tide of economic change triggered by the World Wide Web. The company has grown from a small firm staked out in the far reaches of New York's Alphabet City to a publicly-traded company with offices stationed across the globe, from Los Angeles to Helsinki. With clients ranging from the funky shopping service Petopia to the financial giant Charles Schwab & Co., Inc., Razorfish helps companies strengthen their BRANDS and conduct fast, secure, and emotionally satisfying transactions on-line.

Among Razorfish's most prominent projects has been the total redesign of Schwab's vast Web site. Starting in 1998, Razorfish's work helped Schwab be a leader in on-line personal finance, customer service, and trading.

Razorfish's approach can be seen in the redesign of Schwab.com's Customer Center, a secure environment where account holders can place trade orders, manage their accounts, track their portfolios, and research potential investments. The old site design was dependent on an unwieldy and poorly structured list of more than twenty-five links along the left side of the screen. In the redesigned site, a series of "file tabs" runs across the top; a concise group of main options are always visible, with a second level of sub-categories beneath them. Supplementing the tab system is a series of "Quick Links," enabling users to call up information that is contextually relevant to a particular page. Scrolling has been eliminated from pages such as trading forms, where even a few extra seconds can impede the ease of financial transactions.

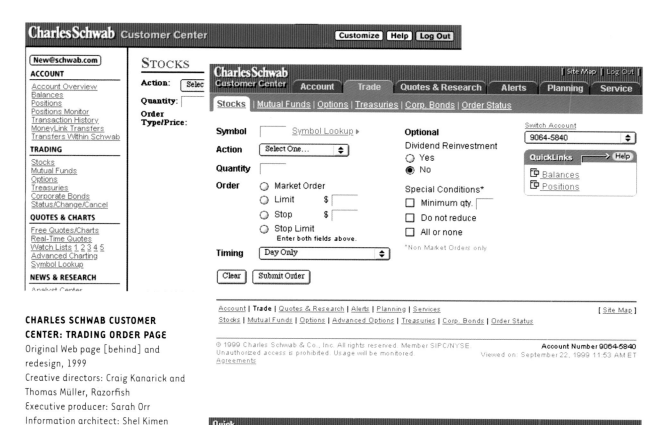

CHARLES SCHWAB CUSTOMER CENTER: TRADING ORDER PAGE
Original Web page [behind] and redesign, 1999
Creative directors: Craig Kanarick and Thomas Müller, Razorfish
Executive producer: Sarah Orr
Information architect: Shel Kimen
Interface designer: Olle Strondahl
HTML developer: Audie Panganiban
Client: Charles Schwab & Co.

Color, typography, and layout serve to enhance the Web site's function and convey Schwab's brand to the on-line community. Pinstriped fields of blue convey a sense of authoritative experience and measured, even conservative, financial thinking, energized with sharp, bright areas of gold. Paler yellows and grays guide the eye through columns and rows of data, while black type and white backgrounds maximize legibility.

The Razorfish team worked with Schwab to maintain industry leadership in the increasingly democratic, customer-oriented field of on-line investing. The site functions as a powerful marketing device that actively demonstrates Schwab's services, providing a digital place of business equipped with reliable and understandable tools.
E.L.

PETOPIA
Web page, 1999
Creative director: Cindy Steinberg
Team: Andrea Turner (producer),
Jayson Elliot (information architect),
Dom Sillett (interface designer), Brennan
Babb, John George (html developers)
Client: Petopia

narra(

Visual narrative has colonized the public landscape.
Themed environments have moved beyond the
amusement park to reshape restaurants, hotels,
shopping malls, and even city streets. This sense of
theater has turned dining and shopping into
performances, making consumers both players and
spectators. At the same time, costumes and sets for
theatrical productions and films have become crucial
to the identity and action of many contemporary
dramas. Cartoon characters inhabit the imaginations
of children and adults, animating not only the page
and screen but the vast culture of licensed goods
as well. The field of exhibition design has enabled the
creators of museums and monuments to tell complex
stories in immersive environments using objects,
images, and texts.

RALPH APPELBAUM B. 1942

Ralph Appelbaum Associates
New York City

Ralph Appelbaum's work signals the powerful forces that are transforming contemporary exhibition design and practice. Since 1993, when his firm's emotionally charged United States Holocaust Memorial Museum opened in Washington, D.C., to enormous acclaim, Appelbaum has been a favorite choice of museums that regard culture as big business. Appelbaum's exhibitions are NARRATIVE experiences rather than artifact-centered displays. Few who visit the Holocaust Museum, for example, can forget the multistory hall hung with photographs of former inhabitants from a single village obliterated by the Nazis.

The potential extinction of life on earth inspired Appelbaum's 1998 installation for the 11,000-square-foot Hall of Biodiversity at New York's American Museum of Natural History, designed with architects James Stewart Polshek & Partners and Niles Eldredge, curator of the museum's Department of Invertebrates. Appelbaum's exhibition design was inspired by Eldredge's intention to "hit people right away with the abundance and variety of life....They would learn about mass extinction due to such natural factors as climactic changes and meteorites....At the exit, they would find out what they could do about it."[1]

Like Appelbaum's best work, the installation features grandly scaled, memorable architectural set pieces. In the center of the gallery sits a 2,500-square-foot recreation of a portion of the Dzanga-Ndoki Rainforest in the Central African Republic, a physical manifestation of biodiversity's delicate balance. Digital imagery and three-dimensional scenography immerse the visitor in the sounds, smells, and movements of the forest. The exhibition's most

memorable element, however, is the softly backlit, 100-foot-long Spectrum of Life wall, featuring close to fifteen-hundred specimens and models from the museum's collections. For sheer theatrical sweep, the design—potentially a dry display of taxidermy—fulfills Appelbaum's hope to "create an environment where people enter with a sense of wonder and awe at how beautiful and diverse the world is."[2]

Positioning his design expertise within the context of fundraising, public relations, and other forms of marketing, Appelbaum acknowledges that today's museums must compete with other forms of leisure-time entertainment for their visitors' attention. As a result, a recent Appelbaum commission—the Glass Innovation Center at the Corning Museum of Glass in Corning, New York—employs special effects, high-tech computer software, theatrical lighting, as well as role-playing and other interactive games. These shape a new generation of institutions focused on subjects and issues outside the scope of traditional museums. Appelbaum also realizes that the subjectivity of personal experience is often more critical to museum visitors' hearts and minds than the cool objectivity of a collection of masterpieces. With this in mind, Appelbaum addresses big stories that engage people's everyday lives. D.A.

1. Quoted in Roger Yee, "To Life!" *Contract Design* (Sept. 1998): 61.
2. Quoted in So-Chung Shinn, "Live from New York!" *Interior Design* (Sept. 1998): 62.

AMERICAN MUSEUM OF NATURAL HISTORY: HALL OF BIODIVERSITY
New York City
Photographs, 1998
Principal in charge: Ralph Appelbaum
Design associate/project director:
Melanie Yae Ide
Team: Miranda K. Smith (Senior content coordinator); Marianne E. Schuit (Project manager); Elisabeth Hartman Cannell (Senior designer); Shari Berman (Senior graphic designer); James Jeffries, Jacob Barton, and Dominique Ng (Designers); Nancy Hoerner (Illustrator); Ayako Hosono (Graphic design and production); Eliot Hoyt (Content coordinator); Mia Hatgis (Junior coordinator); Sylvia Juran (Editor); Mark Sweeney (Graphic production)
Exhibition fabricators: Rathe Productions Inc. and Showtime Exhibit Builders

DANTE FERRETTI B. 1943

Rome

After seeing Dante Ferretti's highly stylized decors for films such as *The Adventures of Baron Munchhausen* (1989) and *Interview with the Vampire* (1994), Julie Taymor realized that she had found the ideal, arguably the only, film set designer for *Titus*, (1999), her new adaptation of Shakespeare's *Titus Andronicus*. Ferretti, who also designed the sets of Federico Fellini's last films in the late 1970s and 1980s, brings the operatic theatricality of the great Italian director to contemporary movie narratives. Now the favored production designer of Martin Scorsese, Ferretti created a Gilded Age New York for *The Age of Innocence* (1993), a Las Vegas of the popular imagination for *Casino* (1995), and a resplendent Tibet (on stages in Morocco) for *Kundun* (1997). *Dino*, their planned upcoming collaboration, will recreate the postwar, Rat-Pack Palm Springs of Dean Martin and Frank Sinatra.

Ferretti's most ambitious recent project, *Titus*, meets our contemporary thirst for deadly glamorous spectacle. Taymor's inaugural feature film comes in on the heels of the enormous success of *The Lion King* (1997), her Broadway mega-hit blending African rhythms, Western pop tunes, puppetry, and dance. Taymor regards William Shakespeare's *Titus Andronicus*, which depicts the darkest facets of human nature, as deeply relevant to today's violent world. To visually express the play's currency, Ferretti fashioned a cinematic style that transgresses time and space. Created on soundstages at the legendary Cinecittà Studios outside Rome as well on locations throughout the surrounding region, Ferretti's sets for *Titus* weave a cultural narrative about Rome, a city where diverse histories and cultures crash in a fragmented collage of Roman, Renaissance, and modern

KUNDUN: TIBETAN NOBLEWOMEN
Costume sketch, 1996, watercolor on paper
Designer and delineator: Dante Ferretti
Director: Martin Scorsese
Producer: Touchstone/ The Walt Disney Company

structures. In the film, the Senate Building is just such a time-colliding hybrid. To create it, Ferretti reclaimed the Palazzo della Civitá del Lavoro—an urban stage-set of arcaded marble walls built by Benito Mussolini as a fascist imitation of ancient Roman grandeur—and dressed it with heraldic black banners. Under Ferretti's direction, the building conveys something of the alienation depicted in the paintings of Giorgio de Chirico.

Rendered in somber colors including rust-red, burnt-ocher, and smoky-black, Ferretti's sets depict a hedonistic Rome, circa 400 A.D., on the brink of collapse as Gothic barbarians storm the gates. Violent juxtapositions in palette, scale, and lighting evoke a base, tribal society where rape, dismemberment, and cannibalism are sport. Ferretti's design, part classical splendor, part tough contemporary chic, suits

Taymor's objective to make Shakespeare relevant to modern audiences. "Everyone will know it," she says, "when they see it."[1] D.A.

1. Quoted in Alexandra Stanley, "Taymor's Encore (It's Not Disney)," *The New York Times*, 20 December 1998.

TITUS: SENATE EXTERIOR AND SENATE INTERIOR
Set sketches, 1998,
charcoal and pastel
on paper
Designer and delineator:
Dante Ferretti
Author of *Titus Andronicus*:
William Shakespeare
Director and adapter
of film: Julie Taymor
Producer: Clear Blue Sky
Productions

DAVID GALLO B. 1966

New York City

"Scenery wants to dance," says set designer David Gallo, "just like everything else." Gallo's fluid transitions of space, time, and scenery animate a play's NARRATIVE. His designs for *Jackie: An American Life* (1997), playwright Gip Hoppe's postmodern meditation on contemporary celebrity and the former first lady, demonstrate Gallo's style as well as his funny and slightly skewed sensibility. The play's rapid scenic changes comment on the modern phenomenon of the fifteen-minute celebrity. Set within rows of arches that telescope into a false perspective tunnel, the play presents paparazzi-captured flashes from Jackie's life in the form of overscaled, cartoon-like elements: a stylized yacht owned by Aristotle Onassis, a giant puppet of Joseph Kennedy, Sr., and a Greek chariot heaped with jewels and clothes from one of Jackie's shopping trips. The quick

movements of the play also reflect the short attention spans of contemporary writers, directors, and audiences who have been raised on movies, television, and music videos.

Peripatetic like many young theater designers, Gallo is on the cusp of a major career breakthrough. He has recently mounted shows in New York, Chicago, Washington, and Los Angeles, and is now designing London's *Theater of Blood*, one of a handful of multimillion-dollar musicals on his schedule. Throughout his twelve-year career, Gallo's style has ranged from the wildly colored cartoon aesthetic of Broadway's *You're a Good Man, Charley Brown* (1999) to the down-on-its-heels urbanity of August Wilson's *Jitney* (1998) and the somber chiaroscuoro of the Roundabout Theatre's revival of Arthur Miller's *A View from the Bridge* (1998). To suggest the oppressive working-class environment in which

EPIC PROPORTIONS: CLEOPATRA'S BARGE
Helen Hayes Theater,
New York City
Model, 1999, scale 1/2":1', illustration board,
foam core, foam, and acrylic paint
Set designer: David Gallo

Authors: Larry Coen and David Crane
Director: Jerry Zaks
Producers: Bob Cuillo, Brent Peek, Robert Barandes, Matthew Farrell, and Mark Schwartz
Model fabricators: Kevin Cwalina and David Swayze

IN WALKS ED
Cincinnati Playhouse, Cincinnati, Ohio
Photograph, 1997
Set designer: David Gallo
Author and director: Keith Glover
Producer: Ed Stern

Miller's characters struggle, Gallo surrounded the actors with a semicircular backdrop evocative of the Brooklyn waterfront. He designed the stark, black-and-white drop by collaging a photographic image of the Queen Mary with repeated silhouettes of cranes. Gallo's design for James Goldman's *The Lion in Winter* (1999) features a perfect representation of his quick-change style: a curving metal-mesh stage curtain demarcates different scenes and spaces as it opens and closes or becomes more or less transparent, depending on how it is lit.

The diversity of Gallo's output illustrates his desire to create designs tailored to the specific character of each script. *Epic Proportions*, a 1999 production, presents a comic view of the media's looming presence. The play follows the exploits of two Hollywood extras struggling to

succeed within the overscaled decor of a 1930s Biblical epic, which Gallo realized with DeMille-scaled pieces of scenery, from an Egyptian barge to classical columns and statuary. For Keith Glover's *In Walks Ed* (1996), Gallo's glossy black and gun-metal gray sets suggests the play's barbaric view of urban life. The shiny, monochromatic color scheme mirrors the saturated, day-glo palette of the

lighting design and allows the costumes, in Gallo's words, "to scream." In their willingness to step aside and let the narrative speak, Gallo's diverse stage productions reveal his sole impulse to give audiences a maximum theatrical jolt.
D.A.

JITNEY
The Huntington Theatre, Boston
Photograph, 1998
Set designer and photographer: David Gallo
Author: August Wilson
Director: Marrion McClinton
Producer: Huntington Theatre Company

**A VIEW FROM THE BRIDGE:
RED HOOK DOCK YARD**
Roundabout Theatre, New York City
Painter's elevation for backdrop, 1998, scale
1/2":1', photocopies, black gesso, paper
correction fluid, and acetate

Set designer and delineator:
David Gallo
Author: Arthur Miller
Director: Michael Mayer
Producer: Tod Haymes

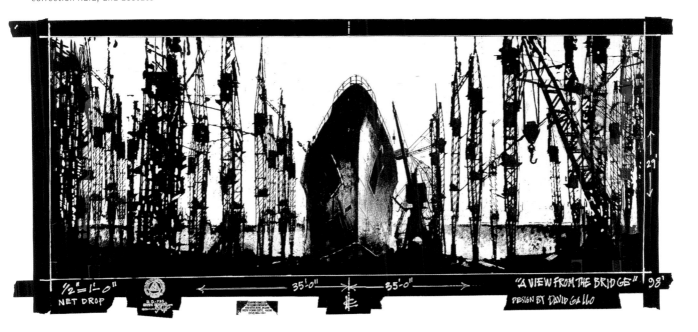

RODNEY ALAN GREENBLAT B. 1960

Center for Advanced Whimsy
New York City

In the innanely violent world of video games, several attempts have been made to create interactive games that celebrate humanity, humor, and sensual pleasure over mass destruction and ruthless competition. Designer Rodney Alan Greenblat has collaborated in the production of a series of spirited video games with Sony Playstation that have proven to be commercially successful as well as good-natured and warm-hearted. As electronic games become an increasingly dominant NARRATIVE form in our culture—replacing television as the constant companion of many school-age children—the arrival of games that attract the imagination with non-violent content is a welcome event.

Greenblat had already made a name for himself as the author of children's books (*Uncle Wizzmo's Used Car*, 1990) and interactive CD-ROM's for young audiences (*Dazzeloids*,

1994) when he began working on the Playstation product *Parappa the Rapper*, in which a musically inclined dog invites users to learn a series of increasingly complex beats, tapped out on the Playstation controller. A player who reaches the highest level of the game—"rapping cool"—is able to improvise in response to the established rhythm of the game.

The characters Greenblat created for *Parappa the Rapper* (1997) and its sister game *Um Jammer Lammy* (1999) are at once wholesome and hip. Rendered in bright, flat colors and endowed with open, wide-eyed personalities, they wear street-wise clothes and walk with a hip-hop beat. Greenblat has added just enough gothic elements—such as the skull-and-crossbones in the *Um Jammer Lammy* logo—to undercut the sweetness of his digital worlds. The games have proven enormously appealing to young people—not just

PARAPPA THE RAPPER
Video game character, 1997
Designer: Rodney Alan Greenblat
Game concept: Masaya Matsuura
Producer: Masaya Matsuura
Publisher: Sony Computer Entertainment

PARAPPA THE RAPPER
OFFICIAL SPACE AGE 1 TOASTER
Toaster, 1997, metal
Surface designer: Rodney Alan Greenblat
Producer: Vacuum Records Inc.

to children, but to adults in their late teens and early twenties. Over two million copies have sold worldwide, attracting an especially vast following in Japan.

Video games spawn huge profits not just in the sale of the games but in the proliferation of licensed goods, and a branded product empire has sprung up around Greenblat's characters. The glowing screen-based world extends into the realm of physical objects, from the usual key chains and stuffed toys to the unexpected Parappa the Rapper Official Space Age 1 Toaster (1997), a full-scale working appliance designed to burn Parappa's face onto slices of bread. The toaster was created for sale in record stores in Japan.

The electronic environments of Rodney Alan Greenblat are almost nostalgic in their loopy, happy sense of fun, and yet they are perfectly

attuned to the beat of popular culture. In Greenblat's words, "I have to create a cozy candy-colored cartooniverse that spreads joy like peanut butter over the burnt toast of so-called reality."[1]   E.L.

1. Quoted in Steven Heller and Elinor Pettit, *Design Dialogues* (New York: Allworth Press, 1998).

UM JAMMER LAMMY
Video game, 1999
Designer: Rodney Alan Greenblat, Center for Advanced Whimsy
Game concept: Masaya Matsuura
Producer: Masaya Matsuura and Sony Computer Entertainment
Publisher: Sony Computer Entertainment

A pioneer in twisted, raucous animation, John Kricfalusi was born to tell stories. One-time protégé of animation legend Ralph Bakshi (*Fritz the Cat*), he leapt to prominence after creating *The Ren & Stimpy Show*, only to break with the Nickelodeon television network that broadcast it after two years. Drawn to the Internet, Kricfalusi founded the animation studio Spumco with partner Jim Smith, and set out to make his characters Web-worthy.

His first "webtoon," *The Goddamn George Liquor Program*, focused on the antics of its namesake—along with the characters Sody Pop and Jimmy the Idiot Boy—through a Thomas Pynchon-like lens of unapologetic exaggeration. Eyes bulging, veins pulsating, George is a study in coiled bitterness perpetually waiting to explode in righteous indignation. Paranoia is balanced with misanthropic behavior. Jimmy is George's terminal project, a ne'er-do-well nephew with a tortured innocence and dazed personality. Episodes are enlivened by Sody Pop, a female alter-ego to Kricfalusi, with big eyes, a form-fitting wardrobe, and pliant, Lolita-like body language.

Spumco actually got its start working on webtoons after the Microsoft Network commissioned a series titled *Weekend Pussy Hunt*. It's hard to imagine Bill Gates authorizing this, and, not surprisingly, only a few episodes were ever made. Since that time, Kricfalusi has launched a series of Web-based animations, and Spumco has branched out to create commercials for clients including Nike and Old Navy and a music video for the Icelandic pop singer Bjork.

Kricfalusi designs his Web animations by feel, using intuition to find the right balance between bandwidth-intensive explanatory detail and quick-loading white space.

JOHN KRICFALUSI B.1955

Spumco, Inc.
Glendale, California

TURTLE FOOD COLLECTOR
Comic book, 1995
Designer: John Kricfalusi,
Spumco

Employing a variety of sophisticated drawing programs, Kricfalusi creates smooth, fluid lines that compare favorably to televised cartoons.

Committed to re-energizing the possibilities for wonder and comedy he believes are intrinsic to cartooning, Kricfalusi turned to the Internet, which offers the chance to do edgy, even raunchy work that pushes technical and cultural boundaries. It also offers the freedom to birth a vision and shape its evolution as a live audience responds immediately to what it enjoys. S.S.H.

THE GODDAMN GEORGE LIQUOR PROGRAM, EPISODE 7 "BABYSITTING THE IDIOT"
[left to right: Sody Pop, George, and Jimmy the Idiot Boy]
Animated series, 1998
Designer: John Kricfalusi, Spumco

BIG BAD WOLF
Commercial, 1996
Designer: John Kricfalusi, Spumco
Client: Nike

GARY LLOYD B. 1943

Reallybigskies, Really Fake Digital,
and Sky Drops
Los Angeles, California

In the seventeenth century, baroque artists painted putti-filled skies on church ceilings under which Catholic penitents enacted sacred rituals of redemption and salvation. Gary Lloyd and his team of scenic artists have updated this tradition for secular purposes. Lloyd's studio designs and paints trompe l'oeil "sky drops" for film, television, and still photography. They also create sky ceilings for theme environments including casinos, restaurants, and shopping malls, enhancing these fantasy versions of reality with architectural NARRATIVES of the great outdoors.

Lloyd and his scenic artists are able to capture subtleties of light, shadow, and mood. Measuring as long as 450 feet in length, the equivalent of more than two city blocks, the sky drops simulate a wide range of effects, from ominous storms to red-orange sunsets and clear blue skies. Lloyd claims diverse

sources for his designs, including the Sistine Chapel's frescoes, anamorphic painting techniques, and light sculptures by artists James Turrell, Robert Irwin, and Maria Nordman. Aiming to visually eliminate the ceiling in his architectural commissions, Lloyd developed special paints with light-sensitive pigments to enhance the illusion of an open sky. Large-scale models are used to help the designers analyze the ceiling's perspective from the spectator's point of view.

Casinos in Las Vegas and Reno, Nevada, are among Lloyd's most loyal clients. The painted sky at the Silver Legacy Resort Casino (1995) in Reno—a hemisphere with a diameter of 200 feet—is accompanied by a day-to-night lighting change that occurs during a two-hour period. Projected stars and a sound-track featuring the sounds of rain, thunder, and insects complete the illusion. The simulation

of nature—the painted sky—leads visitors to almost believe they are outdoors; they often report that the air actually seems fresher within Lloyd's spaces.

His sky ceilings are integral parts of new Las Vegas mega-hotels and casinos such as the Venetian (1998), where he worked with Karen Kristin, and the Aladdin, which opens in the spring of 2000. The hyper-real confluence of art, architecture, and entertainment in Lloyd's work is perfectly attuned to an economically booming America as well as to contemporary Las Vegas, a steroid vision of the city celebrated (with irony) by architects Robert Venturi, Denise Scott Brown, and Steven Izenour in their 1972 polemical classic *Learning from Las Vegas*. Lloyd's skies, along with scenographic architecture and HVAC (heating, ventilation, and air-conditioning) technology, create stage sets for fantasy. Liberated from the norms of time and space, they remove visitors from the daily concerns of real life. People stay longer and spend more money, enacting a modern-day version of the gambling ritual with the promise of financial redemption.

D.A.

THE NEW FRONTIER
Fashion photograph, *New York Times*, 1999
Backdrop designer: Gary Lloyd/Sky Drops
Photographer: Cleo Sullivan
Stylist: Elizabeth Stewart
Fashion designer: Ralph Lauren

More dreamlike than real, David Rockwell's fantasy environments use cinema and theater as their starting points to weave spatial NARRATIVES about subjects as diverse as Native-American traditions and Hollywood legends. Rockwell's New York-based firm creates these hyper-charged, artificial environments for companies such as Sony, Disney, and Planet Hollywood. Like the fusion cuisine served in Rockwell-designed restaurants, his interiors offer their visitors artfully crafted melanges of nostalgic references, popular icons, and cultural allusions.

An enthusiastic lover of theater and set design, Rockwell starts each project by reading its program like a script and designing scenarios rather than spaces. Like movies and plays, Rockwell's interiors lead people on time-based adventures. For example, the Star Theatres (1997) outside Detroit, a suburban prototype

for future retro-urban movie theaters, features a vintage streetscape to evoke the era when the city's automotive industry had sway over American culture. For Vong (1992), an upscale restaurant in midtown Manhattan, he created a chic, Indo-French colonial environment.

The 500,000-square-foot Mohegan Sun Casino in Uncasville, Connecticut (with phased openings in 1996 and 2001), is the most fully realized example of the Rockwell Group's backlot aesthetic of cultural reclamation. The design is the product of extensive research and consultation with tribe members. Hidden behind a starkly utilitarian facade—not unlike those of movie soundstages—faux rocks, real waterfalls, weather machines, and features like glass ceilings decorated with corn husks recreate the rituals and natural world of the Mohegan tribe. The project's second phase is organized along a

DAVID ROCKWELL B. 1956

Rockwell Group
New York City

MOHEGAN SUN CASINO (PHASE I)
Uncasville, Connecticut
Photograph, 1996
Concept and interior architect:
Rockwell Group

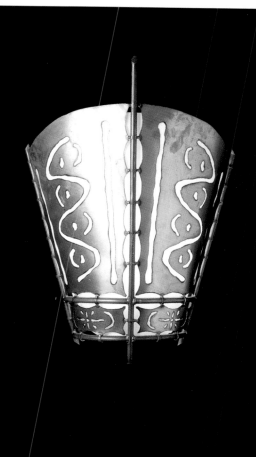

MOHEGAN SUN CASINO (PHASE I): LIGHT FIXTURE
Uncasville, Connecticut
Prototype, 1997, rusted steel and parchment
Concept and interior architect:
Rockwell Group
Prototype fabricator:
J. Frederick Studio

serpentine "Life Trail" representing the tribe's eastward migration across the Great Lakes to their ancestral home on the land now occupied by the resort. Visitors enter stores, restaurants, and casinos along the path, which is punctuated by crystalline mountains, colored-glass canyons, and "memory piles." These are recreated versions of places where Mohegans left stones and other artifacts to memorialize a significant event, honor a death, or ensure luck in the hunt.

Mohegan's narrative promenades resurface in Rockwell's future Hollywood theater for the Academy of Motion Picture Arts and Sciences. Long passages and sweeping stairways will offer tourists on a daily basis the once-a-year Oscar-night experience of running a press gauntlet. Whether Rockwell's fantasy interiors trade on memories of popular culture or historical legend, going to them puts

visitors into the last scene of Billy Wilder's classic 1950 film *Sunset Boulevard*: in Rockwell's interiors we are always ready for our close-ups.
D.A.

[above]
MOHEGAN SUN CASINO (PHASE II): LIFE TRAIL PROMENADE
Uncasville, Connecticut
Sketch, 1999, watercolor on paper
Delineator: Curtis Woodhouse
Concept and interior architect: Rockwell Group

[left]
MOHEGAN SUN CASINO (PHASE II): LIFE TRAIL PROMENADE
Uncasville, Connecticut
Model, 1999, scale:1/4":1',
basswood and museum board
Concept and interior architect and model fabricator: Rockwell Group

B. 1952

New York City

"I demand the audience goes with me," Julie Taymor says of the *terra incognita* she explores in her plays, films, and operas. Best known as the director and costume designer of Disney's popular Broadway musical *The Lion King* (1997), Taymor has just directed her first feature film, *Titus*. But the eponymous hero of an earlier avant-garde stage project, *Juan Darién* (1988–96), functions as the best metaphor for Taymor's unique and mercurial career, which has crossed the spectrum of contemporary culture. Subtitled "A Carnival Mass" and based on a South American NARRATIVE of compassion and revenge, *Juan Darién* tells the story of a mythological creature with remarkable transformative powers— a mirror for Taymor's own diverse talents. Not only did she design the drama's puppets and masks, but she served as its director, co-author (with composer Elliot Goldenthal), and co-

set and costume designer (with G. W. Mercier).

Throughouth her career, Taymor has been drawn to mythic, larger-than-life stories that challenge the public emotionally as well as intellectually. She never panders to her audiences—an easy trap she avoided in *The Lion King* by completely reimagining the animated film and, in the process, reinventing the moribund Broadway musical form. Whether adapting Walt Disney or William Shakespeare, Taymor delves deeply into a work's soul, visually depicting it in compelling, sometimes shocking, metaphors and media. To express the humanity of the film's beasts on the stage, Taymor and co-puppet and mask designer Michael Curry created an astonishing array of animal headdresses worn above the actors' faces, creating hybrid stage creatures part Disney, part African, and part their own.

THE LION KING: MUFASA
Headdress prototype, 1997, carbon fiber, acrylic paint, balsa wood, ethafoam,
and peacock feathers
Sculptor: Julie Taymor
Mask and puppet co-creators:
Julie Taymor and Michael Curry

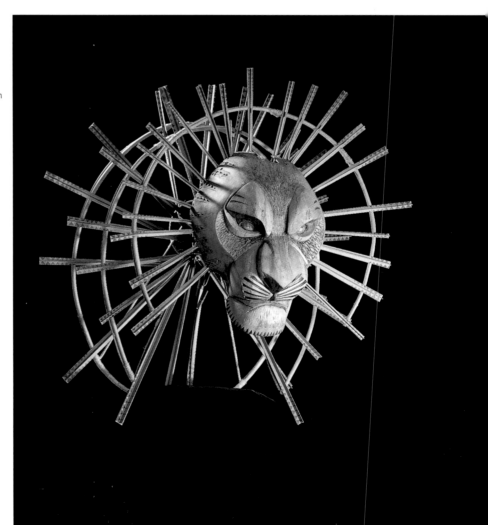

As director-designer, Taymor invents visuals that match her work's unique language. Shakespeare's dialog in *Titus Andronicus* is both poetic and direct, shifting, she notes, between "graphic, base emotions and ephemeral, mythic revelations."[1] As a result, the film version, designed by Dante Ferretti, juxtaposes naturalistic and stylized imagery. *Titus* combines scenes that were filmed in actual locations—a Roman amphitheater in Pula, Croatia, for example—with five dream sequences she calls Penny Arcade Nightmares. These function as "haikus," Taymor says, that mimic the film's violence in grotestque ways, like distorting mirrors in a circus funhouse.

Titus and *The Lion King* also reveal Taymor's unique capacity to move fluidly between stage and screen, bringing cinematic devices to the theater and unexpectedly poetic stylizations to the medium of film.

A broader message for our time may be drawn from Taymor's fusion of media and transgression of boundaries. Fostering a borderless, egalitarian world, her democratic art unites avant-garde and popular audiences, film and theater, Western and non-Western styles into a rich global community.   D.A.

1. Eileen Blumenthal and Julie Taymor, *Julie Taymor: Playing with Fire* (New York: Harry N. Abrams, 1999), 219.

THE LION KING
[general credits]
Director: Julie Taymor
Costume designer: Julie Taymor
Scenic designer: Richard Hudson
Lighting designer: Donald Holder
Sound designer: Tony Meola
Hair and makeup designer: Michael Ward
Producer: Walt Disney Theatrical

THE LION KING: TRICKSTER
Sketch, 1997, watercolor on paper
Mask and costume designer and sketch
delineator: Julie Taymor

THE LION KING: SCAR
Headdress prototype, 1997, carbon fiber,
acrylic paint, balsa wood, ethafoam, chicken
feathers, and turkey feathers
Sculptor: Julie Taymor
Mask and puppet co-creators:
Julie Taymor and Michael Curry

187

The desire to be a comic artist fuels many youthful urges to draw, paint, and write. It is a calling that few can turn into a viable pursuit. Chris Ware has done just that. Over the past decade, he has emerged as a startling new voice in the competitive world of comics. His serial publication the *Acme Novelty Library* features an odd assembly of comic strips that Ware conceives, writes, illustrates, letters, and designs himself. Running counter to the fantasy escapes that dominate the genre, his unnerving NARRATIVES feature seemingly normal people and strangely ordinary landscapes.

Ware's gentle sense of color, agile draftsmanship, and rhythmic layouts recall various comic precedents—from Winsor McCay's *Little Nemo in Slumberland* to George Herriman's *Krazy Kat*. Yet while reclaiming aspects of a venerated comic tradition, Ware skews his seemingly familiar settings with an

aura of emotional dysfunction.

One of his stories unfolds in a small town in mid-century America, rendered cold and lonely rather than nostalgically reassuring. The story focuses on Jimmy Corrigan, "The Smartest Kid on Earth," who appears in various stages of life—from childhood to old age. In one sequence, a deer-crossing sign triggers a string of thoughts in the mind of Jimmy, who, seeing a mail truck, converts "deer" to "dear" and begins to compose in his mind a pathetic letter to a lost father. "Dear Dad..." he writes. "You might not remember me...." Embedded among the panels depicting an icy suburban landscape is an interior view invoking a psychological state: a tiny Jimmy is engulfed by a giant armchair, where he struggles to write to his father with larger-than-life writing instruments.

Many comic artists treat lettering as a secondary element. Ware, however, is fiercely attached to his

CHRIS WARE B. 1967

Chicago, Illinois

ACME NOVELTY LIBRARY
Comic book, 1996–1999, offset lithograph
Designer, illustrator, and author: Chris Ware
Publisher: Fantagraphics Books

literary content and the visual form it takes. The *Acme Novelty Library* mixes various styles of lettering and typography, from traditional comic-book handwriting to geometric characters, three-dimensional title blocks, and decorative Victorian scripts. One issue has a wholly typographic cover, a heretical statement in such a picture-oriented medium. Included as well are fake advertising pages and news items whose obsessive density recalls the typographic texture of old commercial catalogs and nineteenth-century magazines and contribute to Acme's self-consciously fabricated brand identity. Ware produces most of his lettering—and all of his images—by hand, later scanning them for digital reproduction.

Ware has revived old traditions and rescued abandoned styles, transforming them into his own unsettling vision of the world. This young artist seeks to dignify a popular narrative form for the next century. E.L.

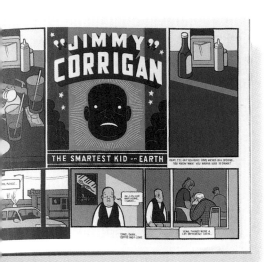

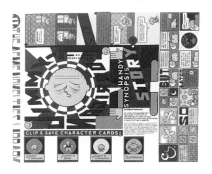

Since 1976 Lebbeus Woods has expressed his visionary ideas about architecture through complex, fantastic drawings. Depicting future worlds of vast machine-like cities in the process of growth and decay, Woods has attracted the attention of an avid circle of avant-garde architects and critics, as well as Hollywood studios (he served as conceptual architect for the 1992 science-fiction thriller *Alien3*). Woods has recently begun to translate his visionary architectural concepts into built projects. In 1998 he designed an outdoor performance space—the Hermitage—in Eindhoven, the Netherlands, and in the spring of 2000 his design for a large millennial exhibition will open in Berlin. In both projects, dense, serpentine forms and labyrinthine spaces demonstrate the architect's conception of contemporary civilization caught in a continual process of accumulation. In Woods's spatial NARRATIVES, things, ideas, and relationships come together in our culture in ways that are random and arbitrary. And the future, according to Woods, will only intensify the effect.

Woods's theory of random accumulation carries through his processes of design and fabrication. Woods develops his ideas in ever-expanding notebooks that freely intersperse small, intense ink drawings of visionary projects with studies of real buildings as well as speculative commentary. He establishes a flexible, stylistic framework for a design that invites his collaborators—modelmakers, engineers, and fabricators—to apply their own interpretations and ideas, allowing the design to evolve in unexpected ways. Computer-aided fabrication techniques liberate Woods's imagination and permit him to create any form he chooses.

LEBBEUS WOODS B. 1940

New York City

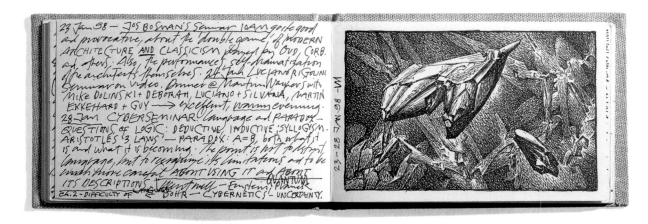

[above]
NOTEBOOK
1998, ink on paper
Delineator: Lebbeus Woods

[right]
SEVEN HILLS: IMAGES AND SIGNS OF THE TWENTY-FIRST CENTURY EXHIBITION: CIVILIZATION SECTION
Martin Gropius Bau, Berlin, May–October 2000
Model, 1998, scale 1:50, painted polystyrene
Architect: Lebbeus Woods
Team: Dwayne Oyler (Design and model),
Christian Axt (Production and construction),
Andreas Glücker (Production and construction assistant)
Chief curator: Bodo-Michael Baumunk
Curator: Dr. Thomas Medicus

In Eindhoven, the design's steel rods and plates seem to grow like organic vines against the rigidly formal facade of a renovated factory.

Woods's exhibition in Berlin encloses visitors in a maze of sinuous steel trees and branches. Entitled *Civilization*, it is one of seven components comprising a vast exhibition *Seven Hills: Images and Signs of the Twenty-First Century*. Unlike typical world's fairs, which tend to present the future as cheery and optimistic, Woods's view of tomorrow is reflective and critical. Topics include transient hotels for newly mobile populations, construction of the self through cyborg-like implants and prostheses, and the all-encompassing role of digitized images.

Randomness is built into the exhibition in many ways. The curator will select models and objects, without Woods's input. The space takes the form of a jungle-like landscape of objects, randomly displayed on walls, on the ceiling, and under a glazed, ramped floor. A late twentieth-century version of a baroque cabinet of curiosities, the design shows the future as increasingly arbitrary and unmoored from stable truths. D.A.

[above]
HERMITAGE PERFORMANCE SPACE
Eindhoven, The Netherlands
Photograph, 1998
Architect: Lebbeus Woods
Team: Dwayne Oyler (Design and model),
Jos Bosman (Coordination)
Fabricator: Werner Schippers
Engineer: Leon Mevis
Sponsor: MU Art Foundation, Ton van Gool (Director)

unbelievable

Some of the most spectacular design projects of our time exist in the realm of the imaginary. The objects and environments found in movies, television, and interactive media often strain credulity—they are unbelievable. These are the deliberately unreal, postcredible objects of our moment. Product designers strive to imagine a world transformed by digital technologies that will change our experience of reality yet remain linked to the human and natural worlds. Designers working with digital special effects create fantastic creatures and imaginary environments that are familiar, yet not quite like anything we have seen before.

RICHARD WATSON B. 1963
JASON SHORT B. 1971
AND TEAM

FITCH
San Francisco, California

Known for interdisciplinary research performed in the service of product definition, Fitch is now bringing together teams of industrial and interface designers to conceive of digital devices in which the physical aspects of the object function in a dynamic way with its electronic software. An example of such an interdisciplinary effort is the Mobile Computing and Communication Appliance (MoCCA), a product developed for and with the Digital Equipment Corporation in 1997.

The MoCCA was intended to demonstrate how different types of computers might be integrated in the near future. The Fitch team, led by Richard Watson and Jason Short, envisioned a device for which the voice would be the primary medium of interaction—no buttons, keyboards, or pens. The end result is UNBELIEVABLE: a translucent device barely 4 inches square, a computer that can be worn, hand-held, or used on a desktop. A soft rubber grip that conforms to the shape of a semiclosed hand contains a speaker, a small earphone, and an antennae for wireless communication. Its square displays rotate on any 90 degree axis, allowing the interface to swivel and change direction as the user desires. A centrally-located camera lens is the dominant element in the design and relays gestures to a processor programmed to recognize physical movements. The MoCCA also responds to physical movement: tilting the unit, for example, causes it to scroll information; shake the object, and the screen will erase. The MoCCA offers a synthesis of technologies that simplify the user's experience.

MoCCA represents the possibility of merging visual, vocal, and tactile interaction to release the latent potential of the computer. In

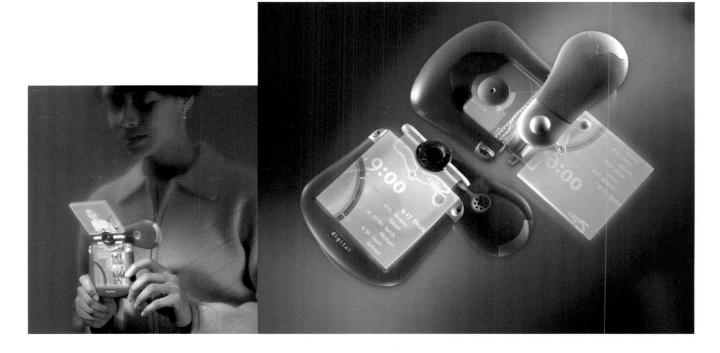

developing an object that would have been inconceivable only a few years ago, the Fitch team has advanced an idea of the computer as a functionally rich and visually mutable piece of technojewelry. s.s.h.

MoCCA (MOBILE COMPUTING AND COMMUNICATION APPLIANCE)
Prototype, 1997, cast urethane, molded rubber, and acrylic
Designer: Richard Watson and Jason Short, Fitch, and Bob Hanson, Digital Equipment Corporation
Client: Digital Equipment Corporation

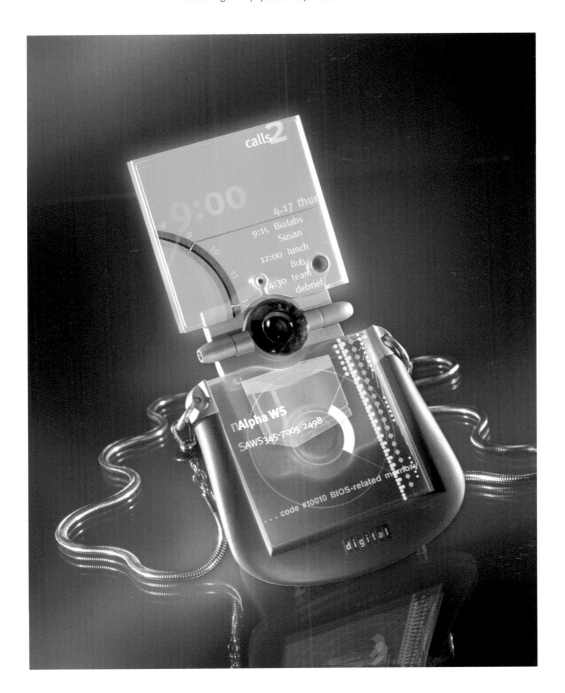

Every year, Herbst Lazar Bell's Mark Dziersk challenges his design team to take on a conceptual project that, if realized, will help people feel more comfortable with technology. Zuzu's Petals (1998) is a souped-up personal digital assistant inspired by a regenerating flower in the film classic *It's a Wonderful Life* (1946). Zuzu aims to break the black-box paradigm typical of today's electronic gadgetry by creating an almost UNBELIEVABLE expressive and sculptural cyber-creature.

Zuzu's central "stalk" is a docking station for a collection of small digital components—petals. Each petal acts as an interface between the user and the world at large: one petal is a digital camera; another is a digital voice recorder; yet another fans out to facilitate satellite access and solar charging. Each petal can be removed for remote use—to be worn on a lanyard—and then replaced. Seeded with memory modules—"digital dirt"—at its base, Zuzu is a powerful information tool with a playful, tongue-in-cheek attitude.

Gooru was designed the following year in an effort to enhance children's learning experiences while relieving pressure on overburdened school systems and working parents. Intended for children between seven and eleven years of age, Gooru consists of two main components: an interactive communications device—the "Gooball"—and a backpack equipped with a flexible screen (the backpack also supplies memory and power for the system, along with storage for odds-and-ends). Each Gooru has its own electronic "personality," and provides the child with educational advice, personal guidance, and entertainment. Soft geometric forms counterbalance the unit's technical complexity, fostering a friendly, unintimidating presence.

HERBST LAZAR BELL
Chicago, Illinois

Though meant for children, it has the potential for broader applications, offering a new paradigm for the so-called "laptop," which is rarely used in a lap. By successfully recasting the interface between people and machines, it offers a welcome vision of technology merged with humanity. s.s.h.

[left and below]
GOORU
Conceptual prototype for customizable educational system, designed in 1999 for the year 2015, digital goo, flexible polymer LCD screen, recycled natural fibers, recyclable polymers, and neoprene rubbers
Designer: HLB Gooru Team: Stefan Andrén, Jason Billig, and Jason Martin (Product design, concept and model-making); Pete Kopec and Mark Witt (Concept and model-making); Steve Remy (Concept, model-making, and engineering); Elliot Hsu (Graphic design)
Manufacturer: Herbst Lazar Bell

[above]
ZUZU'S PETALS
Conceptual prototype for personal digital assistant, 1998, injection-molded plastic (ABS), thermoplastic, elastomer (Santoprene), metal accents, and translucent polypropylene; PDA screen: woven hologram
Designer: HLB Vision Team
Product design and model-making: Josh Goldfarb, Simon Yan, and Jon Lindholm
Manufacturer: Herbst Lazar Bell

Some of the most conceptually resonant student work of the 1990s was conducted by Gary Shigeru Natsume, a student at the Cranbrook Academy of Art. Under the aegis of Peter Stathis, chair of Cranbrook's three-dimensional design department, Natsume seamlessly blended hardware with software to make the UNBELIEVABLE seem possible. Natsume's Bound Packet Computing (1997) and Data Pond/Hyper Personal Assistant (1997) use transparency and dematerialization to express the profound effect that digital culture is having on the things around us. In Natsume's hands the boundaries, hard edges, and boxy shapes of technology dissolve before our eyes.

Bound Packet Computing is a proposal for a "recombinant customizable laptop" computer that would allow the user to visually and functionally tailor a machine to his or her taste. The system is comprised of five components (displays, keypads, memory, media drive, and battery system) to be sold as self-contained "packets." Users choose from a variety of different packet types, and then stack these modules onto a spine-like hub. The system is then inserted inside a simple casing of the user's choice: clear or opaque, leather or plastic, nylon or fabric—again allowing for individual preference. By keeping the casing simple and the packets easily interchangeable, Natsume envisioned a machine that would not become obsolete with every new advance in technology.

Another conceptual project, the Data Pond (1997), created a literal metaphor for the flood of information we face every day: a reservoir in which individual pieces of information are represented by digital fish. A roughly 4 by 2-foot, furniture-sized information storage unit for the

GARY SHIGERU NATSUME B.1969

Cranbrook Academy of Art
Bloomfield Hills, Michigan

frog
New York City

BOUND PACKET COMPUTING
Prototype, 1997, hard foam, acrylic glass, ABS, steel, aluminum, automotive paints, vinyl, and plastics
Designer: Gary Shigeru Natsume, Cranbrook Academy of Art
Academic Advisor: Peter Stathis

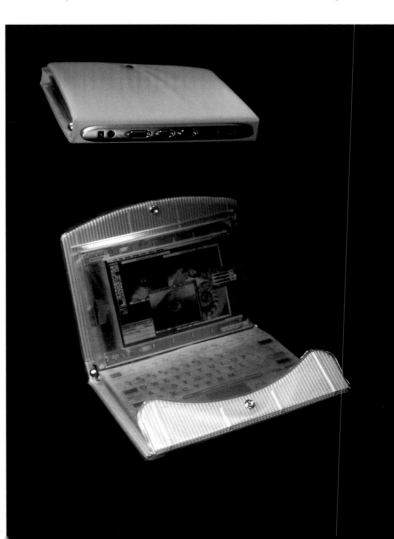

home, it is housed in a gelatinous case that responds to pressure from the hand. Users physically interact with the screen through touch, just as a fortune teller massages a crystal ball. To access the Data Pond, a user must be equipped with a Data Cell, which can capture but not transmit information. Transmission requires the addition of various "Hyper Components," each having a single specific function: digital camera, infra-red transmission, satellite uplink. The Data Cell, along with a selection of Hyper Components, are held in the hand while a "matrix skin" is wrapped around the entire group and sealed through heat and radiation. The resulting object—a Hyper Personal Assistant—is different every time it is assembled. The skin serves as protection, as the electric connection for all of the components within, and as an LCD-like screen for display.

Natsume explores design and technology on a genetic level, imagining malleable machines that respond to a rapidly changing information-based society. Rejecting the sterility of so much of today's computer technology, Natsume relies on tactility and metaphor to instill a personalized relationship between man and machine—a truly brave new world. s.s.h.

DATA POND AND HYPER PERSONAL ASSISTANT
Prototype, 1997, acrylic glass, steel, aluminum, resin, brass, vinyl, plastics, and automotive paints and finishes
Designer: Gary Shigeru Natsume, Cranbrook Academy of Art
Academic advisor: Peter Stathis

A mix of spiritual amazement and intellectual rigor animate David Small's typographic research. Small, who is both a graphic designer and computer scientist, uses three-dimensional and dynamic typography to display complex bodies of information. His visionary explorations of digital text have yielded UNBELIEVABLE results—stunning in appearance and rich in conception. His projects, many of them produced at MIT's Media Lab, attempt to display complex bodies of information within digital landscapes that users can intuitively navigate.

Awe and intellect converge with special intensity in the Talmud Project (1998–99). The Talmud is a collection of sacred writings on the Torah, in which Biblical passages are embraced by a series of commentaries. Small's Talmud Project displays a portion of the Talmud and builds additional links to an essay by the modern French philosopher Emmanuel

Levinas, a text that is itself an extended commentary on a section of the Talmud. Small's project envisions a new narrative space in which distinct but linked texts can be simultaneously available in their entirety.

The Talmud Project employs shifting scale, focus, line spacing, and transparency to allow texts to move in and out of the reader's primary field of attention. To alternate between Levinas's French essay and its English translation, for example, the reader controls the spacing between the French and English lines, expanding and contracting them in order to shift from one language to another or to display them simultaneously. A page from the Torah might be in full focus, while the referring page from the Talmud appears to hang behind it, blurred just enough to maintain the legibility of the main text. As one passage comes forward, another

DAVID SMALL B. 1965

Small Design Firm
Cambridge, Massachusetts

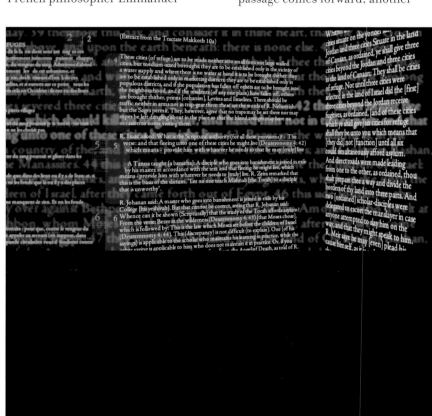

moves back; as one becomes sharp, another becomes hazy.

Even when individual lines become illegible, the architectural features of the text remain apparent, such as paragraph and section breaks. Small aims to design for both the reading scale, where five hundred or a thousand words can be displayed at one time, and for what he calls the "contextual scale," where a million or more words can be visible but not legible. By allowing text to appear as a body—whole yet indecipherable— Small builds sublime typographic spaces, in which written language imposes its vastness upon the senses as well as upon the intellect.

To be sublime is to be unbelievable: to invoke awe and amazement within a context of rational structure. Such is the effect of Talmudic study, expanded into other dimensions in this profound typographic project. E.L.

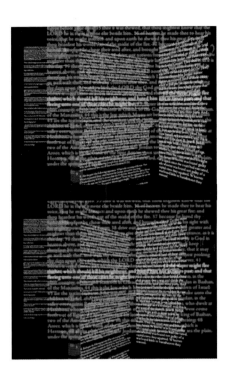

TALMUD PROJECT
Prototype for interactive book, 1998–99, software and electro-mechanical interface
Designer: David Small, Small Design Firm
Produced at the MIT Media Lab's Aesthetics and Computation group, under the direction of John Maeda. Project is part of David Small's MIT Doctoral Thesis, "Rethinking the Book," January 1999; advisor, William J. Mitchell

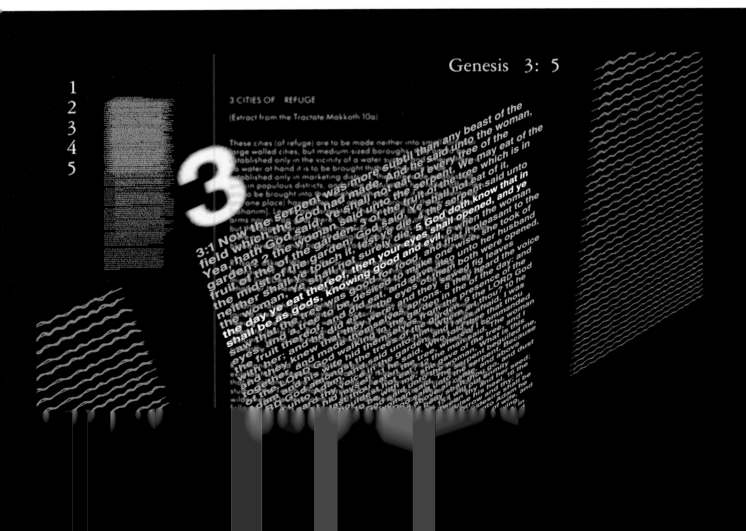

PAUL PIERCE B. 1964
DENNIS ERBER B. 1950
AND TEAM

THOMSON CONSUMER ELECTRONICS
Indianapolis, Indiana

Experts in conceptual provocation, the in-house design team at Thomson Consumer Electronics has developed some of the more imaginative concept products that attempt to bridge the gulf between high technology and the people who use it every day.

Inspired by Pablo Picasso's depictions of a bull drawn with just a few strokes of the pen, designer Ronald Lytel created the Picasso Internet Radio (1998) with a minimum of form and an economy of means. The unit's two large "horns" accommodate compression-driver technology, which, as in early horn-shaped speakers, requires little power to produce high sound levels. The main body houses a subwoofer to reinforce lower frequencies. Aesthetically, the radio harkens back to the days of the phonograph, but in a stylized manner with a touch of anthropomorphic cool.

The idea for Thomson's E-Buzzz (1998) personal digital assisstant came when designer David Schultz realized that the current crop of PDA's suited the needs of thirty-something office workers rather than students in their teens and early twenties. Schultz proposed a device with a wireless Internet connection, enabling the student to receive the teacher's assignment after leaving the classroom via a wireless transmitter. The bug-like E-Buzzz integrated a removable stylus, an interactive touchscreen, and a simple one-button interface with a rugged, playful aesthetic.

The most fantastic of Thomson's recent conceptual devices are undoubtedly Demetrius Romanos's Io and Esmerelda portable information systems (1998). Worn on a belt (the more masculine Io) or as a purse (the more feminine Esmerelda), the two "digital snowglobes" have liquid

ESMERELDA PORTABLE INFORMATION SYSTEM
Conceptual prototype, 1998, acrylic and resin
Designer: Demetrius Romanos, Thomson Consumer Electroncs
Manufacturer: RCA

crystal displays (LCD) and can be personalized through the selection of a variety of casings—"skins." Users can access information—both graphic and audio—by using a control key to scroll through icons and then shaking the unit to choose the desired function. When not on the move, the units can be linked to a desktop computer to download music and data. Io and Esmerelda would hang on a "data hook" that would connect the PDAs to a computer like any other peripheral.

Thomson's experimental products provide much-needed diversity to the consumer electronics industry. Although the Picasso, E-Buzz, and Io and Esmerelda are still in the realm of UNBELIEVABLE experiments, each proposes to personalize the digital encounter through style, convenience, and whimsy while adding unique visual character to otherwise neutral devices. S.S.H.

IRIS ORGANIC HOME WORKSTATION
Conceptual prototype, 1998, ren-shape, acrylic, wood, and perforated metal
Designer: Joshua Maruska, Thomson Consumer Electronics
Manufacturer: RCA

EBUZZ STUDENT'S ASSISTANT
Prototype, 1998, acrylic and resin
Designer: David Schultz, Thomson Consumer Electronics
Manufacturer: RCA

PICASSO INTERNET RADIO
Conceptual prototype, 1998, SLA resin and aluminum
Designer: Ronald Lytel, Thomson Consumer Electronics
Manufacturer: RCA

PHIL TIPPETT B. 1951
CRAIG HAYES B. 1963
AND TEAM

TIPPETT STUDIO
Berkeley, California

After working as an animator and creature designer on the first three *Star Wars* films, in 1983 Phil Tippett left George Lucas's famed Industrial Light + Magic to found his own visual effects studio, Tippett Studio. Two years later, while working on the sci-fi classic *RoboCop* (1987), Tippett met Craig Hayes, who was designing the live-action prop that Tippett was animating. This meeting marked the beginning of a collaboration between Tippett and Hayes (now Tippett Studio's creative director) that has been responsible for innovative effects in such films as *Willow* (1988), *Honey, I Shrunk the Kids* (1989), *Armageddon* (1998), and the breakthrough *Jurassic Park* (1993). For this last film, Tippett truly animated director Steven Spielberg's voracious dinosaurs, creating an effect of realism that thrilled audiences worldwide (Tippett won an Academy Award for the effort).

For the interstellar war picture *Starship Troopers* (1997), which chronicled an undermanned group of soldiers as they battled an armada of insect warriors, Tippett Studio designed live action and computer generated battle sequences, some featuring thousands of digital bugs. The team storyboarded scenes, and Hayes designed six different bug types—each a different rank in the bug army. Bug models were created and then digitized along with hundreds of photorealistic paintings—complete with dust, reflections, and elaborate surfaces. To create injured bugs, the team designed a series of digital "wound decals" to be applied as needed.

Virus (1999) is the story of a marauding extraterrestrial life form that seeks to eradicate humanity. For the film, Tippett Studio constructed a digital replica of the full-scale puppet invader, "Goliath." Modeling a

STARSHIP TROOPERS
Digital special effects, 1996-97
VFX supervisor: Phil Tippett
Client: Sony Pictures Entertainment

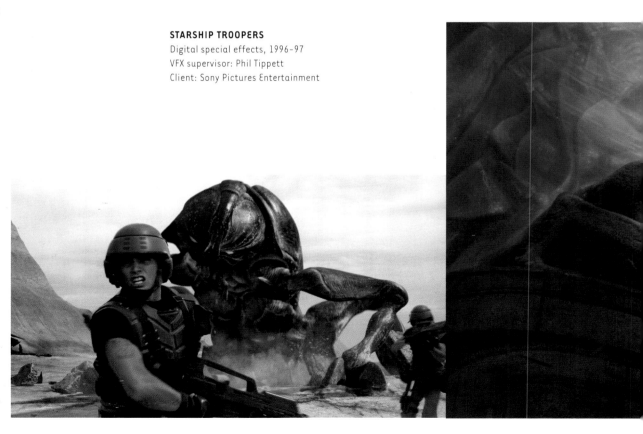

creature with more than eleven-hundred moving parts was no easy task, but the team's diligence resulted in a convincing—and exceptionally malevolent—space monster.

Tippett Studio broke new ground in the computer generation of photorealistic hair and fabric—materials that pose the greatest challenges for digital animators—for Jan de Bont's 1999 horror thriller *The Haunting*. In one scene, the heroine combs her hair in front of a mirror and watches in shock as it takes on a supernatural life of its own. In another, a ghost child enters a bedroom through an open window, billowing a digitally-created silk curtain and then gliding under a computer-generated satin sheet toward the dozing damsel. The team produced dynamic ripples that make it appear as if the child were moving through the satiny sheet, leaving folds and gathers in its wake.

While many of Tippett Studio's effects rely on state-of-the-art computer techniques, the team has by no means abandoned traditional hand animation and old-fashioned puppeteering. Their common-sense approach is to take the best aspects of each method and combine them in the service of visually and emotionally convincing storytelling—to make the UNBELIEVABLE seem frighteningly real. S.S.H.

THE HAUNTING
Digital special effects, 1998-99
Co VFX supervisors: Phil Tippett and Craig Hayes
Client: Dreamworks

UNBELIEVABLE

Known as a strategically-minded industrial design firm, Ziba has steadily moved its focus from how products should look to what products should be. Driving this change is a growing emphasis on the integration of research into the creative process and an effort to combine anthropologically-derived insights with technologically driven, minimal designs.

In their recent work with Intel, Ziba was asked to think outside the box—the beige box. Recognizing that today's personal computer is still a cumbersome, frustrating, and visually unappealing object, the Ziba team created a series of concept computers that are just the opposite: easy to use and hard to forget. The result was the idiosyncratic Simple PCs.

While the Simple PCs were never intended for production, the chipmaking giant hoped that these UNBELIEVABLE proposals would set the design standard for a new generation

of machines. If, as Ziba founder Sohrab Vossoughi has noted, "the traditional PC was designed to look like a scaled-down version of a supercomputer," the Simple PCs were intended to be approachable, sculptural, and colorful.

While design studies of this ilk are often nonfunctional models, Ziba was asked to create fully-operational prototypes in order to illustrate just what can be achieved when designers and engineers commit to changing paradigms. Although the Ziba team was not able to create an instant-on machine like the common TV or telephone, they did make substantial progress. The 1999 Aztec model— silver, metallic orange, shaped like a truncated pyramid with an aluminum crown—has a single power button, two LED indicators ("power" and "email"), and three peripheral connectors. An ancient symbol of strength and a contemporary symbol of stability,

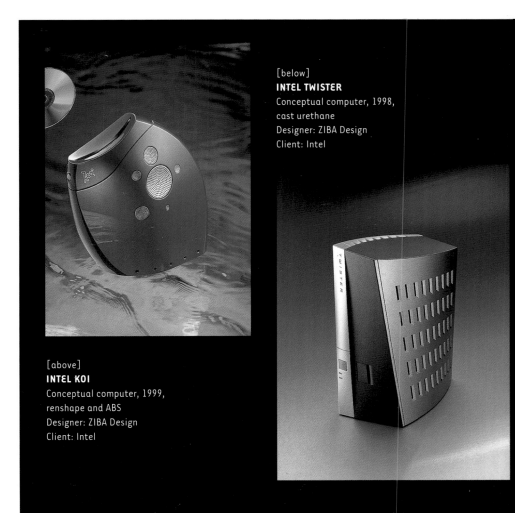

[above]
INTEL KOI
Conceptual computer, 1999,
renshape and ABS
Designer: ZIBA Design
Client: Intel

[below]
INTEL TWISTER
Conceptual computer, 1998,
cast urethane
Designer: ZIBA Design
Client: Intel

the pyramid is a simple and
memorable shape. The most light-
hearted of Ziba's design solutions is
the Koi (1999). Its simple, fish-
derived form directs the user to its
disk-drive mouth, in the process
humanizing technology by calling
attention to the active intelligence
behind its making.

By eliminating cumbersome user
manuals and elaborate set-up rituals,
the Simple PCs aim to create an
environment that minimizes hassle.
Ziba's work foretells a future where
a playful approach to storing,
processing, and sharing information
will be the norm. s.s.h.

INTEL AZTEC
Conceptual computer, 1999, cast
urethane and aluminum
Designer: ZIBA Design
Client: Intel

BIOGRAPHIES

ACCO | Tim Parsey, Peter Pfanner, Tim McKeown, Scott Wilson, and team
ACCO Brands, headquartered in Wheeling, Illinois, was founded in 1903 by Fred J. Kline as the Clipper Manufacturing Company. The firm was eventually renamed the American Clip Company and, following a string of mergers, took on the name ACCO. Today, the firm is a leader in the manufacturing and design of office and computer products.

Erik Adigard and Patricia McShane | M.A.D.
Graphic designers Erik Adigard and Patricia McShane founded McShane Adigard Design (M.A.D.) in 1989. The firm has since designed Web sites, multimedia installations, and print publications. Adigard and McShane were the recipients of the Chrysler design award in 1998. Their work has been published in magazines such as *Novum, Graphis,* and *Communication Arts*.

Marwan Al-Sayed | Marwan Al-Sayed Architects
Marwan Al-Sayed established his firm in 1997 in Phoenix, Arizona. With Janet Fink he was a principal in the firm Al-Sayed Fink Architects in New York City and Phoenix from 1991 to 1997, and was a senior associate at Tod Williams Billie Tsien and Associates in New York from 1987 to 1996. He was a winner of the Architectural League of New York's Young Architects Forum competition in 1996.

Ralph Appelbaum | Ralph Appelbaum Associates
Ralph Appelbaum founded his eponymous firm in 1978 to provide interdisciplinary communications and design services to museums. His work for the United States Holocaust Memorial Museum won the Presidential Award for Design Excellence in 1997 and the Federal Design Achievement Award from the National Endowment for the Arts in 1995. The firm's fossil halls at the American Museum of Natural History in New York won a Design Excellence Award from the Industrial Designers Society of America [IDSA] in 1996.

Apple Computer
Apple Computer was founded by Steven Jobs and Steven Wozniak in 1976. The company helped propagate the personal computer revolution with the Apple II of 1977 and the Macintosh of 1984. Apple computers can be found in numerous museum collections, including the Museum of Modern Art, New York and the Whitney Museum of American Art. The Apple Industrial Design Team, led by Jonathan Ive, received the Chrysler design award in 1993.

Boris Bally
Boris Bally is a metalsmith and jewelry designer based in Providence, Rhode Island. His work has been included in numerous exhibitions and can be found in the permanent collections of the American Crafts Museum in New York, the Brooklyn Museum of Art, the Carnegie Museum of Art in Pittsburgh, and the Victoria & Albert Museum in London.

Julie Bargmann | D.I.R.T. Studio
Julie Bargmann founded D.I.R.T Studio, a landscape consultancy, in 1992. Recent projects include the landscaping of the Massachusetts Museum of Contemporary Art in North Adams, and Riverside Park South and the Hudson River Park in New York City. Bargmann is an assistant professor at the University of Virginia School of Architecture. She was the 1990 recipient of the Rome Prize in Landscape Architecture.

**Kadambari Baxi and Reinhold Martin
Martin/Baxi Architects**
Martin/Baxi Architects was founded in 1992. Recent projects include the interactive installation and CD-ROM *Entropia*, a residence in Union Vale, New York, and a loft renovation in collaboration with the artist Lothar Baumgarten in New York City. Martin and Bax were selected as winners of the Architectural League of New York's Young Architects Forum competition in 1996.

Geoffrey Beene | Geoffrey Beene Inc.
The first American designer to show his fashions in Milan, Geoffrey Beene has won numerous awards, including the Council of Fashion Designers of America Lifetime Achievement Award in 1998. His thirtieth anniversary as a designer, in 1993, was celebrated by an exhibition at the Fashion Institute of Technology in New York City and the publication of the monograph *Geoffrey Beene: Unbound*.

Ayse Birsel | Olive 1:1
Ayse Birsel founded Olive Design, now Olive 1:1, in 1997 after studies at the Middle East Technical University in Ankara, Turkey, and at the Pratt Institute as a Fulbright Scholar. The firm designed the Authentics exhibition space at the 1998 Chicago Gift Fair and the Resolve office system for Herman Miller in 1997. Olive 1:1 won the Best of Competition award at the NeoCon 99 contract furniture show in Chicago.

**Constantin Boym and Laurene Leon Boym
Boym Design Studio**
Constantin Boym and Laurene Leon Boym founded their design studio in 1986. Recent projects include products for Alessi, Swatch, and Vitra, and exhibitions for Cooper-Hewitt, National Design Museum and the National Building Museum in Washington D.C. Their work has been featured in such publications as *Domus, Metropolis,* and *Met Home,* and is included in the permanent collection at the Museum of Modern Art, New York. Both are members of the faculty at the Parsons School of Design in New York City.

Wendell Burnette | Wendell Burnette Architects
Wendell Burnette founded his Phoenix-based firm in 1996 after three years as an apprentice in the Taliesin Fellowship and more than eleven years in the office of William P. Bruder, with whom he co-designed the Phoenix Central Library. Recent projects include the Arboretum Park at Arizona State University and numerous residences and commercial interiors. Burnette was selected as an Emerging Voice by the Architectural League of New York in 1999 and won a Record Houses Award from *Architectural Record* in 1996.

Cannondale | Mario Galasso, Tod Patterson, Chris Peck, and team
Cannondale, based in Bethel, Connecticut, was founded by Joe Montgomery in 1971 with the production of the first bicycle trailer. The company introduced its first bicycle in 1983, and now manufactures more than fifty models at its factory in Bedford, Pennsylvania. The company began production of motocross motorcycles in 1999. Cannondale has won awards for innovative design from *Bicycling* magazine, *Popular Mechanics,* and IDSA/BusinessWeek.

Eric Chan | ECCO
Eric Chan, a graduate of the Cranbrook Academy of Art, founded ECCO Design in 1989. The firm has designed for such firms as Herman Miller and

Bausch and Lomb, and has won numerous awards, including an *I.D.* magazine Annual Design Award. ECCO designs are included in the permanent collections of the London Design Museum, the Museum of Modern Art, New York, and Cooper-Hewitt, National Design Museum.

Art Chantry

Art Chantry founded his design studio in 1980, and has since received over 350 design awards. Based in Seattle, he is the author of *Instant Litter: Concert Posters from Seattle Punk Culture* (1985). His poster design was the subject of a retrospective at the Seattle Art Museum in 1983. The the Denver Art Museum, the Museum of Modern Art, New York, the Rock and Roll Hall of Fame, in Cleveland, and the Cooper-Hewitt, National Design Museum,have exhibited and collected his work.

Coleman Coker and Samuel Mockbee
Mockbee/Coker Architects

Mockbee/Coker Architects was founded in 1986 in Canton, Mississippi and Memphis, Tennessee, by Samuel Mockbee and Coleman Coker. Samuel Mockbee is currently on the faculty of Auburn University, where he directs the Rural Studio. Coleman Coker, a recipient of the 1995 Rome Prize from the American Academy in Rome, is the director of the Memphis Center for Architecture. Together, they are authors of *Mockbee Coker: Thought and Process* (Princeton Architectural Press, 1995).

Sheila Levrant de Bretteville | The Sheila Studio

Since the formation of The Sheila Studio in 1980, Sheila Levrant de Bretteville has designed numerous permanent, site-specific, community-based installations. Most recently, in 1999 she completed *At the start...At long last...* in the terminus of the A subway line in the Inwood neighborhood of New York City. She is currently Director of Graduate Studies at the Yale University School of Art.

Neil M. Denari | Neil M. Denari Architects

Neil M. Denari is Director of the Southern California Institute of Architecture and principal of the Los Angeles-based architectural firm Neil M. Denari Architects (formerly known as Cor-Tex Architecture), founded in 1988. In 1986 he was a winner in the Architecture League of New York's Young Architects competition. His models and drawings can be found in numerous museum collections. Denari is the author of the monograph *Gyroscopic Horizons* (Princeton Architectural Press, 1999).

Emigre | Rudy VanderLans, Zuzana Licko

Emigre is a digital type foundry that was founded in 1984 by Rudy VanderLans and Zuzana Licko to exploit the freedom of personal computer technology and desktop publishing. In addition to creating type forms, Emigre publishes the critical design journal that also carries the firm's name. In 1994 Licko and VanderLans received the Chrysler design award.

Stephen Farrell | Slip Studios

In 1992 Stephen Farrell created Slip Studios, a graphic design firm and digital type foundry based in Chicago. He has won awards from the American Center for Design, the American Institute for Graphic Arts, the Type Directors Club, *Adobe* magazine, and *Letter Arts Review*. Farrell is on the design faculties of the Illinois Institute of Art and the Art Institute of Chicago.

Edward Fella

After thirty-odd years as a practicing commercial artist, Ed Fella returned to academia to study graphic design at the Cranbrook Academy of Art in 1985. He is currently a professor of graphic design at the California Institute of the Arts, where he produces experimental typography, graphics, and photography. Fella received the Chrysler design award in 1997. His book, *Edward Fella: Letters on America*, will be published by Princeton Architectural Press in 2000.

Dante Ferretti

Dante Ferretti, born in Macerata, Italy, began his film career in 1960. He worked as an art director with Pier Paolo Pasolini on such films as *Medea* and *The Decameron*, and later with Federico Fellini on *The City of Women* and *Ginger and Fred*. Recent credits include Martin Scorsese's films *The Age of Innocence, Casino*, and *Kundun*.

Fitch | Richard Watson, Jason Short, and team

Fitch is an international design firm that for almost forty years has specialized in packaging, product, retail, and environmental design, corporate identity, and branding. Fitch clients inlcude 3M, British Telecom, Chrysler, Compaq, Ellesse, and General Electric.

Fluke

Fluke came to life in the basement of founder John Fluke's home in Springdale, Connecticut in 1948. Now headquartered in Everett, Washington, the firm designs and manufactures electronic test tools. Now led by George McCain, Fluke's award-winning design department, was established in 1965.

Frog

Frog was founded as an industrial design studio by Hartmut Esslinger in Germany in 1969. The firm moved to the United States in 1983, and now has offices in New York City, Sunnyvale, California, and Austin, Texas. Frog provides product and graphic design, engineering, and new media development services for such clients as Lufthansa, Logitech, Oracle, Packard Bell, Acer, and Compaq.

Funny Garbage | Peter Girardi

Funny Garbage, a design and production company, was founded in 1996 by Peter Girardi, a former graffiti artist. The firm has developed Web sites, CD-ROMs, title graphics, and print campaigns for such clients as The Cartoon Network, Compaq, Nike, the Rock and Roll Hall of Fame, and *I.D.* magazine. Girardi received a 1999 Daimler/Chrysler design award.

Michael Gabellini | Gabellini Associates

Michael Gabellini, a graduate of the Rhode Island School of Design, worked for Kohn Pedersen Fox Associates before founding his own practice in 1991. Recent projects include exhibitions for the Solomon R. Guggenheim Museum, the Marian Goodman Gallery, and the Council of Fashion Designers of America. The firm received a P/A Award from *Architecture* magazine for the redesign of the Piazza Isolo in 1999.

David Gallo

David Gallo, based in New York City, has designed sets for more that 150 professional productions over the past eleven years. His designs for *A View From The Bridge* at the Roundabout Theatre received an American Theater Wing Award nomination. Off-Broadway, he has designed the sets for *Blue Man Group/Tubes* at the Astor Place Theater, and *Machinal* for the New York Shakespeare Festival. Recent projects include the Broadway revival of *You're a Good Man, Charlie Brown*.

Frank O. Gehry | Frank O. Gehry & Associates

Toronto-born Frank O. Gehry has been a leading figure on the architectural scene since he established his practice in 1962. His Guggenheim Museum in Bilbao (1997) has been celebrated as one of the masterpieces of twentieth-century architecture. Gehry received the Pritzker Prize for architecture in 1989, the National Medal of the Arts in 1998, and the American Institute of Architects Gold Medal in 1999.

Alexander Gelman | Gelman
Educated at the Moscow Art Institute, Alexander Gelman became the creative director of Access Factory in 1993 and founded his own studio, Design Machine, in 1997. He has worked on corporate and brand identity programs, ad campaigns, and packaging for Absolut, Chanel, Dell, Exxon, MTV, and IBM, and created a series of watches for Swatch. Gelman has won many design awards, and his work is found in the collections of the Museum of Modern Art, New York and Cooper-Hewitt, National Design Museum.

Richard Gluckman | Gluckman Mayner Architects
Richard Gluckman studied at Syracuse University and started his own practice in 1977, now known as Gluckman Mayner Architects in partnership with David Mayner. His projects include the Dia Center for the Arts in New York, the Andy Warhol Museum in Pittsburgh, Pennsylvania, and the Georgia O'Keefe Museum in Santa Fe, New Mexico. Other recent projects include the Second Stage Theatre with Rem Koolhaas in New York, and the Deutsche Guggenheim in Berlin.

Rodney Alan Greenblat
Center for Advanced Whimsy
Founded by Rodney Alan Greenblat, a graduate of the School of the Visual Arts in New York, the Center for Advanced Whimsy produces learning games and interactive animated software products for children. Greenblat is also the author of several children's books, including *Uncle Wizzmo's Used Car* (1991).

Tinker Hatfield | Nike
Tinker Hatfield trained as an architect at the University of Oregon and joined Nike in 1981 as a designer of offices, apparel showrooms, and retail outlets. He later became a product designer and then Creative Director for Product Design, helping to create the Air Trainer, the first "cross-training" shoe. As he oversaw the company's output, he designed annual versions of the Air Jordan shoe and a variety of other sneakers.

Haworth | Office Explorations Team
Founded in Holland, Michigan in 1948, Haworth—then known as Modern Products—began as a small manufacturer of office furniture. In an attempt to bring a new sense of vitality and innovation to the design of office environments and in response to recent theories of cognitive ergonomics, Haworth formed a research and development department in 1996.

Herbst LaZar Bell
Founded in 1963 and headquartered in Chicago, Herbst LaZar Bell is a consulting firm that offers research, strategic planning, industrial design, mechanical and electrical engineering, and prototype services for the design and development of industrial, medical, and consumer products. Clients include Motorola, Kodak, Hewlett Packard, Compaq, Sunbeam, Craftsman, Gillette, and Electrolux.

Steven Holl | Steven Holl Architects
Steven Holl studied at the University of Washington before establishing Steven Holl Architects in New York in 1976. Recent projects include the Museum of Contemporary Art in Helsinki, the Knut Hamsun Museum in Norway, and the Chapel of St. Ignatius in Seattle. His work has been the subject of exhibitions at the Museum of Modern Art in New York and the Walker Art Center in Minneapolis. Holl has received numerous awards for his architecture, and is the author of *Anchoring, Intertwining,* and, most recently, *The Chapel of St. Ignatius* (Princeton Architectural Press, 1989, 1996, 1999).

Walter Hood | Hood Design
After working for the National Park Service and various landscape architecture firms, Walter Hood established his own practice in 1992. Recent projects include the Courtland Creek Park and Lafayette Square in Oakland, California, Macon Yards in Macon, Georgia, and the Underground Railroad Museum in Cincinnati, Ohio. He is the author of *Urban Diaries* (1997) and is chair of the Department of Landscape Architecture and Environmental Planning at the University of California, Berkeley.

IDEO
The largest industrial design firm in the United States, Ideo was founded by David Kelley and Dean Hovey in 1978. Based in Palo Alto, California with offices in Asia, Europe, Israel, and the United States, the firm's recent clients include Amtrak, Apple Computer, Hewlett-Packard, Motorola, Logitech, Proctor & Gamble, and Deutsche Telekom.

Imaginary Forces | Kyle Cooper and team
In 1996 Kyle Cooper founded the studio Imaginary Forces, based in Los Angeles, with Peter Frankfurt and Chip Houghton. He has directed live action sequences for feature film titles, broadcast projects, and commercials, including title designs for *Wild Wild West, The Mummy, Seven, Mission Impossible, Twister, Quiz Show,* and *The Avengers,* and has directed live action commercials for AT&T, Target, Reebok, and Charles Schwab.

Carlos Jiménez | Carlos Jiménez Studio
Born in San José, Costa Rica, Carlos Jiménez established his practice in Houston, Texas, in 1982. Recent projects include the Spencer Studio Art Building at Williams College, Williamstown, Massachusetts, and a proposed addition to the Nelson-Atkins Museum of Art in Kansas City, Missouri. Jiménez's work has been recognized by *Architecture* magazine, *Architectural Record,* and the Architectural League of New York. He is the author of *Carlos Jiménez: Buildings* (Princeton Architectural Press, 1996).

Sulan Kolatan and William Mac Donald
Kolatan/Mac Donald Studio
Sulan Kolatan and William Mac Donald established their firm after attending architecture school at the Columbia University Graduate School of Architecture, Planning and Preservation. Recent completed projects include a corporate residence in the Hotel des Artistes and an extension of the Angelika Film Center, both in New York City. They received a 1997 P/A Award from *Architecture* magazine and a fellowship from the New York Foundation for the Arts in 1996. Both are on the faculty of the architecture school at Columbia University.

John Kricfalusi | Spumco
John Kricfalusi began his career in cartoon animation working on such animated classics as *Mighty Mouse* and *The Jetsons.* After leaving Hanna-Barbera, where he first directed cartoons, Kricfalusi joined the studio of Ralph Bakshi, and subsequently designed and directed the animation for the Rolling Stones' video, *Harlem Shuffle.* With Jim Smith, he created the television series *The Ren & Stimpy Show* (1991) and founded the animation studio Spumco.

B. J. Krivanek | B. J. Krivanek Art + Design |
Community Architexts
B. J. Krivanek founded B. J. Krivanek Art + Design in 1983 and Community Architexts, of which he is artistic director, in 1993. His body of public, environmental art work seeks to integrate text into architecture and its urban context. He has taught at the California Institute of Arts and UCLA, and has won numerous awards for his work.

Lewis.Tsurumaki.Lewis
Paul Lewis, Marc Tsurumaki, David J. Lewis
Paul Lewis, Marc Tsurumaki, and David J. Lewis, graduates of the Princeton University School of Architecture, began their architectural collaboration in 1992. The firm has designed and fabricated office and exhibition spaces for the Van Alen Institute, Princeton Architectural Press, and Happy Mazza Media Company. They are the

authors of *Pamphlet Architecture 21: Snafu* (Princeton Architectural Press, 1999), and have received three *I.D.* magazine design awards.

Bruce Licher | Independent Project Press
Bruce Licher established Independent Project Press in Los Angeles in 1984. Now based in Sedona, Arizona, the firm has created album and CD packages for such artists as Cracker, R.E.M., Savage Republic, Stereolab, and Hank Williams, Jr. Licher has also designed magazine covers for *Emigre* and *Plazm*.

Gary Lloyd
Reallybigskies, Really Fake Digital, and Sky Drops
Gary Lloyd attended the Art Center College of Design and Otis Art Institute before founding Reallybigskies in 1981. Recent projects include sky paintings in the Silver Legacy Resort Casino in Reno and the Venetian in Las Vegas. Lloyd is the recipient of an Individual Artist Grant from the National Endowment of the Arts.

Loom
Raveevarn Choksombatchai and Ralph Kirk Nelson
Raveevarn Choksombatchai and Ralph Nelson founded the architectural firm Loom in Berkeley, California, in 1991. Their work has since received a P/A Award from *Architecture* magazine, two Minnesota AIA Honor Awards, and been featured in group exhibitions at the Weisman Art Museum in Minneapolis, the High Museum of Art in Atlanta, and the 1991 Venice Biennale.

LOT/EK | Giuseppe Lignano and Ada Tolla
Ada Tolla and Giuseppe Lignano studied architecture at the University of Naples and the Graduate School of Architecture, Planning and Preservation at Columbia University. Recent work by their firm, LOT/EK, includes its studio in New York City and numerous residential spaces. Their work, which includes furnishings as well as architecture, has been widely exhibited.

Lunar Design | Max Yoshimoto and team
The industrial design firm Lunar Design, with offices in Palo Alto and San Francisco, was founded in 1984. Projects completed under the direction of Max Yoshimoto include designs for such clients as Steelcase, Coherent Medical, Xerox, Cisco Systems, Hewlett Packard, and Oral-B Laboratories. Lunar has received numerous design awards, including those from *I.D.* magazine and the IDSA/*BusinessWeek*.

Greg Lynn | Greg Lynn FORM
Greg Lynn studied architecture at Princeton University before founding Form, a "paperless" design studio. He recently completed the

Presbyterian Church of New York in Sunnyside, Queens, in collaboration with Michael McInturf Architects and Douglas Garofalo. He is the author of *Animate Form* (Princeton Architectural Press, 1999) and teaches architecture at UCLA.

John Maeda | Maedastudio
John Maeda studied at the Massachusetts Institute of Technology and Tsukuba University in Japan before forming Maedastudio in 1995. He is the author of *Design By Numbers* (1999), and is the Sony Career Development Professor of Media Arts and Sciences and an Assistant Professor of Design and Computation at MIT.

P. Scott Makela and Laurie Haycock Makela
Words + Pictures for Business + Culture
P. Scott Makela and Laurie Haycock Makela formed their design studio Words + Pictures for Business + Culture as Co-Chairs of the Two-Dimensional Design Department at the Cranbrook Academy of Art. P. Scott Makela (1960–1999) produced film and video work for clients including Nike, MTV, MCI, and Kodak. Laurie Haycock Makela created the graphic identity for the Walker Art Center in Minneapolis, of which she was formerly Design Director, and for which she produced numerous exhibition catalogs. In 1998, the Makelas authored the book *Whereishere*.

Michael Manfredi and Marion Weiss
Weiss/Manfredi Architects
Collaborators since 1987, Marion Weiss and Michael Manfredi formally established their partnership in 1989. Recent projects include the Women's Memorial and Education Center at Arlington National Cemetery in Washington, D.C., and the Olympia Fields Park and Community Center in Illinois. They are the recipients of a 1999 *I.D.* magazine award and a 1998 American Institute of Architects Award of Excellence. Together, they are the authors of *Site Specific: The Work of Weiss/Manfredi Architects* (Princeton Architectural Press, 2000).

Martha Stewart Living Omnimedia
Martha Stewart and Gael Towey
Martha Stewart worked as a stockbroker on Wall Street after graduating from Barnard College. Her reputation as a America's tastemaker grew from the one-woman catering business she founded in Westport, Connecticut in the early seventies. The magazine *Martha Stewart Living* was launched in 1991, and today she leads Martha Stewart Living Omnimedia, of which Gael Towey is Creative Director. Among many honors, Stewart has received two Emmy Awards. Towey received the 1999 Daimler/Chrysler Award.

Bruce Mau | Bruce Mau Design
Bruce Mau attended Ontario College of Art and Design before founding Bruce Mau Design in 1985. He has designed numerous publications, created the graphic identity for the publisher Zone, and is co-author, with Rem Koolhaas, of *S, M, L, XL* (1995). Among many honors, he received the Chrysler design award in 1998. Mau has taught at the California Institute of the Arts, the University of Toronto, and the Getty Research Center for the History of Art and the Humanities.

Roy McMakin | Domestic Furniture
Roy McMakin, a native of Wyoming, attended the University of California, San Diego and founded the studio Domestic Furniture, now based in Seattle, Washington in 1987. McMakin designed the furniture and interiors of the administrative offices at the J. Paul Getty Museum in Los Angeles, and has designed for numerous residences across the United States.

Pablo Medina | Pablo Medina Graphic Design
Pablo Medina, who studied graphic arts at the Pratt Institute, began his design career as a high-school fanzine publisher. The New York-based typographer now finds inspiration in hand-crafted lettering found in Latino communities. His clients include the National Hockey League, Time Warner, and ESPN. His font designs are available from Plazm Fonts.

Rebeca Méndez
Rebeca Méndez Communication Design
Rebeca Méndez, born and raised in Mexico City and trained at the Art Center College of Design in Pasadena, founded her design studio in 1998. She has designed publications for the Getty Center, the Los Angeles County Museum of Art, and the Whitney Museum of American Art, and developed the graphic identity program for the UCLA Department of Architecture and Design. She has been on the faculty of the Art Center College of Design since 1985.

Montgomery Pfeifer
Herbie Pfeifer, Paul Montgomery
Located in San Francisco, Montgomery Pfeifer is a design consultancy that specializes in product design and graphic identity programs. The firm's clients include Apple Computer, Sun Microsystems, Pronet, and Lufthansa. The firm has received awards from *I.D.* and *PC* magazines, among others, and its work has been featured in such publications as *Wired, Online Design,* and *Macworld*.

Motorola
Scott Richards, Frank Tyneski, and team
Motorola was founded in 1928 by the brothers Paul V. and Joseph E. Galvin as the Galvin Manufacturing Corporation. The company's first product was a device that allowed battery-operated home radios to operate on ordinary household current. With the production of the first affordable automobile radio in 1930, Paul Galvin renamed the company Motorola, linking the words motion and radio. Motorola has since grown into a global corporation producing a vast array of electronic communications devices.

Gary Shigeru Natsume
Born in Japan, Gary Shigeru Natsume has studied environmental design at the Aichi Prefectural University of Fine Arts, the Parsons School of Design, and the Cranbrook Academy of Art, and has worked for such design firms as IDEO, frog, and the Maruzen Corporation. His work won the 1998 Students Design Distinction Award from *I.D.* magazine and the Grand Prize at the Design Nagoya 92 Design Competition.

Arlen Ness and Cory Ness
Arlen Ness Enterprises
Arlen Ness began customizing Harley Davidson motorcycles in 1967. Together with his wife Bev Ness, he opened his first shop in 1970 in Oakland, California. Now based in San Leandro and working in collaboration with his son, Cory, Ness continues to produce customized motorcycles and accessories. In 1992, Arlen Ness was inducted into the National Motorcycle Museum and Hall of Fame in Sturgis, South Dakota.

Oakley | Colin Baden
Oakley, founded in 1975 by Jim Jannard, is a design and manufacturing company based in Foothill Ranch, California. From its inception, the firm has brought together new materials and methods of production to create sunglasses, goggles, and high-performance eye-wear for athletes. Oakley has since extended its product lines to include apparel, outerwear, backpacks, sunglasses, footwear, hats, and watches.

Palo Alto Products International
Founded in 1983, the design firm Palo Alto Products provides comprehensive product development services, including industrial design, mechanical engineering, and production. The company has designed products for Dell, Intel, Ericcson, and Sun Microsystems, and has won numerous awards, including those from *I.D.* magazine, the Chicago Athenaeum, and IDSA/ *BusinessWeek*.

Stephen Peart | Vent
Stephen Peart, a graduate of Sheffield Polytechnic and the Royal College of Art in London and a former design director at frog, formed the design consultancy Vent in 1987. Based in Campbell, California, Vent provides a broad range of design services to clients such as Apple Computer, Nike, Herman Miller, The Knoll Group, Sun Microsystems, and Santa Cruz Skateboards.

Post Tool Design
Gigi Biederman and David Karam
The studio Post Tool Design was founded in 1993 in San Francisco by Gigi Biederman and David Karam. Recent work includes the California College of Arts and Crafts Web site, an interactive environment for children at the Getty Information Institute, and a Web site for the organization Amnesty International. Biederman and Karam are winners of a 1999 *I.D.* magazine award for interactive media. Both are on the faculty of the CCAC.

Karim Rashid | Karim Rashid Inc.
Karim Rashid, a native of Cairo, studied at Carleton University in Ottawa. Rashid founded his eponymous design firm in 1992, and has since produced furniture, installations, lighting, housewares, and products for Black and Decker, Fujitsu, IMAX, Issey Miyake, Umbra, and Sony Electronics. He recently won a competition held by Con Edison to redesign manhole covers for New York City, and is currently on the faculty of the University of the Arts in Philadelphia.

Razorfish
Jeffrey Dachis, Craig Kanarick, and team
Razorfish is a two-year-old Web-design company founded in New York City by Jeffrey Dachis and Craig Kanarick. Its client list includes America Online, ABC Television, IBM, Pepsi, and Sony Electronics. Recent projects include Razorfish Studios, conceived to generate original content for on-line sites, and *The Blue Dot*, the company's own on-line magazine.

David Rockwell | Rockwell Group
David S. Rockwell established the New York-based Rockwell Group in 1983, and has since pioneered the field of "entertainment architecture." Clients include Planet Hollywood, the Official All Star Cafe, the Motown Cafe, the Walt Disney Company, Sony/Loews Theaters, and the Academy of Motion Picture Arts and Sciences. Rockwell was named Designer of the Year by *Interiors* magazine in 1998.

Stefan Sagmeister | Sagmeister
Stefan Sagmeister worked for M&Co, Leo Burnett, and Muir Cornelius Moore before forming his own studio in 1993. He has created CD covers for the Rolling Stones, Aerosmith, Lou Reed, Pat Metheny, and David Byrne. Current work includes an identity program for the Kunsthalle Tirol in Austria, catalogs for Lipanje-Puntin Gallery in Trieste, Italy, and a lyric book for Lou Reed. He is the subject of *Stefan Sagmeister: A Designer's Life* (1998) and the recipient of four Grammy Award nominations and numerous design awards.

Jim Seay | Premier Rides
Jim Seay is the President of Premier Rides, a roller-coaster and amusement ride design and engineering firm founded by Peter Schnabel. Seay guided the design and installation of Linear Induction Motor (LIM) roller coasters at numerous theme parks in the United States, Europe, and Japan. Premier Rides, based in Millersville, Maryland, has won numerous awards, including the International Association of Amusement Parks and Attractions Best New Technology and Best New Attraction awards in 1995 for roller coasters at Kings Island in Ohio and Kings Dominion in Virginia.

David Small | Small Design Firm
Designer David Small earned B.A., M.S., and Ph.D degrees from the Massachusettes Institute of Technology, and taught at MIT's Media Lab with Muriel Cooper from 1990 to 1994. In 1998 he created the interactive typographic installation *Stream of Consciousness* with Tom White. Previously, Small designed the animation for Tod Machover's interactive *Brain Opera*, which premiered in 1997 at New York's Lincoln Center.

Kate Spade | Kate Spade New York
Kate Spade formed the handbag company that bears her name with husband Andy Spade and partners Elyce Cox and Pamela Bell in 1993. Spade entered the design world after leaving *Mademoiselle*, where she served as the magazine's Accessories Editor. The Council of Fashion Designers of America awarded her its Perry Ellis Award for New Talent in 1995.

Specialized Bikes | Robert Egger
Based in Morgan Hills, California, Specialized was founded in 1974 by Mike Sinyard. From its inception, the company has focused on the design and manufacture of high-performance mountain bikes, tires, and accessories.

Jennifer Sterling | Sterling Design
Jennifer Sterling founded her San Francisco design studio in 1996 and has since created packaging, product design, graphic design, and identity programs for such clients as Calvin Klein, Levi Strauss, the San Francisco Museum of Modern Art, and the State of Florida. Sterling was featured in a recent Absolut Vodka advertising campaign, and has received numerous design awards. Her work is in the permanent collections of the San Francisco Museum of Modern Art and the Library of Congress.

Julie Taymor
Julie Taymor won Tony Awards for both direction and costume design for the musical *The Lion King*. *Juan Darién*, a collaboration with composer Elliot Goldenthal, received five Tony nominations including that for Best Director. New projects include her first feature film, an adaptation of Shakespeare's *Titus Andronicus*, and the opera *Grendel* (also in collaboration with Goldenthal). Her work is the subject of the books *Julie Taymor: Playing with Fire* (1995 and 1999) and *The Lion King: Pride Rock on Broadway* (1997).

Thomson Consumer Electronics
Paul Pierce, Dennis Erber, and team
Elihu Thomson founded the Thomson-Houston Electric Company in the late nineteenth century with a fellow high school science professor, Edwin Houston. One of the most prolific inventors of the era, Thomson was granted 696 patents for such innovations as arc lights, electric welding machines, and X-ray tubes. The 1892 merger of Thomson-Houston and Thomas Edison's Edison General formed General Electric. Today, Thomson Consumer Electronics and Thomson Multimedia are among the largest consumer electronics companies in the world.

Tippett Studio
Phil Tippett, Craig Hayes, and team
Tippett Studio, an animation and visual effects studio based in Berkeley, California, was founded in 1983 by Phil Tippett, the former head of animation at George Lucas's Industrial Light and Magic, and Jules Roman, a film producer, editor, and postproduction supervisor. In partnership with designer Craig Hayes, Tippett Studio has worked on such films as *Honey, I Shrunk the Kids*, *Ghostbusters 2*, *Robocop 2*, and *Jurassic Park*. Tippett Studio has received six Academy Award nominations.

Martin Venezky | Appetite Engineers
Martin Venezky founded Appetite Engineers in 1997. He has designed the books *Hot Rod* and *Bordertown*, *Speak* magazine, and graphics for the 1998 Reebok Supershow Trade Exhibit.

Current projects include exhibition catalogs for the California College of Arts and Crafts and the San Francisco Museum of Modern Art, and signage for the San Francisco Lesbian and Gay Community Center. His designs have won awards from the AIGA, *I.D.* magazine, and the American Center for Design.

Chris Ware
Chris Ware studied at the University of Texas at Austin, the Skowhegan School of Painting and Sculpture, and the School of Fine Art at the Art Institute of Chicago. He was a cartoonist for *The Daily Texan* from 1986 to 1991 and, since 1992, has drawn a weekly cartoon for the *Newcity* newspaper. He initiated the comic book periodicals *The Acme Novelty Library* in 1983, and *The Rag-Time Ephemeralist* in 1988. His book *Jimmy Corrigan: The Smartest Kid on Earth* will be published in 2000.

Tod Williams and Billie Tsien
Tod Williams Billie Tsien Associates
Tod Williams and Billie Tsien established their practice in 1986 and have since designed the Neurosciences Institute at the Scripps Institute in La Jolla, the Student Arts Center at Johns Hopkins University, and the Natatorium at the Cranbrook Academy of Art. Their Museum of American Folk Art in New York is scheduled for completion in 2001. Williams and Tsien have won four awards from the American Institute of Architects and were the recipient of a Chrysler design award in 1998.

Lebbeus Woods
Lebbeus Woods studied architecture at the University of Illinois and Purdue, worked in the office of Eero Saarinen, and established his own practice before co-founding the Research Institute for Experimental Architecture in 1976. He has since published numerous books, including *OneFiveFour*, *War and Architecture*, and *Radical Reconstruction* (Princeton Architectural Press, 1989, 1993, and 1997). Among many honors, Woods received the Chrysler design award in 1994. His works appear in major museum collections throughout the world.

Ziba Design
Ziba Design is an industrial design firm founded by Sohrab Voussoughi with offices in Portland, San Jose, Taipei, and Tokyo. Its clients have included Black and Decker, Microsoft, CD Medical, Cleret, Coleman, Intel, and Fujitsu. Ziba has received awards from IDSA/*BusinessWeek*, the Design Zentrum, Industrie Forum Design Hannover, *I.D.* magazine, and the Chicago Athenaeum.

THE AUTHORS

Donald Albrecht
Donald Albrecht is an independent curator as well as adjunct curator for special projects at Cooper-Hewitt, National Design Museum. He is exhibition director and catalog editor for *Charles and Ray Eames: A Legacy of Invention* (1997), organized by the Library of Congress and the Vitra Design Museum. Other projects include the exhibition and catalog *World War II and the American Dream* (1994), for the National Building Museum, and the book *Designing Dreams: Modern Architecture in the Movies* (1986).

Ellen Lupton
As adjunct curator of contemporary design at Cooper-Hewitt, National Design Museum, Ellen Lupton has produced numerous exhibitions, including *Graphic Design in the Mechanical Age: Selections from the Merrill C. Berman Collection* (1999), *Mixing Messages: Graphic Design in Contemporary Culture* (1996), and *Mechanical Brides: Women and Machines from Home to Office* (1993), each accompanied by a book of the same title. Other book and exhibition projects include *The ABCs of* ●■▲*: The Bauhaus and Design Theory* (1991), *The Bathroom, the Kitchen, and the Aesthetics of Waste* (1992), and *Design/Writing/Research: Writing on Graphic Design* (1997). She received the Chrysler design award in 1993.

Steven Skov Holt
Since 1992, Steven Skov Holt has been the visionary and director of strategy at frogdesign, where he has been involved with building the company's identity through new media, print publications, and the design of the US offices. He has led many of frog's conceptual, future-oriented studies, and has participated in select graphic design and industrial design projects. Since 1995, he also has been chair of the industrial design program at California College of Arts and Crafts (CCAC) in San Francisco. Previously, he was a partner of Zebra Design (Cologne); a designer at Smart Design (New York); and editor of *I.D.* magazine.

PHOTOGRAPHY CREDITS

Arthur Bagen 191
Carmina Besson 56
Danny Bright 136 (left)
Shawn Brixey 80–1
Eric Chang and Srdjan Weiss 107
Coleman Coker 150
Erika Barahona Ede, © Guggenheim Museum
  Bilbao. All rights reserved. 41
Effective Images 42–3
Rick English 47
Chris Faust 81 (top)
Louis Fliger 100 (left)
Brooks Freehill 66
Hunter Freeman 31 (top)
Matt Flynn 69 (left), 76–7, 88 (right), 116-7,
  162 (left, center), 176 (right), 177 (bottom),
  178, 184 (right), 185 (bottom), 186–7
Jeff Goldberg, © Esto 139
Beverley Harper 114, 115 (both)
Timothy Hursley 151
Gordon Joseph 126 (left)
Kristine Larsen 130
Lavrisha Photography 88
Mike Litchner 57
Peter Mauss, © Esto 172–3
John Mazey 157
Mazy & St. John 156
John McCallum 28-29

Dan Meyers 60–1, 85, 98–9, 128–9, 188–9
Michael Moran 44 (left), 93 (right)
Mariano Pastor, Herman Miller 33
Jeff Kurt Petersen 154
Jock Pottle, © Esto 106 (right), 138
Tom Powell 106 (left)
Phoenix 79 (far right)
Dave Rubin 123
Ilan Rubin 59
SandBox Studios 46
Craig Saruwatari 52–3
Tom Schierlitz 84
Mark Serr 198
Ken Skalski 33
David L. Smith 122
Mark Steele, Fitch Inc. 194–5
Ezra Stoller, © Esto 135 (left)
Marcus Swanson 206–7
Lewis Tanner 152–3
Tom Vack 64
Paul Warchol 102, 137 (top), 184 (left)
Whamo Inc. 126 (right)
James Wojcik 127 (left)
Mark Woods 112–3
Joshua White 40

INDEX OF DESIGNERS AND FIRMS

COLOPHON

Book design
Ellen Lupton

Cover design
Karim Rashid

Editor
Mark Lamster

Editorial assistants
Megan Searing and Kristina Kaufman

Special thanks
Ann Alter, Eugenia Bell, Jan Cigliano, Jane Garvie, Caroline Green, Beth Harrison, Mia Ihara, Clare Jacobson, Leslie Ann Kent, Anne Nitschke, Lottchen Shivers, Sara Stemen, and Jennifer Thompson of Princeton Architectural Press—Kevin C. Lippert, publisher

Typefaces
Filosofia, Tarzana, and Base Monospace, designed by Zuzana Licko, Emigre Fonts